The Wizard of Milton Brodie

By the same author:

A.E. WAITE: Magician of Many Parts

THE GOLDEN DAWN: Twilight of the Magicians

THE MAGICAL MASON: Forgotten Hermetic Writtings of W. Wynn Westcott

THE SORCERER AND HIS APPRENTICE: Hermetic Writtings of S.L. MacGregor Mathers and J.W. Brodie-Innes

REVELATIONS OF THE GOLDEN DAWN: The Rise & Fall of a Magical Order

THE GOLDEN DAWN COMPANION: A Guide to the History, Structure, and Workings of the Hermetic Order of the Golden Dawn

The Wizard of Milton Brodie

The Esoteric Papers of J.W. Brodie Innes

Edited by
R. A. Gilbert

THOTH PUBLICATIONS
Loughborough, Leicestershire

Copyright © R.A. Gilbert 2023

All rights reserved. No reproduction, copy or transmission of this publication may be made without written permission. No paragraph of this publication may be reproduced, copied or transmitted save with the written permission or in accordance with the provision of the Copyright Act 1956 (as amended).

Any person who does any unauthorised act in relation to this publication may be liable for criminal prosecution and civil claims for damages.

The Moral Rights of the Author have been asserted.

A CIP catalogue record for this book is available from the British Library.
Cover design by Tabatha Cicero

Cover photo of *J.W. Brodie Innes and his wife, Frances* and photo of *J.W. Brodie Innes and his dog at Milton Brodie* copyright © R.A. Gilbert.

ISBN: 978-1-913660-38-3

Published by Thoth Publications
64 Leopold Street, Loughborough, LE11 5DN
Web address: www.thoth.co.uk
email: enquiries@thoth.co.uk

Contents

Preface ix
Introduction 1

Psychic and Spiritual Papers

1. Some Psychic Memories 21
2. A Haunted Church in Munich 33
3. Divers Hauntings: An Attempted Classification 45
4. Concerning Obsessions 57
5. The Cloud upon the Sanctuary 71

Witchcraft and Folklore

6. Some Celtic Memories 75
7. Witchcraft 89
8. Witchcraft Rituals 99
9. On Witchcraft in Scotland 109
10. An Egyptian Ritual Against Apophi and its Relationship to Modern Witchcraft 113
11. Ethnological Traces in Scottish Folklore 123
12. Bluebeard and the Maid of Orleans: A Study in Fifteenth Century Sorcery 135

Occultism and Divination

13. The Hermetic System 151
14. Occult Symbology in Relation to Occult Science .. 157
15. The Esoteric Teaching on the Origin and Significance of the Zodiac 165
16. Remarks on the Lecture on the Zodiac 177
17. The Tatwas: Four Lectures 181
18. The Science of Numbers — Kabalistic and Hermetic 215
19. The Tarot Cards 223

Magic and the Golden Dawn

20. MacGregor Mathers: Some Personal Reminiscences 235
21. Concerning the Revisal of the Constitution and Rules
    of the Order R.R. et A.C. 241
22. Some Notes on the First Knowledge Lecture 247
23. Essay on Clairvoyance and Travelling in the Spirit Vision . . . 251
24. Notes of an Experiment in Exorcism 257
25. Letters and Notes Relating to the Solar Order
    (The Cromlech Temple) 261

Novella

The Old House in the Canongate 269

J.W. Brodie Innes and his dog at Milton Brodie

Preface

When Samuel Liddell Mathers effectively destroyed the Golden Dawn in 1900, some of the members sought to rebuild the Order in its original magical form. Prominent among them was John William Brodie Innes, who was also – if we set aside W.B. Yeats as a special case – the most prolific of the literary magicians. But his writings, which extended far beyond the boundaries of occultism, are today little known. This is due, in no small part, to his being seen as nothing more than an acolyte of Mathers, basking in his master's reflected glory.

Such a perception is grossly unfair. Brodie Innes could often be dogmatic in his views, but he lacked both the mean-spirited arrogance and the paranoia of Mathers, and his work deserves to be presented to a wider readership. Some of his papers were collected in an earlier anthology, *The Sorcerer and his Apprentice* (1983), in which Brodie Innes's work was subordinated to that of Mathers. The present collection aims to discard the image of Brodie Innes as a junior partner and to redress the balance by giving Brodie Innes the prominence he deserves.

The fifteen previously published papers are all reprinted here, with the addition of a further fourteen. All of the papers now drawn together are grouped thematically under four headings – Psychic and Spiritual; Witchcraft and Folklore; Occultism and Divination; and Magic and the Golden Dawn – with a coda in the form of his novella, 'The Old House in the Canongate', which offers a heady mix of the occult and the psychic. For each contribution the original source is given.

Two of the contributions on the Golden Dawn have not been easily accessible and two others are previously unpublished. These will be welcomed by students and members of the Order. Other unpublished, historical material relating to the Golden Dawn has not been included: the correspondence of 1903 between Brodie Innes and A.E. Waite is largely dull and uninspiring, and would be of interest only to earnest students of the historical minutiae of western esotericism. It would also have been necessary, for the correspondence to make sense, to include Waite's letters – an unwelcome prospect for both men, who would make very uneasy bedfellows.

Other potential contributions have also been excluded. The lengthy, controversial letters and comments on disputed points of Christian history and doctrine that appeared in various issues of the theosophical journal *The Vahan* are bewildering rather than enlightening, and they, too, would have needed the other sides of the various debates to be printed. A final exclusion has also been felt desirable because of Brodie Innes's regressive views on the Highland Clearances, and for the offensive tone (and overt racism) of 'Theosophy and Modern World Problems', an article he published in *Theosophical Siftings* in 1890.

We should remember, however, that Brodie Innes was a child of his times and that our world is very different from his – but his work in the esoteric sphere, in its broadest sense, deserves greater recognition, and it is with this hope that we present it to a new generation.

Introduction

Without question John William Brodie Innes was a complex and many faceted man. For the avid reader of fantasy fiction he was a story-teller who should have written more, or perhaps less, of his supernatural romances; for the local historian he is a marvellous resource for the byways of Morayshire history and of the murky story of witchcraft in Scotland; for the law student he is the malign author of a thousand page work comparing English and Scottish Law; for theosophists he remains an enigma; and for historians – especially ill-informed historians – of occultism he was a great figure in the tale of the Golden Dawn.

This last perception has been due, to a large extent, to the assumed influence upon him of his occasional mentor, Samuel Liddell Mathers, although there is another, and more egregious, myth about Brodie Innes and the Golden Dawn that needs to be exploded. According to Ithell Colquhoun, Mathers's biographer, Brodie Innes was 'Dion Fortune's model for the 'soul-doctor' in *The Secrets of Dr. Taverner*', and she also claims that,

> One is fairly safe in identifying him [i.e. the character 'Z' in *Psychic Self-Defence*] with Brodie-Innes, whom she elsewhere acclaims as her first *gourou*: Z's magical techniques are certainly those of the GD, and Brodie-Innes was reputed to use such hypnotic powers as she describes.[1] (pp. 150-151)

Alas, this is all nonsense, but the myth persists and is believed by all too many. Dr. Taverner, and Dion Fortune's first teacher, were one and the same man, Theodore Moriarty. He was not Brodie Innes and there is no known connection of any kind between the two men.

It should also be emphasised that Brodie Innes was much more than a supposed acolyte of Mathers, under whose shadow he has lain too long, and his work has a greater appeal for a far wider readership – even within the confines of the supernatural. This new collection of his writing is aimed at demonstrating the breadth and value of his work, which

---

1. Ithell Colquhoun, *Sword of Wisdom. MacGregor Mathers and 'The Golden Dawn'.* 1975

reflects the many aspects of his life. To introduce his work, and to set it in context, we must examine both the public and private lives of the *real* J.W. Brodie Innes.

The Lawyer and the Laird

The first point to be noted about this Scottish laird is that he was English, as was his father before him. The Revd. John Brodie Innes was born in London on Boxing Day of 1815. He came from a family of landed gentry who could afford to educate him at Oxford, and in 1839 he graduated from Trinity College. In the same year he entered the Church, being ordained a Priest in 1842. From 1846 to 1871 he was Vicar of Downe in Kent, and Charles Darwin was thus one of his parishioners. The two men were widely different in outlook, and yet Brodie Innes noted, 'On my last visit to Down, Mr. Darwin said, at his dinner-table, "Brodie Innes and I have been fast friends for thirty years, and we never thoroughly agreed on any subject but once, and then we stared at each other, and thought one of us must be very ill"'. Darwin repeated these sentiments in a letter to the elder Brodie Innes: 'We often differed, but you are one of those rare mortals from whom one can differ and yet feel no shade of animosity.'[2]

It was into this almost idyllic rural atmosphere that his only son, John William Brodie Innes, was born on 19 March 1848. The young Brodie Innes was first educated at Bradfield (where, in the 1920s, Ellic Howe, the great historian of the Golden Dawn, would also be a pupil), but left in 1861 when his father succeeded his cousin as heir of the estate of Milton Brodie, a house originally known as 'Windy Hills', in Morayshire, tucked between Forres to the West and Elgin to the East. The house retained some of its pre-Reformation structure, with continual additions up to the 19th century, and it was here that Brodie Innes developed his enthusiasm for folklore, archaeology, ecclesiology and the less admirable pursuit of shooting wild life. His education continued briefly at Bonn University, then from October 1866 to March 1869 at Pembroke College, Oxford, before moving to St. John's College, Cambridge, where he read Mathematics, and graduated BA in 1872.

He next turned to the law, and began his studies at Lincoln's Inn in November 1872 until he was called to the Bar on 28 June 1876.

---

2. Francis Darwin (Ed.), *The Life and Letters of Charles Darwin*. 1898 Vol. 2, p. 83.

Brodie Innes had Chambers in New Court, Lincoln's Inn, but he initially supported himself by journalism. Three years later, on 4 June 1879, he married Frances Annesley Voysey at the fashionable church of St. George's, Hanover Square. His wife was also a clerical child, albeit one of four sisters and four brothers, a daughter of the Revd. Charles Voysey (1828-1912), who was notorious for having been deprived of his living in 1871 for preaching and propagating heresy. Voysey's particular wickedness was to be a non-believer in the divinity of Christ.

Voysey had the means and the inclination to establish a Theistic Church, in Swallow Street, Piccadilly, but it could not survive without its charismatic leader and this curious Church faded away after Voysey's death in 1912. Long before this Brodie Innes continued his association with the eccentric *avant garde*. The newly married couple moved to Milton House (3, The Orchard), at Bedford Park in west London: a consciously designed community for artistic and literary minded professionals that was home to such prominent future members of the Golden Dawn and the Theosophical Society as Florence Farr, Henry Paget, John Todhunter and W.B. Yeats. It stimulated not only Brodie Innes's interest in occultism, but also his literary and artistic ambitions (he was a more than competent draughtsman).

Brodie Innes and his wife divided their time between England and Scotland, but the birth of a son, John Stuart, in 1887, followed by a daughter, Gwendolyn Mary, led them to settle in Edinburgh[3] where Brodie Innes studied Scots Law and was admitted to the Faculty of Advocates on 13 March 1888. He still maintained his London practice and travelled frequently, but with two small children his wife was tied to Edinburgh and Milton Brodie.

Frances Brodie Innes did not restrict herself to domestic concerns. She was actively involved in esoteric affairs, having become a Fellow of the Theosophical Society in 1890 and a Neophyte in the Isis-Urania Temple of the Golden Dawn in 1893. In the public sphere her involvement mirrored her husband's social and political attitudes. She became an Associate of the English Church Union on New Year's Day, 1892 and three months later was enrolled as a Dame of the Primrose League. On the fringes of political reality she espoused lost Royalist causes, probably encouraged by the Jacobite pretensions of S.L. Mathers. Thus she

---

3. They lived first at 14 Dublin Street, then at 15 Royal Circus, Edinburgh.

maintained a friendship and frequent correspondence with Princess Eugénie Paleologue, who was a claimant to the throne of Greece, and in July 1895 she was admitted as a Companion of the Jacobite legitimist Order of St. Germain. Her certificate for this Order is countersigned by Mathers's cousin Walter MacGregor Stoddart.

In October 1894 the Revd. John Brodie Innes died and his son inherited the Milton Brodie estate. This cemented his position as an establishment figure and it is appropriate at this point to consider his social and political attitudes and activities. He was, like his father, a High Churchman, of pronounced Tory views, a keen country sportsman and possessed of reactionary social attitudes. But he should not be seen as all bad. He maintained his estate with care – including such delights as a rare red-berried elder that figured in local folklore,[4] and a graft from the Glastonbury Thorn – and was concerned to preserve the ruins of Kinloss Abbey, to which the original house at Milton Brodie had belonged. His public lectures and their printed versions, on the abbey, and on local history and local legends, seem to have been much appreciated.

Brodie Innes was a Justice of the Peace in Morayshire and in 1905 he was appointed Deputy Lieutenant in and for the Shire of Elgin: appointments that he took seriously and attended to as scrupulously as he did his legal duties as Chancellor of the Diocese of Argyll and the Isles, a post he held from 1892 until his death in 1923. He also turned his skills to the benefit of other churchmen, and in 1901 he prepared a long legal Statement for Bishop Douglas of Aberdeen and Orkney that brought success to the Bishop in a very complex case.[5] His enthusiasm for ancient churches led, in 1917, to correspondence with Frederick Bligh Bond about the position of the altar in medieval abbey churches. It is thus possible that the Glastonbury Thorn at Milton Brodie was presented by Bligh Bond.

---

4. This was grown from a cutting at Lochcarron Kirk taken by John Brodie Innes in 1869. He was impressed by the legend that a catastrophe would follow the growth of the tree above the height of the old church walls, and he identified it with the Franco-Prussian war of 1870.

5. *Statement of facts on behalf of ... the Honourable Arthur Gascoigne Douglas, Bishop of the United Diocese of Aberdeen and Orkney; in answer to appeal to ... the Episcopal Synod of the Episcopal Church in Scotland by the Reverend Frank Powell Williamson, James Reid Sutherland and John Milne, against the ... Bishop of Aberdeen and Orkney* [for his refusal to reinstitute the Rev. F. P. Williamson to the Pastoral Charge of St. Margaret's, Aberdeen] 1901 22pp.

As a 'sportsman' Brodie Innes supplied a chapter on 'Grouse Moors and Deer Forests' for *Bird Life in England* (1887), a book written by Edwin Lester Arnold, better known as the author of *Phra the Phoenician*, a curious novel of reincarnation. The chapter demonstrates Brodie Innes's enthusiasm and justification for the Highland Clearances. He claims that the natives had overpopulated the Highlands, refers to 'the natural indolence of the Celtic temperament', fulminates against 'Radical agitators' and states that,

> To assert, as is often done now, that the glens were cleared of men to make room for sheep, is to display the sheerest ignorance or wilful perversion of fact regarding the economic conditions. ... the people went voluntarily, or, if removed, it was to save them from a life of wretched dependence on charity, in a land which could no longer support them, even though they had it for nothing. (p. 250)

All of this is on a par with his inflammatory statements in a lecture on *Theosophy and Modern World Problems* delivered in 1890 to a theosophical audience. It constitutes an attack on Socialism and all other 'panaceas of social and political quacks', including the emancipation of women, temperance, opposition to blood sports and vivisection. Brodie Innes argues against the belief that 'all human beings should be born free and equal' (he uses Karma as excuse), and insists that a differing future for the various human races is inevitable. It is all very eloquently put, and he is fully aware that 'It is more than likely that what I have to say may bring down the wrath of many worthy members of the T.S.'[6] This would prove true also of some of his subsequent writings.

The Writer

From the time of his first forays into journalism Brodie Innes was a prolific writer, producing dramatic poetry and fiction, historical and critical studies of folklore, demonology and witchcraft, legal texts, mystical and esoteric theology and the whole gamut of theosophical and occult speculation. His later works received a mixed reception, but no

---

6. Published as *Theosophy and Modern World Problems* (1890) *Theosophical Siftings*, Vol. 3, No. 6.

comments have survived about his drama *Thomas A'Becket* (1877) or his satirical verse *Legends of the Leading Cases* (1881).[7] Much of his literary output was slight, but his one major legal work, *Comparative principles of the laws of England and Scotland. Courts and Procedure* (Edinburgh, 1903) ran to 978pp, was four inches thick and weighed seven pounds! Perhaps as a relief from such a meticulous study, Brodie Innes produced a series of supernatural novels from 1908 onwards. Four of these, *Morag, the Seal* (1908), *Old as the World* (1909), *For the Soul of a Witch* (1910) and *The Devil's Mistress* (1915), are concerned with Scottish folklore and legend, Scottish witchcraft trials and demonology. All of them were praised by reviewers, but only one – *The Devil's Mistress*, which he dedicated to the memory of his friend Bram Stoker – is truly memorable. It is the story of Isabel Goudie, a real witch of the 17th century, and it involves Patrick Innes, one of Brodie Innes's own ancestors. When it appeared Brodie Innes informed his readers that the Devil in question 'was not the Devil of theologians, or of the Bible, but rather a species of Pan, the personification of the Powers of Nature'. Despite its appearance in the middle of the war, it proved to be a great success.

Much earlier, in 1890, he had published an 'occult' novel – 'The Old House in the Canongate' – in serial form in *Lucifer*, but it has not, until now, been reprinted. It is a powerful, atmospheric and darkly supernatural novel, and superior to his final published novels, *The Tragedy of an Indiscretion* (1916) and *The Golden Rope* (1919), which are both more social than supernatural. One further fantasy novel, *The Curse on Bally na Bride*, was begun in 1914 but Brodie Innes died before he finished revising the text. It was finally published, in a very limited edition, in 2003.[8] Its theme, of confronting and overcoming ancient evil, is similar to that of 'The Old House in the Canongate'.

Most of Brodie Innes's non-fictional writing on the occult and the supernatural appeared in various periodicals. He produced only two

---

7. *Thomas A'Becket. A play, in four acts* [and in verse] [London : Printed for private circulation, 1877], 48pp. His second work was pseudonymous: *Legends of the Leading Cases: or, Law and Laughter*, by Touchstone. 1881. A further satirical work in verse was *Ye Papyrus Roll-Scroll of Ye Sette of Odd Volumes*. (O. V. Miscellanies. vol. 19), 1888, 23pp.
8. *The Curse on Bally na Bride*. Edited by Ethan Barlass [i.e. George Locke], Lamorna: Cove Press, 2003.

books in this field: *The True Church of Christ Exoteric and Esoteric* (1892), and *Scottish Witchcraft Trials* (1891),⁹ a short historical study written for the 'Sette of Odd Volumes', a club for bibliophiles and book collectors, of which he was an active member.

Brodie Innes was a keen book collector and built up a splendid library, although the contents are known only in part from the somewhat sketchy inventory prepared for insurance purposes in 1908. It was certainly a mixed collection: law, theology, local and church history, archaeology, folklore, literature and occultism are all present, and there are rare early books of great value. Two are of particular note: Eliphas Lévi's copy of Khunrath's *Amphitheatrum Sapientiae Aeternae* (1596), and an otherwise unrecorded copy of William Blake's *Marriage of Heaven and Hell*, an 'original hand coloured copy in good condition', which may have been printed at any time between 1793 and 1825, and which was then valued at £80. What happened to this is unknown, but its fate is worth pursuing for its rediscovery would be an event of major importance in the academic world.

The Convinced Christian

Brodie Innes was born into the Anglican Church and remained a High Church Episcopalian throughout his life. He never wavered in his deeply held Christian faith, never doubted its central doctrines and loved the ceremonial of traditional liturgies – especially that of the Scottish Prayer Book. Growing up as the son of a socially and intellectually well-connected priest, Brodie Innes moved in clerical circles of the establishment and became a respected ecclesiastical lawyer in Scotland, and in England he knew Dr. J.M. Neale, church historian, theologian and authority on the Eastern Churches, as a family friend.

When he strove to present Christian orthodoxy to the members of the Theosophical Society he was able to call on the work of Dr. Neale, who had been a close friend of Brodie Innes's father, to refute the arguments of his hostile, theosophical critics. They had risen up against him because he had the temerity to write a book that A.E. Waite described as 'a treatise which is essentially hostile to their position' while yet being

---

9. *Scottish Witchcraft Trials. Read before the Sette at a meeting held at Limmer's Hotel, on Friday, 7th November, 1890.* London, 1891 [Privately Printed Opuscula Issued to Members of the Sette of Odd Volumes] 66pp, 245 copies printed.

'a singularly well pleaded brief for the defence of the Christian Church' by a man 'who recognises above all things the mystic side of Christianity'.

The *True Church of Christ Exoteric and Esoteric* was published in 1892, perhaps in the cause of even-handedness, by the Theosophical Publishing Society, having first appeared in the journal *Lucifer*. In the book Brodie Innes presents a robust defence of the Church and of its universal doctrines, *i.e.* those accepted by the Ecumenical Councils, which is what he maintained 'constituted the teaching of the Church', and gave a detailed refutation of popular misconceptions about the Church and Christian theology. *The True Church of Christ* also demonstrates clearly that Brodie Innes held a deep and abiding traditional Christian faith, which he yet managed to reconcile with an eclectic spectrum of esoteric doctrines and with his magical practices. His attempt to reconcile and harmonise true Theosophy with true Christianity was a forlorn exercise, as orthodox Christians who were not attracted to Theosophy or other esoteric paths would never have accepted, as he did, such concepts as Karma and the astral body, or have agreed that 'The idea of the Buddhist or Theosophical Nirvâna and the Christian Heaven is precisely the same, and necessarily so, for both are true.'[10]

He explained his own position in the introduction: 'I write not for those who have been *truly* trained in the faith and doctrines of the Church ... not for the indifferent ...not for the avowed enemies of the Church ... Those for whom I write are the seekers after truth, pledged to no positive opinions which may prevent their accepting it, those whose inner eye is sufficiently open to understand that there are mysteries in heaven and earth which the bodily senses cannot grasp, and the logical brain cannot fathom, but of which the Divine intuitive faculty of the seer in moments of ecstasy may obtain fleeting glimpses.'[11]

Most theosophists did not like his views. Those of them who had rejected, or never accepted, Christianity did not like what they called his 'strong language' and bitterly attacked his thesis. They had a champion in G.R.S. Mead, the editor of *Lucifer* and of *The Vahan*, the house journal of the Theosophical Society. At the time Mead was an enthusiastic theosophist (in the Blavatsky sense), but he was also a real scholar,

---

10. *The Vahan*, Second Series. No. 3, October 1891, p. 4.
11. *Lucifer* Vol. 8, No. 43, May 1891, p. 23.

well versed in both patristic and Gnostic writings. He criticised *The True Church of Christ* at great length in *Lucifer* and to a degree beyond the capacity of almost all his readers, except Brodie Innes, to understand.

Mead also supported those readers of *The Vahan* who opposed the orthodox views, especially those on the doctrine of Atonement, expressed by Brodie Innes in his answers to questions about Christian doctrine and theosophy posed in the journal. Mead supported the hostile readers by agreeing with them that 'Atonement' meant expiation and not reconciliation, thus seeming to justify the 'orthodox' theosophical view of the God of the Bible as an angry and vengeful being. The theosophists of his day had no intention of letting Brodie Innes's mildly unorthodox Christianity slip inside the fortress of militant neo-Buddhism. But they would never shake his faith.

Spiritualist, Occultist and Theosophist

Despite his commitment to the Christian faith, Brodie Innes was fascinated by the supernatural and by occultism, but how, when and why he came to take up his various esoteric pursuits is not clear. Towards the end of his life he stated that,

> My interest in the subject [*i.e.* Spiritualism] began many years ago, when I was an undergraduate, and there was much talk of physical manifestations. I was neither a believer nor an unbeliever, I simply wanted to know.[12]

He accepted an invitation to a 'materializing séance', 'in a disused chapel somewhere in Bloomsbury'. It was not an impressive affair but it led him to consider a 'new theory', that 'a strong thought, or imagination, could actually create a .visible and tangible image.'[13]

This initial sitting, which took place in the early 1870s, was followed by other séances and by a meeting with the Scots medium David Duguid, at which they discussed psychic photography. Brodie Innes was not convinced that the phenomena were due to spirits, but he did have other psychic experiences, including a prophetic dream in 1916 in which he seemed to be involved in a great naval battle, ending in what seemed to be his death. A week later he received news that his son-in-law had

---

12. 'Some Psychic Memories', in *The Occult Review,* Vol. 31, No. 5, May 1920, p. 269.
13. *ibid.* p. 271.

been killed at Jutland in exactly the circumstances of his dream.[14] While this was a personal tragedy, other experiences were far more horrible. Early in 1895 Frances Brodie Innes had suffered a severe attack of influenza and Brodie Innes notes that,

> her recovery was followed by a great exhaustion, an exhaustion which ultimately I came to share. I considered this exhaustion, which seemed more than natural and it came to me that this was the obsession of some vampirizing elemental.[15]

Brodie Innes determined to cast out the elemental, which he perceived as 'a most foul shape, between a bloated big-bellied toad and a malicious ape', and immediately became aware of a powerful adept in spirit form who had come to assist him. Calling up 'the foul thing that had troubled me', he exorcised it, under instruction from the adept, by smiting it in 'the Name of the Lord Jesus' and thus disintegrating it. After this he notes that 'Both my wife and myself rapidly recovered our full health', although 'Afterwards, a message came to me that 'the unclean spirit is gone out, but it remains to purge away his traces from the house of life.' (see pp. 255–258, below)

In a later encounter with evil, about 1909, in a vast, disused church in Munich, Brodie Innes let discretion get the better part of valour. The very proximity of the building gave him 'a sensation of something horrible and uncanny', and he entered it with great reluctance. Once inside 'the whole place seemed filled with a ghastly emanation, oozing from the floor and walls as of a charnel house', and he wrote that 'the very fear of death came over me irresistibly, and a feeling of sudden weakness and collapse'. He escaped with difficulty and 'felt the evil influence of that church all the time I was in Munich'.[16] Brodie Innes later discovered that the church had been the home of the Inquisition in Munich and

---

14. 'Psychic Help for Soldiers and Sailors', in *The Occult Review*, Vol. 27, No.4, April 1918, p. 219. Lieut. Percy Strickland, RN, had married Gwendolyn Brodie Innes on 10 December 1913. They had one daughter.
15. This episode was circulated within the Second Order of the Golden Dawn as 'Flying Roll' No. 34. One version is printed in Francis King (Ed.), *Astral Projection, Ritual Magic and Alchemy*. Revised and expanded edition, 1987, pp. 40-41. It differs, but not significantly, from the version printed here (pp 255–258).
16. 'A Haunted Church in Munich', in *The Occult Review*, Vol. 30, No. 3, September 1919, pp. 138-147.

in pre-Christian times had been the site of 'very depraved Mithraic worship, and of various abominations of the corrupt later Empire'. More significantly, when the church was closed there had been no proper exorcism performed and the place became the prey of elementals: 'subtle forces operating behind the veil of matter.'

His concern with exorcism differed markedly from that of the occultists whom he would meet in the Golden Dawn, and of those who became his colleagues in the Theosophical Society. It is not clear when Brodie Innes joined the society, but it is most likely that he became aware of theosophy while living at Bedford Park and he was probably already a member when he joined the Scottish Lodge in 1889, by which time he seems already to have had his own Master. It seems to me to be possible that the unseen 'powerful adept' was the spirit of the Master about whom he wrote, but did not identify, in a reply to a question in *The Vahan* in 1892.[17] He refers there to 'an instruction' given to him by 'My own Master ... long ago'. This 'Master', I would suggest, is most likely to have been an esoterically minded priest of the Anglican Church, definitely a firm believer in the Church Militant, and utterly unlike the putative Himalayan Master of H.P. Blavatsky.

Mrs. Brodie Innes soon followed her husband into the Scottish Lodge, receiving her certificate of Fellowship in the Theosophical Society on 27 January 1890. It is duly signed by HPB and by W.R. Old ('Sepharial' who was then the General Secretary), and countersigned by J.W. Brodie Innes as 'President of the Scottish Lodge'. He was not a perpetual president, but his influence on the lodge was distinct. Under Brodie Innes's tutelage the Scottish Lodge, which had been founded in July 1884 and was wholly independent of the European Section, and thus of control from London, developed into one of the foremost intellectual and academic branches of the society. His faith also coloured the lodge's outlook, so that in 1892 it could be stated that,

> The Leaders of the Scottish Lodge are all Christians, and are proud of the title. Of necessity they must think Christianity to be the highest and the fullest expression of the universal truth.[18]

---

17. *The Vahan*, Vol. 2, No. 5, December 1892, p. 2. Brodie Innes was replying to a question about 'the esoteric interpretation of the cursing of the fig-tree by Jesus'.
18. 'The Scottish Lodge – A Retrospect and a Prospect', in *The Transactions of the Scottish Lodge of the Theosophical Society*. Part IV, 1892, p. 50.

The writer, most probably Brodie Innes, went on to state that 'Theosophy is not necessarily precisely the same as the esoteric philosophy,' and 'Those who have the power and wish to become practical occultists' can obtain training within the lodge, although 'this is quite apart from Theosophy, and is a path open only to the few'.

What Brodie Innes meant by this would soon be made clear, but he continued with what might be termed 'orthodox' theosophical work for some years. He produced papers for *Lucifer* and for the series of *Theosophical Siftings*, supplied many of the answers to queries in *The Vahan* – at least until 1896, when he was elbowed out by the Annie Besant and C.W. Leadbeater axis – and was the mainstay of the *Transactions* of the Scottish Lodge. But Brodie Innes was always something of a square peg in the round hole of the Theosophical Society. His particular interests, in such subjects as astrology, Kabbalah and the Tarot, were not widely shared and he did not endear himself to Annie Besant when, in 1895, the Scottish Lodge declared itself strictly neutral over the schism between W.Q. Judge and the Adyar Society.

To an outside observer it seems odd that Brodie Innes did not find an alternative to Theosophy within Freemasonry. He had a penchant for High Church ceremonial and for amateur dramatics in his family circle, so he might have been expected to take up the ritual dramas of Freemasonry with some enthusiasm. Why he did not is unclear, for while Scottish Freemasonry may have seemed prosaic and classless to him, the ingrained social snobbery of the English Craft ought to have had a strong appeal. One explanation is that he knew enough of Freemasonry to realise that it had no esoteric content in either its ceremonies or its philosophy. Thus it was that he turned to magic.

The Magician

Brodie Innes's enthusiasm for magic was not derived solely from a historical interest in witchcraft, sorcery and demonology. He was fascinated by both the ceremonial workings of magic and by the esoteric philosophy that underpinned its rituals. As a boy he had 'determined to try a black magical formula, out of an old book picked up, Heaven only knows where, but which certainly I ought not to have had access to.'[19] The process involved names written in blood, notably '*Asmodeus Szathan*', and

---

19. 'Witchcraft Rituals', in *The Occult Review*, Vol. 25, No. 6, June 1917, p. 329.

the calling up of a familiar spirit. Brodie Innes followed the instructions faithfully, but nothing happened. At first. Then came terrifying success. He woke at night feeling that 'some dark form seemed pressing upon me, and long tentacles were round my throat.' He broke free only after a violent struggle and a desperate recital of the Lord's Prayer, and burned the blood written parchment. He was, he records, 'properly scared, and [I] left black magic severely alone for some time.' His return to it was only ever in an academic and literary manner, although he did have in his library,

> a MS of the names and characteristics of over a hundred evil spirits with their seals (i.e. the geometric symbols whereby they might be invoked or commanded) taken from the Great Grimmoire, from Trithemius, and other works on black magic. Also the formulae whereby they might be exorcised, or cast out.[20]

It was not the only black magic manuscript that he had seen. In 1888,

> When all London was startled with horror at the crimes of Jack the Ripper, the late Mr. Bernard Quaritch [a prominent bookseller] showed me a MS. he was then wishing to buy of black magical formulae. .... Inter alia, the very formula on which Jack the Ripper seemed to have been working, the very mutilations, were minutely described, and the desecration of Christian emblems.[21]

He goes on to note that 'if the sites of the murders be marked on a map of London, they form, viewed from the west, an inverted cross, … the Mitre Square murder was probably exactly on the site of the High Altar of Holy Trinity Church, Whitechapel.' Then he adds, 'A man trying to work the formula of that old MS. could not have done it with more painstaking accuracy', and suggests that 'if the evil spirits invoked did verily obsess the murderer it would account for many things.' After such frightfulness the rites and ceremonies of the Golden Dawn must have seemed rather tame. But perhaps that is precisely why Brodie Innes took them up.

---

20. 'Concerning Obsessions', in *The Occult Review*, Vol. 35, No. 2, February 1922, p. 81.
21. 'Bluebeard and the Maid of Orleans', in *The Occult Review*, Vol. 27, No. 1, January 1918, p. 28.

The story of the Hermetic Order of the Golden Dawn can be briefly summarised.[22] It was founded in London in 1888, the creation of Dr. William Wynn Westcott, Dr. William Robert Woodman and Samuel Liddell Mathers. The purpose of the Order was to teach aspiring occultists the various aspects of Western esoteric philosophy by way of a graduated series of ceremonies based upon the Sephiroth of the kabbalistic Tree of Life. These ceremonies were worked within Temples, established in London, Weston-super-Mare and Bradford. The structure of the Order followed a Masonic pattern, with the furnishings and officers of each Temple modelled on those of various branches of Freemasonry and of the masonic *Societas Rosicruciana in Anglia*. It did not, however, demand that its members should be masons, and it was open to both men and women. In practice most of the men who joined were Masonic Rosicrucians, and most of the women were either their female relatives or members of the Theosophical Society – or both.

The rituals, which were eclectic to say the least, had been expanded from outlines found in a series of manuscripts in cipher that were almost certainly the work of Kenneth Mackenzie, a noted Victorian occultist. Candidates for admission took a Latin, or other motto by which they were known within the Order; the robes and regalia were on Egyptian patterns as perceived at the time; and ceremonies were supplemented by a set programme of study. It is also important to note that the Outer Order was esoteric rather than magical; aspiring magicians needed to progress to the Inner, Second Order: the *Rosae Rubeae et Aureae Crucis*. There they ceremonially recreated the legend of Christian Rosenkreutz and became Adepts, engaged in a demanding round of magical work.

The Golden Dawn survived in its original form for twelve years; it then split into warring factions and the divided Order gently declined for a further fourteen years. Some parts continued for much longer and since 1980 there has been a revival of the Golden Dawn that shows no signs of declining. That, in summary, is the setting for Brodie Innes's Odyssey within the Golden Dawn.

---

22. For further information on the Golden Dawn, see Ellic Howe, *The Magicians of the Golden Dawn*, 1972; R.A. Gilbert, *The Golden Dawn Companion*. New edition, 2021 and Israel Regardie, *The Golden Dawn, an account of the Teachings, Rites and Ceremonies*. Revised edition, 1969.

He was initiated into the Order in its London Temple of Isis Urania in August 1890, taking the motto *Sub Spe* ['Under Hope'] but he did not begin his advance to higher Grades for some eighteen months because of his move to Edinburgh. It was also difficult for him to travel regularly to London, and after his wife also entered the Order, in February 1893, as Soror *Sub hoc Signo vinces* ['Under this sign, conquer'] – and shortly after his guarded statement about 'practical occultism' – Brodie Innes requested the Chiefs of the Golden Dawn to grant a charter for a new Temple in Edinburgh. This was issued on 8 June and on 19 December 1893 Dr. Westcott consecrated the Amen-Ra Temple, reputedly at the headquarters of the Scottish Lodge.

At first the Temple flourished. It began with eleven members,[23] eight more were added in the first twelve months and a further fifteen during 1895. Of the thirty-three members (seventeen men and sixteen women) still active by the end of 1895, twenty-one progressed to the Second Order: a higher proportion than in any other Temple. But the growing dissension within the Order, as a result of Mathers's autocratic behaviour, was reflected within Amen-Ra. In October 1897 Brodie Innes was deposed by Mathers from his role as Imperator (the title given to the head of each Temple) and both he and his wife were 'requested' to resign as Chiefs (i.e. principal officers) of Amen-Ra. The new Imperator was William Peck, the City Astronomer of Edinburgh and an erstwhile friend of Brodie-Innes. This change was welcomed by the artist and occultist Isabelle de Steiger, a prominent member of Amen-Ra, who said that Peck was a 'born occultist', while Brodie Innes was simply one with a 'desire to rule over others and to show forth his knowledge and play the Initiate here among admiring neophytes.'[24] This was a sudden *volte face* for Mme. de Steiger, who only a year before had been delighted to have Brodie Innes's polished and sympathetic Preface to her translation of Eckartshausen's *The Cloud upon the Sanctuary* (1896).

There was now an irrevocable split in Amen-Ra. Brodie Innes and Peck each had about fifteen followers, but Peck held the Temple and Brodie Innes was obliged to transfer his allegiance to the Isis Urania

---

23. These included Brodie Innes and his wife, the astrologer C.W. Pearce and his wife, Dr. George Dickson, William Peck, the City Astronomer of Edinburgh, and Andrew Cattanach, the printer of the Scottish Lodge's *Transactions*.
24. Quoted in Howe, *Magicians of the Golden Dawn*, p. 190.

Temple. Then came the great 'Rebellion' within the Order in 1900, followed by the scandal of Mme. Horos, who had stolen Order rituals, set up a bogus Temple and aided her husband in the robbing and seduction of servant girls. At their trial the Golden Dawn was held up to ridicule and many of the members hurriedly left – including William Peck, who destroyed all his papers, robes and regalia and closed down Amen-Ra Temple.

In the aftermath of all this Brodie Innes sought to take a commanding role and during 1902 he was one of the acting three Chiefs of the Order,[25] although his glory was to be short-lived. He had issued an open letter to the adepti of the Order, *Concerning the Revisal of the Constitution and Rules of the Order R.R. et A.C.* (1902), and because of his legal expertise the members chose to elect him as one of the three Chiefs. But in 1903 his proposed Constitution of the Order was rejected at the Annual Meeting by the members, who had been carefully marshalled by A.E. Waite in a meticulously planned *coup d'état*.

In his autobiography, *Shadows of Life and Thought* (1938), Waite writes that Brodie Innes was 'in a state of white rage'. The account he gives in his private diary is more picturesque:

> It was almost pitiful to notice the change which came over the poor small Pope of Edinburgh and to compare the grandiloquence of his accent when he first spoke with the crestfallen tones … when he found the tables of the previous annual meeting turned upon him.[26]

What followed was a convoluted attempt to mend fences, but neither Waite nor Brodie Innes would give ground and the end result was three divisions of the Golden Dawn: Waite with his Independent & Rectified Rite of the Golden Dawn on a mystical path; Dr. Felkin with his magical Stella Matutina, a host of new Grades, new Masters and new 'teaching'; and Brodie Innes with a rump that would eventually, in 1910, be absorbed into a revived Amen Ra Temple.

By 1912 Brodie Innes had established a daughter Temple, Alpha et Omega, and risen to the exalted Grade of Adeptus Exemptus, with the new motto 'Fidei Tenax'. He was working amicably with Mathers, aiding

---

25. The other two were Percy Bullock (*Levavi Oculos*) and R.W. Felkin (*Finem Respice*).
26. R.A. Gilbert, *A.E. Waite: Magician of Many Parts,* 1987. p. 117.

him in his legal tussle with Aleister Crowley and, in due time, receiving his reward. Mathers died in Paris on 19 November 1918, and, 'In his last moments … he named as his successor and as the Supreme Chief of the Order, representing the Secret Chiefs, the V[ery] H[onoured] Frater "Sub Spe" 5=6, "Fidei Tenax" 7=4.'[27]

Brodie Innes did not retain an active role for long. Mina Mathers returned to London in 1919 and took control of the Alpha et Omega Temple, proving, as it turned out, to be far more autocratic than Brodie Innes and as difficult to work with as her husband had been. But Brodie Innes did have one notable success; in that year he initiated into Alpha et Omega – or as she described it, 'the Southern branch of the Scottish section of the Order' – a young woman named Violet Firth. She took the motto 'Deo non Fortuna' and so Dion Fortune was born and the Golden Dawn was set upon an utterly different path.

It was not quite the end for Brodie Innes. He firmly believed that since 1892 (or even earlier) he had been in regular contact with what he termed the 'Sun Masters' and used the material that they transmitted to him to establish a Solar Order, that ran in tandem with Amen-Ra – a situation that was unacceptable to Mathers, and the probable cause for his dethroning of Brodie-Innes – but survived for much longer. From the beginning it was known as the Cromlech Temple,[28] as he told Westcott in a letter of 16 August 1896 (pp. 261 below).

The material from the 'Sun Masters' was substantial: eight specific Cromlech rituals and a very substantial number of instructional papers, delivered over a period of more than twenty years. These were often given through Mrs. Brodie Innes, who acted as amanuensis. One of them directs each frater to 'regulate his breathing to the four-fold rhythm' and to 'recall in thought the other companions as he & they knelt together at the Shrine of Mithra – holding the red cords of the Veil' while he renews his pledge to the Infinite Supreme. This particular direction does seem a little strange for a man who would later look upon the worship of Mithras as debased, but in occult

---

27. Minutes of the Ahathoor Temple, Paris, for 12 December 1918, translated from the French.
28. Anthony Fuller, in his as yet unpublished doctoral thesis 'Anglo-Catholic Clergy and the Golden Dawn: The Ritual Revival and Modern Magical Orders 1887 – 1940' (2009), gives a very full account of the Cromlech Temple.

matters Brodie Innes was nothing if not inconsistent. He had regularly fallen out and then in with Mathers for some thirty years, and yet he could write a cloying panegyric after Mathers's death that falsely claimed almost every human virtue for his autocratic and vindictive Chief.[29]

Once finally free of responsibility for the Golden Dawn, Brodie Innes turned again to writing. He produced a series of articles for *The Occult Review*, his final novel, *The Golden Rope* (1919), and papers and lectures on Scottish folklore. He also kept up his occasional correspondence with Westcott until 1920, when Westcott left for South Africa. One of his last public acts was to unveil the war memorial at Alves in May 1921. This was a poignant event as the first name on the memorial was that of his son, Lieut. John Stuart Brodie Innes, who had been killed in action on the Western Front in 1915.

John William Brodie Innes died at his home, Milton Brodie, on 8 December 1923 and was laid to rest in the family burying-ground at Elgin Cathedral. He had known and fought for or against almost all the assorted occultists, magicians and Theosophists of his day. Perhaps at the end he was reconciled to their variety while still maintaining the opinion he had expressed many years before in his satirical poem for the 'Odd Volumes':

> "So much for the Mystics! The Priest waved his rod,
> And Pharaoh replied with a satisfied nod,
> "They're deucedly clever – but Odd! very Odd!

R.A. Gilbert,
Tickenham, Somerset, March 2022

---

29. See pp. 235 to 238 below.

Psychic and Spiritual Papers

1. Some Psychic Memories

A strong wave of interest seems to have set in recently concerning the possibility, or otherwise, of communication with those who have passed over, and I have been often asked to record a few, and perhaps not very remarkable, experiences that have occurred to myself. It may well be that the conclusions I have arrived at are not those which would commend themselves to convinced spiritualists. In fact some spiritualistic friends have told me that I have seen enough to convince the most hardened doubter, but instinctively I have always applied the old lawyer's habit of weighing evidence, and where two or three possible explanations present themselves I do not pledge myself to the acceptance of one only and reject the rest. I hold the view of the old friend of my boyhood, Charles Darwin, that it is the duty of an honest investigator to record impartially every fact that he can ascertain, and then state clearly the deductions he draws therefrom, leaving his readers free to accept or reject his theories, but to be sure that he has honestly told them every fact he knows.

My interest in the subject began many years ago, when I was an undergraduate, and there was much talk of physical manifestations. I was neither a believer nor an unbeliever, I simply wanted to know. I wanted to see, as I said then, 'things move about'. I had seen Maskelyne and Cooke, and Pepper's Ghost, and other clever conjuring tricks. I understood from my studies in physics that there might be unknown forces, perfectly material and scientific, accidentally set in motion; and I knew the theories of discarnate entities, whether of the dead, or of non-human beings, who could produce physical results. But wishing to see for myself the manifestations produced, I gladly accepted an invitation to be present at a materializing séance.

This took place in a disused chapel somewhere in Bloomsbury; I forget the address, I don't think it exists now. The sitters were all strangers to me, but I had my introduction and was welcomed. Candidly I expected to see clever conjuring, but was quite prepared for something uncanny, if such should happen. We were directed to sit round a table in the usual way, the lights were turned down, and a hymn or two was sung. For a long while nothing occurred. Then I clearly saw against the gallery opposite to me, a faint light, which gradually took the appearance of a vague face. I know I could easily have imagined it was someone I knew, but as a fact I didn't. I only thought that this was very plainly a gauze mask with luminous paint. Only I didn't quite see how it got there, or how it was suspended. It was near a pillar, and I thought if it would only move a little to the right I could see how it was done. Immediately, as if in answer to my thought, it swayed to the right. This seemed curious, and I began to wish it would move to the left, and then promptly it did so. Rather astonished, I whispered to a lady next to me that it seemed to move with my will. She replied: 'Of course it does. Would you like to see it closer?' I said naturally I would very much, and thereupon it apparently glided down on to the table immediately in front of us, passing over my hand, and feeling like a bit of damp fog. To me the features, so far as discernible, seemed to be those of a bald-headed man with a white beard, but a lady three or four places off declared that it was most plainly her mother's face. Immediately the medium began to speak, in a quavering falsetto, some very trivial matter; a lady declared it was a message from her mother, of the authenticity of which she had no doubt. Other messages were given to various persons present, which appeared to give them great content, but to me the appearance of the face was the striking and unaccountable fact.

After leaving the room I walked a short distance with the lady who had sat beside me, and who seemed familiar with the circle, and the proceedings.

'What was it?' I queried. 'That face we saw?'

'Just a thought-form,' she replied. 'He thought it, and it appeared.'

'But the other lady took it for her mother, and to me it looked like a man.'

'Really it looks like nothing. But any one's thought can mould it. Perhaps her mother's spirit actually took possession of it. Or again perhaps it was her own subconscious mind. Very likely the message was her own memory of something her mother had said in life. That often happens.'

'Then you don't altogether believe in the spirits of the dead?'

'Not altogether. It may be so. But there are other ways of accounting for what takes place. I come as an inquirer, because I am sure there is no fraud in this circle. But I'm not convinced that it is spirits.'

This opened a new theory to me, which I had not previously thought of: namely, that a strong thought, or imagination, could actually create a visible and tangible image. This seemed to be a possible clue to many things, where fraud was excluded. It was a good many years later that this possibility was confirmed by Alfred Capper, the well-known thought reader. He told me that by making his mind an absolute blank (which by long practice he was able to do) he could see materially before him an image that another person thought of with strong concentration. But he could not tell whether this were a material presentment, or a brain wave, a species of telepathy. I made frequent experiments with Capper at that time, both publicly at his entertainments, and privately, for we were near neighbours then in London. I realized also that this power was by no means rare. There was a popular game at that time wherein one person went out of the room, while the remainder decided on a certain card, which he was to guess on his return. My old friend Dr Todhunter, the Irish poet, told me that the first time he was induced to try this he physically, as it seemed, saw the card thought of floating in the air, and others have told me of the same experience.

During the following four or five years I came to know several well-known mediums, and was present at many séances. I saw all the usual phenomena, I read of the test conditions devised by Professor Crookes and others, and I saw the reproductions of the phenomena by Maskelyne and Cooke, and read any amount of arguments pro and con. But judged by the strict rules of evidence I found them all unconvincing, and mentally recurred to the well-known Scottish verdict 'Not proven'.

I wondered, however, whether the phenomena ever took place under circumstances wherein it was humanly impossible for any preparation to be made, and, to test this for my own satisfaction, I decided to try and get a materializing séance in my own chambers, with a select circle of my own friends, all being inquirers, neither deniers nor believers, but merely in quest of truth. I arranged with a medium to come when I should fetch him, not telling him where the séance was to be held. I personally procured the things he wanted, such as a concertina, a tambourine, a bell, a musical box, etc., and when we were assembled I brought him in a cab. He said it was very doubtful if there would be any manifestation under the circumstances, which were very unfavourable. But there were the ordinary phenomena that have been so often described, and need not be repeated. A curious point, however, was that none of us had the slightest feeling of having experienced anything uncanny or supernatural. In discussing it afterwards we were divided in opinion, whether it had been brilliant conjuring, or the manifestation of some strange unknown force which the medium somehow was able to set in motion, and to some extent control. Either hypothesis was unlikely, because in either case the power would have been worth a fortune to the medium, and he would not have been dependent on the comparatively paltry fees he charged. But we could think of no other theory.

Since that time I have seen very little of physical manifestations, of the knocking, moving of furniture, and levitation nature. Once seen they become wearisome by repetition. But the memory of that face seen in the old disused chapel in Bloomsbury, and the suggestion of a thought-form made visible and tangible to a person with no claim to abnormal sensitiveness, remained as a haunting problem, as also did the whole question of messages alleged to have come from the dead. My experiences with professional mediums have been very disappointing in one way, though extremely interesting in another. Trance mediums have given me messages from friends who have passed over, couched in familiar phrases, in the very tone and manner of the person they were supposed to come from, sometimes alluding to events known to me and to no one else. Convincing enough, I have been told. What more could you ask? But never by a professional medium have I been told anything that was not somehow, consciously or subconsciously, in my own mind. It might be a forgotten, or half forgotten, memory of something said long ago. But it was there. Vainly have I asked to be told something that could not be in my mind. This I have had, but not from a medium, nor with any suggestion of communication from the dead.

A very instructive experience occurred to me many years ago in London. When walking casually down Bond Street, where at that time many clairvoyants, diviners, fortune-tellers, and others of the same kidney flourished, I chanced on an advertisement over a door of some Oriental name which I forget, and the title 'Lady Inspirationist' It seemed a promising sobriquet, with some originality about it, and I inquired at the door about the lady. Apparently her role was to exclude, as far as possible, any knowledge whatsoever of her consultants. One could not give a name, or make an appointment. The fee was a stiff one, but if she was disengaged, you just paid it and walked in. But you were particularly requested to say nothing whatever, and as far as possible not even to indicate by gesture whether what she said was correct or not, as she wished to be quite unbiassed. This sounded promising and original, so, as she was disengaged at the time, I went in. The room, as I remember, had none of the usual accessories; there was nothing mystic or symbolic about it, a somewhat sparsely furnished, very ordinary, sitting-room, with a centre table covered with a red cloth, at which I was directed to seat myself. After a short pause the lady came in, a tall handsome woman, rather of the gipsy type, with a curious intentness of gaze. She looked at me steadily in absolute silence for a minute or so, then sat down opposite to me, and looked into a large emerald in a ring she wore. After about three or four minutes she began.

'You have had a strange and romantic career — '

I may have looked surprised, being conscious of nothing of the kind, but I said nothing and tried to be as blank as possible. She went on without a moment's hesitation, telling a story that quite bore out the opening, a wild yarn of romance and adventure, including an elopement or so, and several duels, among other things, lasting I should say about twenty minutes. Then she suddenly stopped, and looking full in my face said — 'Is that correct?'

'Perfectly,' I replied, 'but it's not me.'

'What do you mean?'

'Well,' I said, 'you have told me almost line for line a story I am writing, which is not yet finished, and which no one has seen. It is locked up in my desk.'

'I saw it. Every incident passed before me as though it were your own memory of your past life, up to the present, and I saw no more.'

'I was wondering how I should finish it off neatly. It is just a magazine shocker, with no merit whatever.'

She was greatly interested, and we talked for some time about it. She told me she had the faculty, when intensely concentrated, of seeing around a person a series of pictures, usually that person's memories, or the images of those who strongly affected him or her. But never before had she come across pictures invented, or imagined, by the consultant.

Thought-forms again, I said to myself, but unconscious thought-forms again, for certainly I was not consciously thinking of my story at the time. But two points seemed to be clearly demonstrated.

(1) That the power, whatever it was, was genuine; and

(2) that there was any amount of risk of delusion, if an imagined story could be mistaken for an actual memory of the events of the past. It would have been perfectly easy for my Lady Inspriationist to have told me (and perhaps believed), messages from dead friends, whose faces she might have seen in my memory. In fact some sprirualistic friends have more than hinted that this was what actually happened. She, however, had no belief in spiritualism. Her gift, such as it was, she declared was perfectly natural, merely a kind of telepathy, developed by a power of concentration.

The idea of thought-forms recurred. Was it possible that the disembodied spirit, say of one who had passed over, could create a thought-form, which a medium could see, and thus convey a message? If so a mine of information lay before us of great value. If, for example, my father could recall to me, through a medium, an incident known only to me and himself (which seems to be a frequent experience, and considered a convincing proof of bona fides), why should not my grandfather, who was an Indian merchant, be able to give me details of his own life, that would certainly be interesting, and might be verifiable from documents. If the object is to furnish proof of the reality of the communication, this would be far more convincing than some trivial detail of domestic life known to myself and the deceased. Or again, why should not my great-grandfather, who raised a company of his own to fight in the American War of Independence, be able to give authoritative details? I have sought in vain among professional mediums for some communication of a fact unknown to me, but demonstrable afterwards.

That such communication is possible, however, by other means, was proved in another experience. Some years ago I hypnotized a lady for insomnia, and discovered by accident that under hypnosis she became remarkably clairvoyant, with a peculiar power of recalling scenes of the past. In this way she gave me many details of old world ceremonies, Druidic and others. She was keenly interested in these, though absolutely unconscious at the time, or perhaps I should say retaining no conscious memory of what she had said. But to prove the genuineness of her power, she asked me to put a test, by asking her a question to which neither I nor any one in the house knew the answer, but to which the answer could be readily ascertained for certain. I thought of the title to a small piece of land whose history I did not know, though I knew where the title deeds were. Accordingly when she was in the hypnotic trance, I told her to go to the lawyer's office, and look for a certain charter, and tell me who signed it. She found the charter without difficulty, but was unable to read the signature, which she said was much blurred and rubbed. I then told her to try and go back from this, and see, if she could, the signing of it; she did so after a little pause, and described a Chapter-House, Monks, and the Abbot writing; I bade her look over his shoulder and read his signature. She gave this without hesitation, and the date. A letter to the lawyers proved the correctness of the information.

The experiences of Alfred Capper and others of seeing thought-forms naturally raised the question whether these are in any sense objective, and this again suggested the inquiry, if they are objective is it possible that they could be photographed? I have inquired of Mr David Duguid, of Glasgow, and the late Mr Antonio, a Clerk of Session in Edinburgh, and a strong believer in spirit photography, whether in their experience they had come across any case of a spirit photograph which could not possibly be in the mind or memory of the sitter, or of some person in the room. I wanted to get some evidence excluding the possibility of a conscious or unconscious projection of some thought-form, that might be recorded on the sensitive plate. However, I could hear of none such. I have seen of course multitudes of photographs in which recognizable forms and faces appear. And if one can be produced wherein a recognizable face, unknown to any one present, appears, it would be a valuable piece of evidence. This may seem a far-fetched idea, but in a scientific investigation it is necessary to consider every possible cause of a phenomenon before definitely pronouncing on any one.

I have myself taken photographs in which curious appearances came upon the plate, but in every case except one they could be easily identified as being possibly in the thought of some one present, and even so I am bound to admit they have not been very remarkable or convincing. The one instance, however, is curious enough to be worth recording, especially as I was trying at the time to make a fake-photograph of a ghostly monk. There appeared on the plate a shadowy impress of a gigantic human torso, very dim and hard to trace, but when examined it was perfectly anatomically correct in every muscle. It was like a white cloud, the head and the lower limbs going off in mist. Now this could not, so far as I am aware, have been in the thought or imagination of either myself or of the friend who assisted me and acted the part of the fake-monk, nor have I been able to find any history or legend of the place that could in any way have accounted for it. This could not in any sense be called a spirit-photograph, and neither I nor my friend, so far as I am aware, possessed any mediumistic qualities. So this experience, though curious, has, I think no evidential value. At the same time I am convinced that there are many as yet unexplored mysteries, on which light may be thrown by photography.

It is of course well known that the sensitive plate can record rays and waves invisible to the human eye, and moreover the science of sensitizing plates is yet in its infancy, and we may deem it quite within the regions of possibility that not only thought-forms, but beings and intelligences at present only dimly guessed at, may become objectively known, and scientifically investigated by some form of photography. On the subject of automatic writing I would preserve a very open mind. In common with, I suppose, a vast number of investigators, I have seen such leagues of drivel going under this name, and often regarded by the recipients with an awestruck reverence as being little short of a divine revelation, as to cause one to wonder what kind of discarnate entity could produce such utter banality. And then, occasionally, one meets with communications of real value obtained in this way, such as *The Letters of a Living Dead Man, The Gate of Remembrance,* and others the names of which will readily occur. Whence come these?

One instance is in my memory where the origin of an apparent automatic writing was definitely traced. A doctor who practised a good deal in hypnotism had a very sensitive patient, whom he was able to influence by absent suggestion, telling her for instance to take a dose of a certain medicine, or to go and lie down, or whatever simple action he thought good for her. Occasionally he willed her to write her symptoms, and once, when I was with him, he said he thought he could will her to write from dictation. I questioned whether he could will her to write anything that was not in her mind at the time, and as a test he asked me to write some simple sentences, which he would then try and will her to write. The patient was then living several streets away; I wrote a sentence or two, and the doctor concentrated his will on her, ordering her to write the sentences I gave him. Half an hour later we walked round together to the patient's house. She told us that she had felt a sudden and unaccountable desire to take a pencil and write; she had no idea what she had written, having kept it to show the doctor. It was recognizably the sentences I had written for him, some words were left out, some were transposed, many misspelt, but there was no doubt that it was an attempt to reproduce those sentences. The patient was convinced that it was a manifestation of automatic writing, of which she had heard something, and was very anxious to know what it meant, and what spirit was communicating. The doctor was reticent at that time, I believe he enlightened her afterwards; but she never wrote anything except under the dictation of his will.

I trust that these few fragmentary, and perhaps rather trivial, memories may not be considered iconoclastic. I have personally no doubt of the survival of consciousness and of individuality, or of the power of those who have passed over to communicate with those left behind, under appropriate circumstances and conditions. Indeed I have myself had evidence of such communications, convincing to me, though possibly not to any one else. But the methods have been none of the ordinarily accepted ways of communications. Neither by séances, nor mediums, nor rappings, nor knockings, nor tippings of tables. Not by ouija board, or planchette, or any of the parlour toys. All of these I know, and have seen them work, but so far as messages from the Spirit World are concerned not one has come with evidence to satisfy an old lawyer. Far be it from me to deny that others may have conclusive evidence of messages, obtained through these sources or others like them. The number of able men who have recorded their convictions, after most searching investigation, under strictest test conditions, would render any such denial an impertinence. I can only say that such evidence has not come to me, and until it comes I must preserve an open mind. In conclusion I may perhaps be permitted to record an argument I once heard between a spiritualist and a Roman priest on the subject of Reincarnation, which the priest did not admit, but pursued the Socratic method of questioning his opponent.

'You hold,' he said, 'that between incarnations the soul passes to a kind of intermediate state in which it retains its consciousness, and its interest in those it has left behind.'

'Undoubtedly.'

'And in that state do you say it is active, or is it entirely idle?'

'Unquestionably it is active. After a certain period of rest it is busily engaged in doing the work set it to do.'

'Has this work any connection with this world, and with those whom the soul has known and loved here?'

'We believe that the spirits that have passed over are constantly anxious to help those whom they have loved here. That is the reason they are often so keenly desirous to find some means of communicating. Clumsy and seemingly trivial means they often are, but this is due to our denseness of perception.'

'So then there are two worlds, or planes of existence. May we call them incarnate and discarnate; and the soul alternates between them. Is this a fair statement?'

'Not quite our way of putting it. Still I cannot say it is wrong.'

'Then would you say, practically, that a death on one plane is a birth on the other, and vice versa?'

'It has been so expressed, and it seems a fair analogy.'

'Then the soul that enters into a new-born baby was previously existing on what, I believe, you call the astral plane, and when that baby comes to old age and dies here, it will in fact be born again on the astral plane?'

'It will return to the astral plane. But it won't be a baby there, the conditions are different.'

'So be it. But at any rate it dies here, and is born there, according to the conditions of that plane. I need not say born as a baby.'

'Yes! that would be so.'

'And when its appropriate time comes it dies on that plane and is born on this, according to the conditions of this plane, that is as a baby?'

'Yes.'

'In the intervening time it has been working on that plane, doing good among its comrades, and, we presume, interested in its work. Now have you ever met man or woman who retained the smallest memory of his or her prenatal work on the astral plane? Any desire to communicate with or to help the comrades with whom it had been associated? Any looking back, in fact, to its prenatal conditions?'

'There have been many cases of memories of past incarnations, of work begun in the last incarnation, left unfinished, and taken up again. These have been some of the strongest proofs of reincarnation.'

'Possibly. But that's not the point. Those, even if true, are earth memories, continued on earth. What I am asking for is the astral. You claim that it exists one way, between the dwellers on earth and those who have passed on. Logically it should exist the other way also, between the dwellers on the astral plane and those who have come into incarnation. But of this there seems to be no evidence. If astral dwellers (you see I have to coin words which probably are not your words) look back to their earth lives, why should not earth-dwellers also look back, and watch and help friends and comrades they loved, worked with, and left?'

'Possibly there may be such memories. I never heard of them. I might suggest, that those on the astral plane are higher, purer, nobler, than those left behind on earth, and therefore they require no help, while their friends here may, and do.'

Whether the spiritualist fairly stated his case, or whether there were points he did not make that might have been made, I cannot say. But it seemed to me that the priest had stated a difficulty that I have never yet seen adequately met.

Yet after all the difficulty may not be so great as at first appears, if we take the idea, held I believe by many spiritualists, that it is only for a measurable, and comparatively short time after physical death on this plane, that the spirit remains in touch with this earth, and its former life on earth, and those left behind. After this (I don't know that any definite term has ever been set) it is taken away to higher, and more distinctively spiritual, avocations on the astral plane, or whatever plane it may inhabit, and only communicates with those on the earth-plane on special occasions, and for special purposes. If then the analogy holds good, it would only be in the first years of infancy that the incarnate spirit would remember its astral, prenatal life, its comrades, and its work in that life. And what do we know of the memories or fancies of early infancy, before the knowledge of the conditions of the earth life have fairly dawned on the infant mind? May not Wordsworth's fancy of 'trailing clouds of glory' have some real substantial truth behind it? And the golden dreams of childhood, the child's love of fairy tales, and ready belief in all the beauties behind the outward veil of things, be in fact a memory of the prenatal state, a perception of a deeper truth than our grosser senses of mature life can reach to! Nay! may not the child possibly be giving help and counsel to its former comrades, in a way we cannot comprehend, and the child cannot explain to us, and which pass from its memory as it gradually adapts itself to the conditions of incarnate life?

[Reprinted from the *The Occult Review*, Vol. 31 No. 5 (May 1920), pp. 269-79.]

2. A Haunted Church in Munich

My chief object in writing down the following experience is the hope that perhaps some reader of the *Occult Review*, who is familiar with Munich, may be able to throw some light upon it, or may have had similar experiences. The whole subject of places accursed, for some reason or other, is extremely interesting, but there is always a difficulty in getting accurate details. There is little doubt that there are many places in this country of which grisly tales might be told, but the owners are naturally reluctant that these should become public property, and stories that are told are, for the most part, veiled by initials; and also the temptation to the narrator to touch up and make a good yarn seems well nigh irresistible when the means of verification are excluded. I have, therefore, endeavoured to give a plain and unvarnished account of my own experience, of a place that anyone can find and visit for himself, and those who have the opportunity can examine the history of. The chief importance of the story appears to me to lie in the fact that I stumbled on it by pure chance, knowing nothing of its history, or of anyone else's experiences.

It is, of course, well known that the mediaeval formula of consecration included a curse upon whomsoever should violate, or turn to secular uses, ground or buildings which were solemnly dedicated to the service of God, and Joyce's *Doom of Sacrilege*, continuing and expanding the little work by Sir Henry Spelman entitled *Churches not to be Violated*,[1] contains many instances of the fulfilment of this anathema. But the history of the Munich church seems to go farther and deeper, and to be more akin to the curses invoked on the violators of certain Egyptian mummies. It is certain that experiences of this kind often arise from suggestion. An imaginative or sensitive person, going to a place that has an evil repute, or about which grim tales are told, will feel or perhaps see things that they expect to see and feel. Or, even if there be

---

i.e. Sir Henry Spelman, *De non temerandis Ecclesiis: a Tracte of the Rights and Respect due unto Churches*. London, 1613, and J.W. Joyce, *The Doom of Sacrilege and the results of Church Spoliation*. London, 1886.

no known stories, the mere aspect of a gloomy haunted-looking place will predispose to the sensation of horror, and perhaps to the visions, of ghosts that are imperceptible to ordinary mortals. But these predisposing causes were entirely excluded in this case.

It was about ten years ago that I was in Munich, on the way to the last Passion Play at Oberammergau. I knew Munich superficially, but by no means intimately, and on the first evening that I was there I strolled out, somewhat aimlessly, to explore. The Hans Platz is well known, with the picturesque gateway flanked by two towers with clocks leading to the Neu Hause Strasse. A few hundred yards along this street on the left hand side is the show church of St. Michael. This, however, did not attract me. I knew it of old, and considered it not much more than a museum of some fine pictures and carving. But a short distance beyond was a long bare wall, rising sheer from the pavement, and bearing some torn affiches. A garden wall, I thought. But for some unaccountable reason it gave me a sensation of something horrible and uncanny. I looked up and found that it was of a great height, bare and blank, rising high above the tops of the houses right and left of it. I stepped out into the street to try and see what it could be, and then I saw that it was surmounted by a roof sloping backwards at a vast height from the street. High up were remains of arched windows bricked or boarded up. But beyond the narrow roof rose another wall pierced with gothic windows, their tracery broken and destroyed, some of them boarded, some partially glazed, and above this a high-pitched roof. Clearly it was a vast church, but how it came into that condition there was nothing to show, nor was there any apparent way in. But, as I looked at it, the feeling of horror increased, amounting almost to physical fear, such I have never before felt of anything. The enormous size of it, the desolation, gave it an air of menace, as though it were some great brooding demon threatening the town. I found then that, without a word spoken, my companion had precisely the same feeling. It was an evil place, and we hurried past it as quickly as possible, and felt greatly relieved to be again among the ordinary sights and sounds of Munich.

I was naturally very greatly interested in this building, which I had never noticed before, and on my return to the Hotel Belle Vue where I was staying, I studied maps of the city, and the usually accurate and exhaustive Baedecker, and several other guide books, but could find no notice of this church. The hall porter, generally a mine of information concerning everything of note in the town, was equally unresponsive. No one seemed to know anything about it. There was a Customs warehouse somewhere in that neighbourhood. This was all the information I could get. Next morning I set out again, determined to find an entrance somehow. This time I went alone, and experienced the same sensation of brooding evil, of a vast sinister presence. The entrance, if there were one, must be on the other side away from the Neu Hause Strasse. I skirted round, and finally, after several vain attempts, found the way by narrow by-lanes to the wall of the church, on the other side, and here there was a door. Apparently it was a private way. The place was not open to the public, and I was trespassing. But as it chanced no one challenged me, and I went straight up to the door and went in. Very reluctantly, for I felt a strange force as it were pushing me back, and warning me. Never so far as I remember have I felt such reluctance to enter any building, and it was only by a great effort that I conquered the feeling sufficiently to go in. It was quite obvious what the building was. A huge church had been entirely gutted of its contents, and transformed into a warehouse. Many workmen were employed moving heavy bales of goods, wheeling trolleys, etc., and I could not help being struck with the heavy depressed look of them in the dim light. They might well have stood for the spirits in purgatory, labouring ceaselessly at eternal and profitless tasks. The enormous size and height of the building was even more apparent here than from the outside. The lower windows had been built up, and the walls to the height of some dozen or eighteen feet had once been whitewashed, but now, stained with damp and coated with the dirt of many years, were scrawled over with ribald inscriptions, and blasphemous drawings. Above this the old painting had been left, and some of the religious emblems might still be traced. The upper windows were mostly broken, some boarded up, and their tracery, that might once have been beautiful, was broken and ruined. Whether it were fancy or not I cannot say, but to me the whole place seemed filled with a ghastly emanation, oozing from the floor and the walls as of a charnel house. But above all, the one definite sensation was that of acute physical fear. Without claiming to possess any greater courage or strength of nerve than the ordinary man, I can say truthfully that this is a sensation I very rarely experience, and I was correspondingly annoyed and ashamed, but there it was. No sooner had I walked half a dozen yards into that building, than the very fear of death came over me irresistibly, and a feeling of sudden weakness and collapse, so that I wondered if I should have strength to gain the door again, and the workmen appeared like shadowy fiends rather than solid, material, beer-drinking Germans. It was a distinct effort to gain the door again, and I was right glad to be in the open air, where in a very few minutes all the unpleasant effects disappeared, but I felt the evil influence of that church all the time I was in Munich.

I tried in vain to learn anything of the history of that building. Some people apparently knew something about it which they would not tell, there was a distinct reluctance to speak of it, and all professed ignorance of anything beyond the fact that it had been acquired by the Government for a Customs warehouse. Obviously then there could be nothing of suggestion in my sensations, of which, to tell the truth, I was heartily ashamed, but which I was totally unable to banish.

On my return to London I inquired of a friend who knew Munich well, and who told me at once that he had experienced precisely the same sensations, and, as in my own case, utterly without any previous knowledge of the place. He had been on his way to deliver a lecture, and on passing the church was so overcome by an utterly unreasoning terror, that he had to take a cab to his destination, and could only pull himself together to give his lecture after a stiff glass of brandy. The feeling was much less afterwards, but never wholly left him. He often walked a long way round rather than pass the church. He had noticed also that the passers-by usually went to the other side of the road instinctively, though on inquiry they did not know why. He, however, had found the history of the place in the municipal archives, and elsewhere. According to his researches it had been originally the site of a temple of some very corrupt heathen rites before the Roman times, where human sacrifices had taken place. Afterwards, under the Romans, it had been the scene of the later and very depraved Mithraic worship, and of various abominations of the corrupt later Empire. After Constantine a Christian church was built there, but it was recorded that no proper exorcisms had ever been performed, and some of the Fathers of the Church were greatly perturbed in mind concerning it. The history, however, was a blank till the Middle Ages, when it became a headquarters of the Inquisition, with gruesome stories of torture chambers underneath. It was said that some of the instruments of torture in the Nuremberg collection were brought from there. After this various orders held the great church, but scandals grew and multiplied. Nothing seemed to prosper with the building, and at last it was purchased by the Government for a Customs warehouse. Since that time, my friend told me that statistics proved that among the workmen employed there more cases occurred of insanity and suicide than in any other establishment of the same size in any part of Germany.

So far went my friend's testimony, which I had the fullest intention of attempting to verify by a search in the municipal records of Munich on my next visit, but that visit never came off. Other holiday expeditions intervened, and then the war put an end to all travel in Germany indefinitely. Possibly, however, this brief account may meet the eye of some one more conversant than I am with the history of Munich, who may throw some light on the story of this old church, which apart from anything else is itself sufficiently remarkable from its vast size, and strange desolate appearance, to rouse curiosity.

Later I found that my experience was by no means unique. In the following year, passing through Paris on the way to Brittany, I told the story of my experiences to a friend now dead, who was a mine of quaint stories of the supernatural and occult, in the hope that he might throw some light on it. Of the history of the church he knew nothing, but of its sinister repute he was well aware.

"Have you ever heard," he said, "of the painter Jules Renaud, who died there?"

I had not.

"I'm not surprised," he said. "He was of small account as a painter, and was better known as a blackguard, and the story of his death made a small sensation at the time, but was carefully hushed up. He was chronically hard up, from vice and incompetence, and reduced to most disreputable shifts to get a living, and he had a creature, a poor old Jew, whom he had got into his power by threats of exposure of some misdemeanour, I know not what, nor does it matter."

This Jew he forced to act as catspaw in various rascalities. It was said that the old man made many attempts to get free, but was never able to shake off the bonds of his tyrant. At last there came a time when Renaud got a commission to copy some pictures in the Pinakothek at Munich, and was engaged in some blackmailing scheme in which, as usual, he employed the Jew as go-between. The Jew's hour of vengeance had come. Renaud, it seems, had been more than ordinarily offensive. The Jew by some means had obtained possession of the key of this building, and he induced Renaud to accompany him, on the promise that he would meet a man who would pay him some large sums. My friend had seen a jotting book belonging to the Jew, containing notes of his accomplished vengeance. Apparently he knew something of the Inquisition history of the place, for his entries began with prayers to the God of Israel to avenge the cruelties and tortures that had been practised on His chosen people by the Christians in this place, and invocations of the spirits of murdered Jews to rise and torment this Christian, whom he would deliver to them, even as the Christians had tormented them; wild rhapsodies, and quotations from the minatory psalms, mixed with Hebrew curses, were scrawled seemingly at random, without any coherence or logical sequence. Then a triumphant entry, that God had heard his prayer, and had delivered his enemy into his power. Cupidity had prevailed over caution, and Renaud had consented to accompany him, knowing not whither he was going.

The succeeding notes were written later, and told very briefly what had occurred. They bore all the evidence of the satisfaction of a man whose prayers have been answered, and his desires fulfilled. Renaud had gone with him through the dark and squalid by-streets, growing continually more apprehensive with every step, arid it needed all the lure of gold to restrain him from turning round and fleeing, before ever they reached the door. Fear and avarice waged an almost equal battle in his mind, as the Jew unlocked the door and bade him enter, to meet the man who was to give him large sums, the reward of some nefarious transaction. But scarcely were his feet over the threshold than the heavy door swung to with a crash behind him, and he found himself alone in that awful vastness, or so he imagined, for in fact the Jew had slipped aside into some hiding-place known to himself, to gloat over the torments of his tyrant. He narrated how Renaud strove in vain to open the door, how he beat on the heavy nail-studded panels, and shrieked for help. A dim light came through the upper windows, but all the floor of the church was wrapt in darkness. He felt his way a short distance along the wall, then terror-stricken rushed back to beat again on the door. Then he seemed to fancy there were some people inside who were laughing at him, and he raved, threatened, entreated, promising anything they might ask of him, if only they would come to his aid, but there was no answer. Then he seemed to see great shadowy forms in the dim spaces of the roof, and he cried to them, thinking they were gods or demons that might hear him, and besought them to take away the terrible eyes that were glaring at him, or to save him from the deadly damp oozing from the floor and walls. But there was no answer from any, and he shrieked and writhed on the floor in abject terror, and the Jew from his hiding-place gloated over his agony. At last he crouched against the door, forcing himself into the corner between the door and the stone jambs, and stood there paralysed, as if seeing something yet more horrible, and visible to himself alone, and lurched forward, dead. My friend told me that he had never read such a ghastly account of a death from sheer terror as was described in gloating detail in the Jew's pocket-book. He dragged the body out into the street, where he left it, after carefully locking the door, and there in the morning it was found.

At the time, the death was one of the undiscovered mysteries. It was only long after that the pocket-book came to light, and by that time the Jew had disappeared, leaving no trace. Of course the story entirely depends on the evidence of this pocket-book. Still it may yet be verified. Some may possibly still remember, or be able to discover, some trace of Jules Renaud the painter. At all events it seems to go to prove, even though there be no truth in it, the sinister reputation of the old church, and that its story was known some forty or fifty years ago; which, so far as I can gather, was about the date of Jules Renaud. This Munich church may be taken as a rather definite and well-marked example of a place cursed or haunted, and susceptible of comparatively easy investigation. But the subject is a wide one, and there are many types of hauntings. In the eastern tales, particularly in the Arabian Nights, we read of various kinds of djinn inhabiting particular localities, especially old religious buildings and burial grounds and affecting in some way or other those who come within their influence, and of these the commonest, and in some ways the most terrible, are those that produce fear, paralysing their victims. Other kinds of djinn may be resisted or overcome by counter-spells, by fraud, or cunning, or by prayers to Allah the All-Compassionate. But the demons of fear can no man deal with, and of these demons the Munich church is an outstanding example.

Many of the waters of Germany are haunted by water elementals, but these are mostly of a kindly character.

Not far from Munich the loveliest of all the Bavarian lakes, the Badersee, lies like a living jewel among the mountains, said by the peasants to be the trysting place of the souls of dead lovers. They tell a story there of a young woodcutter somewhere near Innsbruck, whose betrothed died only a week before their wedding, and he declared that she could never rest in her grave in the cemetery, and that she had gone to the Badersee, and rowed there every night by the moonlight. They put him under restraint, but he escaped, and made his way, walking by night and hiding by day, to the lake, and there the peasants say they still see the pair by moonlight rowing a small boat across, attended by a swarm of fireflies. And they say that if any youth will bring his sweetheart there by moonlight, and they see the phantom lovers, that their union will be specially blessed. This is a kindly haunting. But at the Laacher-see, near Andernach, the elementals bring death to all who rashly trespass on a certain corner of the lake. I was told there that even birds flying over would fall dead. Only it was said that when the Jesuit Fathers were there the evil was kept in abeyance. Another death haunting close by was at the castle of Lahneck, on the Rhine, opposite to Stolzenfels, and the story of this was told me by a former owner of the castle.

Long ago, when it was an open ruin, tradition said that owing to some mediaeval curse it claimed a life every year (some said every five years) and the ruins were dreaded by all the country folk. The castle was bought by a Mr. Moriarty, an Irish barrister, who restored the castle and furnished it in exquisite taste. In my own student days I knew him, and remember many pleasant whist parties in the old castle, so I heard the story of what he declared was the last victim claimed by the old tower. It was a mere shell at that time, the floor of one of the upper rooms of the tower had fallen, and brought down with it the winding stair that had led to the roof. Long years after this, workmen came to repair the tower, I think for Mr. Moriarty after his purchase. At all events he knew all about it, and vouched for the truth of the story. At the top of the tower, when they reached it by scaffolding, there lay a mouldering skeleton, crouched against an angle of the battlements, and beside it hidden in a niche and protected from weather partly by the stones, and partly by some fragments still remaining of a dress, or cloak, was a manuscript book barely legible, but legible enough to make out the tragic story. A girl had trysted her lover to meet at Lahneck, and meaning to play a trick on him had run up to the top of the tower, when the stairway had fallen behind her. She saw her lover approaching, and shrieked to him, but he heard not, and she saw him go away, and days passed and she called continuously from the top of the tower, but none ever heard. She had a notebook and kept a sort of diary, as long as she had strength to write; she records how she tied messages to stones, and threw them over, but none were found; in fact all round the base of the tower was wild ground where none ever came, and probably if her cries were heard they were ascribed to the evil spirits that haunted the castle. She wanted to jump and end all, but courage failed her, and she kept on hoping for a rescue, till she was too weak to move, and could write no more. Mr. Moriarty told me that he had verified the story to the extent of identifying the girl who had mysteriously disappeared, after trysting her lover to meet her at Lahneck. The castle had been solemnly exorcised, and I was assured that the evil spirit, or whatever it was, had been wholly banished, and no victim had been claimed since. What has chanced to Lahneck since the war I know not. I have been told that most, if not all, of the Rhine castles were requisitioned by the Government for fortresses, and probably many of the old traditions are lost. Still there may possibly be some in the neighbourhood who remember the old story of the castle.

The idea that a bridge claimed its toll of victims from its builders recurs in almost every land, and seems to be as old as the building of bridges, and is still as prevalent as ever. When the Forth Bridge was built there were naturally some accidents among the workmen, despite the greatest possible care. I lived in Edinburgh at the time and often went over to watch the progress of the work. The Highland workmen expected a given percentage of deaths, and, so to say, ticked off each fatal accident as a payment on account of the toll due, and lessening the danger to those left. Towards the close of the work one of the officials said to me, "The men are growing very careless now. They say the tale of deaths is full, and there can be no more. There is no need to take care." There were in fact no more fatal accidents after this. I have heard the same story about the building of many large bridges. I once pointed out to a Highlander that a bridge had been built across a canal in the west without any fatal result — "Ach !" he said. "Ye ken they'll no kill a man for a wee bit brig like yon. But Sandy got his foot crushed whatever."

One wonders how far the old mythological stories, of which the Minotaur of Thebes is typical, of a virgin tribute that had to be paid periodically, may have arisen from observation of the periodic toll of victims exacted by a building. The great Palace of Cnossus may have had the same fatal influence, vastly greater in proportion to its size, as was ascribed to the castle of Lahneck. We know that human sacrifices have been offered at bridges to appease the elementals, who would otherwise take toll of the passers over the bridge. After the Tay Bridge disaster an old Highland woman said to me: "There was naebody killed at the biggin' o't (building of it) an' that's why." Whether in fact nobody was killed, I know not. But many believed it.

Other types of curses there are on places. On the Spey near to Craigellachie there is a wood that seemed to have a terror for animals, horses passing through it for the first time would shy, and sometimes bolt, dogs would cower to their masters' heels. I have seen both of these phenomena frequently, and my father was very familiar with them, but no explanation was ever forthcoming. There was a vague unauthenticated, story of a murder, but no one that I ever heard of had ever seen anything there, though some sensitive persons have told me they would rather walk a couple of miles round than go through that wood. The animals after a time got used to it, and seemed not to mind it.

On the shore of Loch Freesa there is a stone circle on a trackless moor which bears a very sinister reputation. To go there, or even to see the stones, however accidentally from a distance, is to invite misfortune at certain seasons of the moon; even cattle have been found dead who have strayed there at these times, so the natives say. Though as to this last the laird was sceptical, but he told me that beyond doubt misfortune had come to some men who had rashly gone there at the forbidden times. This circle is almost unknown, for not even a pathway leads to it, and it is out of sight of any road, but those who fish in Loch Freesa can easily find it. It has a remarkable peculiarity, for the great stone, locally called "the king stone," has unmistakable phallic carvings on it. I sent photographs and sketches of this stone to several experts on stone circles, and one and all declared that it was unique, so far as their experience went, and probably pointed to two different faiths occupying the same sacred place, for no trace of phallicism has been found among the remains of the stone circle builders.

Instances of places accursed might be multiplied almost *ad infinitum*, but cases where the history and the legends can be identified and traced are well worth careful investigation. There are family curses, which seem to be lifted if a new family comes into possession, and others again that haunt every possessor of the land; of the latter class are stolen Church lands, concerning which there are many authentic stories. In some cases the alleged curse is no more than an earth-bound astral, but the publication thereof may ground an action for libel, so caution is necessary. But enough are known to indicate that there are some subtle forces operating behind the veil of matter on material planes, to form a very fascinating field for investigation by the student of the occult.

[Reprinted from *The Occult Review*, Vol. 30, No. 3, September 1919, pp. 138-147.]

3. Divers Hauntings: An Attempted Classification

Ghost stories of many kinds have been familiar from the earliest ages, and their character has varied little. The yams that are spun to-day could mostly be matched in ancient Egypt, and probably were chestnuts then. Sir Richard Burton once said to me that there were only twenty-five original stories in the world, and he had heard variants of them in every country he knew. Be that as it may, the ghost stories that I have heard myself, and those that have come within my own experience, seem to fall naturally into well-defined groups, and yet strange to say there has been very little attempt at classification. In trying to trace the origin of various well-known types of hauntings it has occurred to me that in the causes of the appearances, if only we could form some fairly reasonable theory, there might lie the germ of a system of classifying, which might be of some assistance to scientific investigators, and also a help to those who have an interesting experience to relate. I would premise, however, that this is no more than a very rough and crude attempt, as it were, to make a sort of sketch map of a little-known country, in the hope that it may be of some service to future better-equipped explorers.

Perhaps the commonest class of experiences is that in which some dramatic happening, usually a crime, is re-enacted in detail before a clairvoyante; sometimes, indeed, before persons who are not consciously clairvoyant at all; sometimes in waking consciousness, sometimes in dream. The ordinary theory that the unfortunate souls or astrals of the actors were compelled to remain on the scene of the tragedy, perpetually reproducing the drama, seemed to me to present well-nigh insuperable difficulties. For one thing it involved the necessity of the innocent victim being compelled to share in the punishment, and act out his or her part in the story. This was contrary to all one's ideas of justice. And again, did all these poor ghosts remain, always waiting until there was an audience, or what gave them the clue to start? Did they ever perform without an audience? I never heard of anyone arriving late, and seeing only the conclusion of the scene. One well-defined instance of this kind occurred to myself in an old house in Fife, about which there was a somewhat grisly story of an old man who had murdered his daughter's lover, and with his butler's assistance had disposed of the body. The crime had never been discovered, and the story was generally regarded as a mere romantic invention, on which various embroideries had grown. One day, when I chanced to be staying in the house, I was in the garret where the murder was said to have been committed, with a companion who had something of a clairvoyant gift, and suddenly we both saw the whole scene enacted clearly as in a cinema picture. Especially we both saw the girl rush screaming through the room and throw herself apparently through a blank wall. Coming down from the garret we passed a long line of family portraits, and simultaneously stopped before one. "That was the girl," we both said almost at once. The family history was hunted up, and though there was no hint of the tragedy, there was the record of the girl having had a severe accident, and a broken leg, and some grave suspicions of a scandal which had caused her father and herself to go abroad for some years. Subsequently walking in the garden, we saw in the outer wall of the garret the clear marks of a bricked-up window, just where the girl had appeared to throw herself out.

For all that, and vivid as the appearances were, the impression on both our minds was not that of having seen ghosts, but rather pictures as though recorded in some astral cinematograph. I had read some speculations, I think of Sir Oliver Lodge, to the effect that every event that happens in a place gets itself somehow photographed, preserving a permanent record, which, under certain circumstances, may be recovered. I also recalled Camille Flammarion's wonderful speculations in *Lumen*, wherein he shows how, if we could only get a sufficient distance from the earth, we could see an event an hour, or a year, or any given time, after it actually happened, and therefore that there exists a series of pictures like an enormous cinema film extending from any spot on the earth's surface, recording everything that has happened there.

Modern psychologists are great on the subjective consciousness, and its powers of memory and projection and perception at almost any distance. For details refer to almost any recent book on psychology — T. J. Hudson,[1] for example. Now assuming that these two theories which

---

1. Thomson Jay Hudson (1834–1903) was an American psychical researcher, not a psychologist. Brodie Innes is apparently referring to Hudson's book, *The Law of Psychic Phenomena. A Working Hypothesis for the systematic study of Hypnotism, Spiritism, Mental Therapeutics, etc.* (1893)

are already widely accepted be taken as a basis, the origin of this type of haunting becomes simple and scientific. The subjective consciousness contacting at the place the end of what I may venture to call the astral film, would travel along it with incredible rapidity. We may conceive that the pictures of the tragedy would be so striking and so definitely traced as to attract the physical consciousness. The subjective perception, passing rapidly from picture to picture, would produce the same effect as a material film passing through the lantern and projected on the screen, and the impression on the physical consciousness would be that of a moving picture. This theory, it will be seen, involves no suggestion of a ghost, no idea of any participation of the actors, criminal or victim, who have passed over, and may well be taken as one class of hauntings which form the subject of many dramatic tales.

Yet this does not, of course, exclude the possibility of earth-bound astrals of the dead, or of thought forms projected by the memories or the concentrated thoughts of the living. These form an entirely different class, one or two examples of which have come under my own observation. From the concurrent testimony of ages it may be inferred that the process of death is not instantaneous, but very gradual; the spirit leaving the body passes out much as the dream consciousness passes out, or even in deep meditation of waking dream; it appears to itself to have still a body, the counterpart of that which it has left, and this to itself appears as solid and material as in life. In fact, often the spirit does not recognize that death has taken place. Many stories now told of those who have been killed in battle bear this out. Whether this body be in fact the astral of the person, similar in all respect to the physical body, only far more tenuous, or whether it be a thought form projected at the moment of death to be a habitation or clothing for the freed spirit, I do not pretend to say. Either suggestion would account for many of the experiences which we often hear, and also for the very common class of stories of appearances at the moment of death. At all events there seems to be a form sufficiently material to be seen and recognized by certain persons immediately after death. The many well-authenticated stories of appearances of this kind leave no reasonable doubt of this.

Comparing many stories that I have heard of appearances of this kind, the principle seems to emerge that the more material the person in life the more material will the post mortem wraith be; and in cases of sudden or violent death also it is likely to be extremely vivid at first, though soon fading away. There are multitudes of stories of men killed in the War that illustrate this. The appearance of the clothes they wore in life, often as is recorded with the very rags or stains they had, is in favour of the idea of a thought form projected at the moment of death, and forming a temporary habitation of the spirit.

Now considering that it is at least probable that the thoughts, ideals and character of the person largely determine the thought form of himself that he projects, the astral image that is the temporary habitation of his spirit after death, it would seem to follow that the mote material and gross his ideals, the thicker and harder will be the shell in which he finds himself enveloped, and consequently the more difficult to get quit of. And so the spirit becomes as it is called earth-bound, in a species of prison, retaining much of the characteristics of his earth life, especially the most material and earthly characteristics, and therefore often producing the same effect on surroundings, as his earthly body produced, exciting the same attractions and repulsions as he did in life.

A distinct case of this nature came under my own observation in an old house not far from Westminster Abbey. Nothing particular was heard or seen there. Occasional creakings and knockings, sounds that might be footsteps, but equally might be the natural movements of old panelled walls, or of rats behind wainscots. Yet the house was persistently unlucky, persistently undesirable persons were attracted there, and were hard to get rid of, while pleasant and desirable persons were repelled, and either would not come or would not stay. Especially was this the case with domestic servants. At length a clairvoyant contrived to make a figure visible in the dining-room. It was that of an old man in the dress of the later Georges, untidy, dissipated, and thoroughly disreputable in appearance. A communication being established, the ghost confessed that he was in fact the cause of all the trouble in the house. He had been in life an evil and dissipated man, whose associates were like unto himself, and after death he found himself imprisoned in a body like that which he had inhabited in life, and in spite of himself involuntarily he still attracted the disreputable and vicious, and repelled all who were clean and virtuous. Being interrogated as to whether he desired to get away, he replied that he wished this above all things. Further asked if it would hurt him if his astral shell could be destroyed, he replied on the contrary it would be the greatest possible blessing to him if he could be released. A brief formula of exorcism was sufficient, the shell was destroyed, and thereafter the ill-luck that had haunted the house absolutely and entirely ceased. I have been told many similar cases. Some in which the earth-bound spirit was released by an exorcism performed by a priest, according to a formula known and practised in the Roman Church, and contained in old editions of the Ritual, but now I understand only permitted to Bishops, though every priest is still ordained as an exorcist. I have cited this case because it came within my own personal experience, but similar ones are by no means uncommon. In one case, also well known to me, the earth-bound spirit had both the appearance and the odour of a decaying corpse, and though the owners of the house where it appeared, being very material and sceptical people, neither saw nor heard anything, yet perpetual illness utterly unaccountable permeated the house, and every one who entered it felt immediately depressed and uncomfortable for no assignable cause. It will be seen that the earth-bound spirit is entirely in a different category from the astral memory which I have described, and constitutes a second class of haunting. But it may well happen in some cases that the two may be combined. An earth-bound spirit may be imprisoned in some place, and the story of his life and the reason for his being thus imprisoned may be recorded in what I have venture to liken to a species of astral cinematograph. A priest in one of the Western Islands has told me several stories of haunted houses, the history of which he has seen in moving pictures, and the haunting spirits of which he has himself liberated, by the simple and well-known formula of blessing the house with incense and holy water.

A similar instance was given me by the late Mr. Eglinton, who was asked to investigate a haunted house in Belgium, where ghostly footsteps were constantly heard, and weird shrieks and cries sounded at night. He succeeded in seeing the previous history of the house, which had been part of a monastery whose monks had become very corrupt and dissipated, and had contrived to burrow an underground passage to a neighbouring nunnery. A monk and nun being caught in *flagrante delicto* had been walled up alive in the passage, which had been closed and forgotten. Mr. Eglinton indicated the place, and on examination the two skeletons were found. They were given Christian burial, the place was exorcised and blessed, and the hauntings ceased. I cannot vouch for the truth of the story, and merely give it as it was told to me. But it clearly comes under the category of a combination of the earth-bound spirits and the astral cinematograph or memory pictures.

Another and closely allied class is that of the obsessing earth-bound spirit. Assuming the theory that the material husk which imprisons the spirit retains the characteristics of its earth life, it would naturally follow that about this material husk should linger the desires and passions that were rampant in life, but the body whereby those desires might be gratified is gone. Yet these revenants seem to possess a certain volition and consciousness, and a quasi-hypnotic power of influencing some types of weak and sensitive persons. Whether by this means they obtain some kind of vicarious enjoyment or satisfaction, or whether they actually enter into and use the body of the victim, I will not presume to decide. I have heard many arguments for both theories. Certainly some Eastern schools firmly maintain the theory that a spirit can take possession of another body, and use it as its own. Many Oriental tales are based on this idea, and Indian magicians are credited with the power of throwing their own souls into the bodies of other men, and even of dispossessing and casting out the souls of their victims. But all or nearly all the authentic stories of this class can be equally well explained by well-known phenomena of hypnotism. The obsession by a discarnate spirit is a different matter, and as a rule cannot be so easily explained. A clairvoyant seer of the Western Islands told me that he had actually seen the earth-bound spirits lurking about a burial-ground, and had seen one attach itself to a weak dreamy youth who was wandering near by, and as it were melt into his body, and that the boy, though previously exceedingly temperate, almost suddenly became an incurable drunkard. This he maintained without doubt was the reason of many sudden and violent accessions of criminal passions. And he also instanced the well-known fact, that wherever there has been a suicide it is almost certain that others will follow. This he maintained was due to the obsession of the earth-bound spirit of the suicide, driven by some strange force to endeavour to repeat the fatal act.

We find, then, two types of earth-bound spirits: the former though often terrifying and generally unpleasant, yet quite harmless, except it may be to weak nerves; the latter distinctly evil and mischievous. The manifestations of the latter class of obsessing spirits are obscure, being often hard to distinguish from auto-suggestion, or some other known psychic phenomenon, or in many cases deliberate hypnotism.

There is, moreover, a distinct difference in the appearances of these contrasted types, as described by those who profess to have seen them; the latter, the obsessing spirits as described by clairvoyants, being only vaguely human in shape, fragments of grey mist, with distorted heads and faces, but usually with malignant gleaming eyes. Most clairvoyants, especially in the Western Islands, insist strongly on the eyes, "like the eyes of a soul in hell," one old dame said to me once. But the former type, whether of the truly earth-bound spirit, or that which merely lingers here for a short time after death, is generally definitely human and recognizable, even in clothes, peculiarities of action, and such like; suggesting clearly the idea of the thought form. But the question may arise: Whose thought was it that projected the form?

Two markedly illustrative cases occur to me here. One happened in my father's parish in Kent, where two women simultaneously saw the figure of an old man, the father of one and uncle of the other at the moment of his death, of which at the time they were unaware. The daughter saw him drive past in his gig, as he frequently did, and wondered at his not stopping as usual for a chat on his way. The niece saw him in his Sunday clothes, as though going to church, and carrying his Bible in his hand, and wondered if he had mistaken the day, and why he did not stop and speak. Both were convinced that they had seen the old man actually alive, until they heard of his death. The probability seems to be that the discarnate spirit had passed by, rousing the memory of his personal appearance, and each of the two women had projected a thought form of him in the shape that they most clearly remembered. The other case was told me by a lady whose brother was killed in some small native riot in India. She being, as she said, more than half asleep at the time, saw suddenly and distinctly her brother in an utterly unfamiliar dress, lying dead just outside of a bungalow, with a native knife in his heart. She had never seen any picture of the bungalow, but subsequent inquiry demonstrated that the appearance was absolutely correct in every detail. This would seem to be a thought form projected at the moment of death, or possibly some species of telepathy whereby her subconscious mind was momentarily brought in contact with the actual scene. Many cases have also been recorded in the late war of persons at home, who have seen their friends or relatives wounded, and know exactly how it occurred though they have lived and recovered. These must, therefore, be carefully distinguished from the true earth-bound spirits. Both classes seem probably to be thought forms, but while the former are merely temporary vehicles, which may probably for a short while be informed by the newly discarnate spirit, the latter are veritable prisons, presumably built up by the thoughts and ideals cherished in earth life.

We arrive, then, at various sub-classes of this second class of hauntings, to which must be added the note that the thought form or astral appearance is not necessarily that of the person as we know or knew him or her, but sometimes that person's ideal of himself, or what he would wish to be like. This idea is well brought out in George Du Maurier's wonderful romance of *Peter Ibbetson*. I have heard Du Maurier describe to a select company of intimates how he had himself endeavoured to appear to his friends as he thought of himself and wished to be.

These classes are all of hauntings connected with human beings living or dead. A totally different class is connected with the manifestations of sub-human or super-human entities.

Leaving aside altogether the vexed and often debated question of the survival of animal souls, which have nothing to do with hauntings in the ordinary acceptation of the term, it seems impossible, when we consider the almost infinite variety of life upon the earth, to conclude that the astral plane can be peopled only by beings connected with human life. Inevitably, if we postulate life at all, we must postulate as great a variety of nature. If here on earth we see the mischievousness of the monkey, the active malevolence of some kinds of snake, the ghastly cruelty as we should deem it of some creatures, the fidelity of the dog, and multitudes of other variations, not only of form but of character and nature, we naturally assume that some similar variations exist on other planes outside of human experience, and as difficult to contact and comprehend as are animals. The folklore of many races and countries has to some extent classified and described these. The Poltergeist, the Leprechaun, the Banshee, under various names are met with in almost every country. The fauns and nymphs, the nereids and dryads of ancient Greece, have their congeners to-day in pixies and fairies and brownies. But the more terrible forms of were-wolf, ghoul and vampire are more rare, and only met with in certain localities. These all clearly belong to the sub-human types, and of them some seem to be more material, and therefore to manifest more easily, than others. Thus though the fairy type is of almost universal distribution, and every country has its fairy legends, with a marked similarity, they are seldom seen save by special persons; they produce few, if any, material or physical phenomena. On the other hand we meet with constant cases of material disturbances apparently causeless and frivolous, furniture thrown about, articles dragged from their places, sometimes even persons struck and injured by things thrown by no human hand.

This is no uncommon experience in haunted houses, and is sometimes the only evidence of haunting that is alleged. Some well-authenticated stories have appeared in the pages of the *Occult Review*, and have generally been ascribed to Poltergeists, But the nature of a Poltergeist, why or how he plays these seemingly meaningless pranks, or why his activities seem to be confined to certain places, remains utterly obscure. We can only dimly know him by his effects. Yet he is a definite haunting, and may or may not be accompanied by an earth-bound spirit, or other manifestation of human connection. So far as the ordinary stories go, the Poltergeist seems to be invisible and immaterial, at least in our sense of gross ponderable and perceptible matter, and yet to have the power of exerting a physical force, often a very considerable force, and a certain consciousness and will mischievous and purposeless rather than malevolent.

If we assume that to produce a physical effect some physical cause is necessary, and that the recorded pranks of the Poltergeist seem to indicate a definite, if purposeless, intention, the conclusion seems to be that a discarnate being is able to set in motion some unknown force; perhaps the same force which causes levitation in the séance room. Many of us have seen heavy tables lifted and whirled about a room without the contact of a human hand, and many tales have been told of heavy furniture, boxes, etc., having been heard dragged about in empty rooms, and found displaced in the morning. There seems at least a probability that the two classes of phenomena may be connected, and if we assume, as I believe Sir Oliver Lodge assumes, that there may be some force as yet unknown to science, which may be set in motion and to some extent, albeit unconsciously, controlled by human sitters at a séance, it is not a very wild assumption that there may exist a discarnate entity, whose will may equally set in motion and control the same or a similar force.

Granting these assumptions, the Poltergeist falls into line and becomes a recognizable class of haunt.

But the question still remains, why should the Poltergeist manifest only in certain places? the localities being apparently as meaningless as his actions. No satisfactory reason, so fax as I know, has ever been assigned for this type of haunting. It may be a house, or a cave, or a wood; it may or may not have a history behind it; but generally it appears to be quite independent of any human actions good or bad. Yet a possible solution might be suggested in the nature of the unknown force which produces the manifestations.

Many guesses have been made at the nature of this force. The Hertzian waves have been suggested, Radium and the forces of disintegrating atoms, even X-rays have been discussed with a certain degree of superficial learning, but the results have not been convincing. The force remains unknown, save for certain unexplained, perhaps unexplainable, effects. Yet some suggestions emerge which may be productive of a solution of these problems in the future. It is possible to control the motions of a floating vessel from the shore, or the motions of a balloon in the air. It is but a short step from this to move, and control the motions of, a table or chair without any physical contact, and assuming the existence of a discarnate will capable of exercising that control, the problem of the Poltergeist is half solved. But one asks why the manifestations should take place only in certain definite places? why, in fact, should the Poltergeist be a haunt? An ingenious suggestion is that in the places where the manifestations occur there are electric, or magnetic, or other conditions of soil or conformation of the ground, or the like, favourable to the generation of the unknown force (which perforce we must call by this clumsy name till we get a better acquaintance with it). If, therefore, we look on the discarnate will as an engineer or electrician, of mad mischievous mood and a playful disposition, and a particular locality from soil or conformation as the dynamo and engine, we have our Poltergeist full blown, and fully equipped, and even liable to some kind of scientific investigation.

Clearly, then, here we have a totally different class of haunting, as to which it would be useless to try to interrogate what I have called the astral cinematograph, and the Poltergeist and his congeners instead of being among the most inexplicable of phenomena, may ultimately come to be the most nearly within the domain of physical science, and his relation to the phenomena of levitation and other manifestations of the séance room may also be fruitful sources of inquiry; though these may perhaps dethrone some of our pet dreams of spirit hands, and may rob the Poltergeist of some of his terrors.

If there be any truth in this theory of the Poltergeist, the same would be applicable to the more definitely evil and sinister manifestations of the were-wolf, the ghoul, and the vampire. The locality of their manifestation is much more limited than that of the others whom I have mentioned, but the records of their activities is as clear and fully attested, and their haunting, that is to say their practical confinement to a special locality, equally definite.

These sinister and terrible manifestations are, therefore, true hauntings, the basis of which appears to be that of a discarnate will, able to set in motion and control some physical force, whose nature is at present unknown, or only dimly guessed at. But they are distinguished from the activities of the Poltergeist and similar entities, in that they are not merely mischievous with a comparatively harmless mischief, they are malignantly hostile to humanity. And if we may compare the will of the Poltergeist to that of a monkey who snatches a lady's hat, these seem rather like that of the deadly snake who hangs from a tree waiting for its victim, and strikes to kill without any provocation. In this country we have but little experience of these malignant hauntings, and are forced to depend on records from remote places in the Carpathians and elsewhere, which are usually regarded as travellers' tales, and either wholly discredited, or scarcely seriously considered. Yet they are vouched for in many cases by the sworn testimony of well-known and capable witnesses. Some of these are cited by H. P. Blavatsky in the *Secret Doctrine* and may be investigated by the curious.

Moreover, in hauntings of this class there is often a suggestion (if no more) of the earth-bound spirit. Thus, taking the Vampire legend, the basis is usually a corpse preserved in some ghastly half-life by physical blood drawn from living bodies, and conveyed to it by the haunting entity. This is sometimes taken to be the earth-bound spirit that once inhabited that body, but in other tales an obsessing spirit. This materializes at one time in the form of a bat, at another in the form of a body, apparently human, in which form it throws its victims into an hypnotic sleep. The fact that only in certain districts, as for example in the Carpathians, are Vampire legends frequently met with might indicate that some geological formation or some electric or magnetic peculiarity rendered possible the generation of an obscure force in those localities favourable to these special manifestations, even as on the material plane certain localities are favourable to certain types of deadly mosquitoes. Some scientific truth may underlie Bram Stoker's conception in Dracula of the necessity of bringing earth from the Carpathians for the manifestation of his vampire count in England.

With these manifestations may be compared those of certain materializing séances, where the thought form projected seems to draw the material whereby it becomes visible and tangible from the physical body of the medium, leaving him drained and exhausted.

That this effect can take place in a séance room or anywhere distinguishes this phenomenon from a haunting properly so called. But it raises the question how far the conditions favourable to the generation of the force producing the physical effects can be artificially created. Assuming this to be possible, we may have here the clue to yet another class closely akin to hauntings, of curses on lands and on families possessing them, as in all the well-known tales of curses resting on the owners of stolen Church lands. In a former number of the Occult Review I have told the story of a haunted church in Munich, which may well be an example of this class. The converse of this would be the blessing resting on sacred sites, such for instance as Lourdes.

The detailed examination of this class, however, would occupy, and would well deserve, an article to itself. My object in this very rough sketch is merely to indicate some general principles of classification. Without some such principle our ghost stories, and our psychic experiences, lose a great part of their value, and we perhaps too readily accept the popular theory that would explain every psychic phenomenon as the work of some one who has passed over, or as an enthusiastic lady said to me not long since, "the dear spirits, who are always close round us, and trying to talk to us." Personally, I set no value on this attempt at classification, save as an attempt which I hope may induce others of wider experience in such matters to formulate definite categories to which well-authenticated stories may be reduced. I am convinced that such a classification on truly scientific lines would add enormously to the value of the experiences of which we have now such an abundant crop.

[Reprinted from *The Occult Review*, Vol 32, No. 2 (August 1920), pp. 83-94.]

4. Concerning Obsessions

The word is in constant use. But what precisely we mean by it probably many would be at a loss to say. Any strong impulse that we do not personally share is often dubbed an obsession, and generally ultimately attributed to some form of brain-lesion. Political opponents are very commonly said to be obsessed by an idea, the implied inference being that no wholly sane person could hold such views. Yet obsession has its definite meaning, which modern usage seems to have considerably departed from. Originally it meant an investment, or blockade by an enemy, whereby a city or a country lost some part at all events of its freedom of action; and applied to an individual, an investment by some external power, causing the loss of his freedom of action, and this external power was held to be supernatural; something from outside, entering in and dominating the will.

The materialism of a century ago, refusing to believe in external supernatural forces or beings, took refuge in the theory of brain-lesions, or of natural human qualities, such as fear, anger, jealousy, revenge, and the like, temporarily upsetting the sane balance of the mind, and all the supernatural beings in whom our forefathers believed were sent to limbo; and to be possessed of a devil merely meant to suffer from a well-known or unknown type of insanity, and to believe in the old stories of obsession was to be regarded with a certain pitying contempt as a superstitious fool.

But the experiments of Mesmer, and all the array of hypnotists who followed, brought such convincing evidence of some external force that had power to limit or destroy, temporarily or permanently, a man's freedom of action, that popular ideas had to undergo a fresh change, and the word obsession to put on yet another new dress. No external supernatural power could be admitted, but the external power of another human being might control the will and the actions. The citadel of the house of life might be invested and controlled by an external force indeed, but a human one, and by known and scientific means, and thus we were preserved from the superstition of believing in supernatural beings, or admitting their power over us. Materialism was still triumphant.

Spiritualist séances raised further clues and questions. Phenomena that undoubtedly occurred were not to be accounted for by ordinary human agency. Of course fraud was alleged, and unquestionably fraud existed in very many cases. Also hallucination accounted for much, and imagination for even more. Hypnotism also and telepathy explained some things. But after making the fullest allowance for all of these there remained a large quantity of phenomena only to be rationally accounted for on the assumption of entities, whether superhuman or subhuman, having some kind of power of coming into contact with mankind, and these seem to be possessed of a rational will.

This much being granted, the materialist theory vanishes. It never really had much to commend it, being founded mainly on the human conceit which refused to acknowledge that there was anything in the Cosmos imperceptible to man's senses, or to the conclusions of his reason, or any being anywhere higher than man.

When once we recognize that there are probably around us beings imperceptible to our senses of will and power and intelligence, whom we can affect and who can affect us, it is clear that the ideas of old races and old religions cannot be contemptuously set aside as gross superstitions, unworthy of consideration by modem enlightenment. Whether these or any of them be the spirits of human beings who have passed through the gates of death, whether they be friendly or hostile to humanity, whether they be actually discarnate, or clothed in a material form which is usually imperceptible to our senses, and whether in the latter case they are able, or can be compelled, to modify such form so as to be perceptible, or as it is said to materialize, all these are most interesting and important questions, but do not affect the main issue, which is that of the existence of such beings. And this may now be generally conceded.

An analogy here is almost irresistible, between these impalpable, imperceptible beings and the germs or bacteria which we now know surround us continually, and affect us through all our lives for good or ill, but many, if not most of which are utterly imperceptible to our strongest microscopes.

This analogy is extremely useful and far-reaching. I shall allude to it further presently — merely noting in the meantime one point of divergence. Germs or bacteria, however minute and imperceptible from their minuteness, are still material. But we assume that there may be some among the beings or entities of which we are speaking which are wholly discarnate, having no material body, however tiny or tenuous, and which yet have the power to affect, to move, even to rule and dominate material bodies.

And this is not such a wild fancy as some of the last century rationalists would have supposed. For hypnotic experiments have demonstrated that thought, even at a considerable distance, can affect the subject, and well-known phenomena of telepathy prove that ideas may be transmitted for practically any distance, and in both these cases the force is certainly discarnate.

We have then the theory which certainly accounts for a large range of observed facts, that there exist around us conscious and intelligent beings capable of entering into communication with us, and of affecting us in various ways, but not perceptible to our ordinary senses, some with and some possibly without material bodies. And as regards their imperceptibility we have to remember the limitations of our bodily senses. We are only conscious of vibrations. When we say we see a thing, all we know is that certain vibrations impinging on the retina of the eye produce an image which the brain can translate, giving a sensation of colour or of form; but the range of vibrations which the eye can perceive and register is very limited. We know scientifically that vibrations too rapid for the eye to register, or too slow, produce no image at all; and hence we say that the photographic plate can see what is invisible to the human eye. And here and there are abnormal individuals whose eyes can register what is invisible to the normal senses.

Now if these beings have power to affect us, as has been said, it is clearly very important for us to have some knowledge of their nature, of the extent of their power, whether they are friendly or hostile to mankind, and if hostile how we may protect ourselves.

In the case of germs and bacteria, multitudes of diligent workers are continually labouring to investigate, to classify and arrange the known species, to isolate and identify those hitherto only known by their effects. But as to the beings of whom we are now speaking, hardly any real scientific investigation whatever has been attempted. And what there has been has been mainly confined to one point, namely, how far are the observed phenomena due to the discarnate spirits of those who were once in human bodies, and have now passed over. Or how far the incarnate human spirit can emerge from the material human body, and produce material phenomena without ordinary material means.

Valuable results have been obtained in these investigations. But that the scientific side is still in its infancy is proved by the disputes concerning the origin of unquestioned phenomena. Thus a man is perfectly certain that at a séance he has received a message from his son, or brother, or wife, lately dead. We assume there is no question of fraud; another equally well qualified observer is equally sure that the supposed message is nothing but a subconscious memory, either of the recipient himself, or, without his conscious knowledge, telepathically communicated to the medium, who is also unconscious of the process. Another equally positively lays down that a mischievous spook has assumed the image and likeness of the deceased, in order to perpetrate a delusion out of sheer wantonness. Each one seems absolutely certain of his own theory, and refuses to listen to any contrary arguments.

We may leave out of count here the theory of communication from the spirits of those who have passed over, with the remark that hitherto those that have been recorded have added little to our knowledge. They seem merely directed to proving that such communications are possible, and that the survival of the consciousness after death is no fable, but a vital truth, and that the spirits of those we have loved are still with us and able to protect and help us.

This, however, leaves all the question of the subhuman, superhuman, and nonhuman entities unaccounted for. The séance rooms give us phenomena, but little if any scientific knowledge. Evil influences are present, we are told, or good influences. Angels it may be, or demons, or mischievous elementals, but of their nature and character nothing seems to be known, Evil spirits sometimes enter into a man or a woman, driving them to actions foreign to their nature. Psychics speak of obsession. Alienists and doctors familiar with mental cases speak of brain deterioration. But there is no real scientific knowledge.

A personal reminiscence, not very remarkable in itself, will serve to illustrate this part of the subject. It was many years ago when I was a law-student in London, having not long left Cambridge, that I was invited to be present at a private séance at the house of some wealthy Jewish friends. A well-known medium was to be there, who, so it was said, was usually controlled by Red Indians, who at that time seemed to turn up constantly in séance rooms. With me went one of my closest college friends, a medical student, but still more an enthusiastic Highlander, possessing (or so he claimed) the second sight. He was practically a spiritualist, I was simply an interested inquirer, willing to believe, if only I might find evidence clear enough, and in the meantime not only willing but anxious to see and hear for myself everything that was to be seen or heard.

The séance was exactly of the normal and usual type. If any materializations were expected they did not happen. I personally neither saw nor heard anything, except a few taps and creaks such as might well be caused by movement of old panelled woodwork, such as lined the room where we were assembled, or maybe rats, intensified by the darkness and the silence. But gradually and contrary to most of my previous experiences of séances, the atmosphere seemed to grow curiously exciting, and slightly fragrant. Something like the bouquet of good champagne, and something like a draught of good champagne was the effect, exhilarating, stimulating. I forgot all about the séance and what we were supposed to be doing. I was thinking of myself. Why was I, in the prime of youth and strength, wasting all this precious time poring over dull books in dingy chambers, stuffing my brain with learning that was profoundly useless to any human soul, when outside was a world full of joy and adventure? Sport and fighting and romance called loudly. Well, at least the séance had done this much. It had opened my eyes. I would linger no longer, the very next day I would shut up the books and be off and away. Where to I was not clear. Big game hunting (then not so common as it has since become). A commission in the Austrian cavalry, then constantly fighting somewhere, and reputed to be the very heart of adventure and romance. It mattered not. Somewhere! Then I heard the voice of the medium speaking, but speaking in a harsh, rather deep male voice, and with broken English: "The great chief is here — The mighty hunter — He calls on all to join in the war path — to drive the pale faces out of his lands."

Then some strange sounds which we were told was Iroquois Indian, but as no one present knew that tongue, it might have been anything. The great chief had a message for one and another of the circle, but nothing for me. To our host and hostess came a salutation and a promise of good to come. And so we adjourned, and I confess with a feeling of disappointment on my part.

My Highland friend had said little through the séance. But in the evening in my rooms over pipes as we discussed the proceedings, he said: "That medium is just cracked on Indians. That was no Indian."

"You recognized him, then? " I queried.

"Of course I did — he came for me. He was our old family pipe. Didn't you hear our war march? "

"No ! I heard nothing. And he had no message for you seemingly."

"Of course not. The tune was his message. It called me to be up and doing. I have been too lazy."

"Then I felt the effect of it. I wanted to go out for adventure, and truth to tell I want it still, and to-morrow I 'm going to see about it."

"Take my advice and don't. I know our Highland tunes. They are over-heady for a Sassenach. Just do as I'm going to do. Buckle hard to work, that's what the tune says."

To make a long story short, I found the impulse fading on the morrow, though still there, and I took my friend's advice. But the idea persisted. The medium apparently was convinced, so was the Highlander: both could not be right. I took an early opportunity to talk with the daughter of the house, a beautiful, enthusiastic, and romantic young Jewess, full of the glory of the Hebrew people.

"Of course it was no Indian," she said. "Why should an Indian come to us? He came for us. It was the Prince of the Captivity." (She had been reading Disraeli's fascinating romance *Alroy*.) "It was the sign of the deliverance of our people. Oh, if only I might be a Judith, and slay one of our tyrants!" Who or what these tyrants might be was not clear, but at all events the girl's enthusiasm had been aroused at the séance, much in the same way as my friend's and mine.

Some time after I asked him again what he thought of it, telling him the girl's experience.

"I think now," he said, "it was no spirit at all. It was an influence that affected us all. But how evoked or whence it came I have no idea. It was a martial influence, an influence of fighting and adventure, and in each one it produced an hallucination of a typical form, such as we associate with that idea — the great warrior chief to the medium, my own family piper to me, Alroy to Rachel — this is not an unfamiliar phenomenon. It is produced by some drugs, the kif of Egypt, the absinthe of France. These confuse the brain centres, and create delusions. You get something the same in hypnotism. But plainly we can no longer regard the phenomena of séances as always the work of spirits of the dead."

This was a great concession, for intercourse with the dead through the offices of a medium, and the proof it afforded of survival of the soul, had been a cardinal tenet of his faith.

But the phrase "a martial influence" set me thinking. The Romans then had known something of similar influences, and had attributed them to Mars, and of course other types of influences to other gods of their pantheon. Here then was at all events an attempt at classification of forces that could influence mankind from without, and an attribution of those influences to intelligent wills. But the Romans were materialist and unimaginative. Earlier races had higher spiritual development and more elaborate and detailed classification of the forces affecting the children of men from without. Might it not well be that in some of these we might find as careful and systematic a study as our scientists now give us of germs and bacteria? Nay, might not the one illustrate the other, and the study of the old myths come to the aid of physical science?

In an old number of the *Occult Review* I told how an Eastern student of bacteriology professed to identify the germ of Typhus fever with the form of Typhon the destroyer, and worked against him a formula of ancient Egyptian magic, and how the doctor who saw the whole performance was reluctantly compelled to admit that the patient recovered. Egyptian mythology gives us many so-called gods hostile to humanity: Typhon and Apophis, Set and Bes, and multitudes more, all distinctly defined with recognizable shapes and attributes, and all with their prescribed formulae for invoking, and banishing, or destroying, as clearly set forth as are the antitoxins whereby we combat germ-produced diseases to-day.

The analogies are even closer in the Hebrew system, perhaps for the reason that they were not regarded as gods, but merely as non-human beings, considered as good or evil according as their effect was beneficent or maleficent towards mankind, and their worship was strictly forbidden. The classification was exceedingly minute and the names in many cases express the forms. The student of the Qabala will recall the classification of the Qlippoth, the subhuman evil beings, described as the distortion and perversion of the Sephirotb, under which name are classified the emanations of the Divine. And the beneficent powers are classified, among many other classifications, as the Angels of the Schemahamphorasch. We may notice here that the evil forces or entities are for the most part grouped as averse forms of the good: indicating how they are to be met and dealt with — in modern scientific language supplying for every toxin its appropriate antitoxin.

As analogy to the germs which enter into the material body causing sickness and disease, we may consider the Thaumiel or Thomiel. These we are told have no bodies, for they are those who seek continually to unite themselves to other bodies and forms. These are described in the Qabala as "dual giant-heads with bat-like wings." But in a mediaeval Hebrew MS Commentary on the Qabala, shown to me long ago by a learned Rabbi, it was said: "Though described as giants, yet may they make themselves so small, that by reason of their minuteness they cannot be seen by man, and thus more easily they unite themselves to the body of man, and so enter in and unite themselves with him." This certainly reads very like the description of disease germs, as it might be written by a Qabalist. It is true that we are considering now mental rather than physical lesions, but we know that very often brain degeneracy is the result of the infection of physical germs, and some of the perverse forms of human criminality are coupled with perfect sanity: as in the recent case of the boy Jones at Abertillery, pronounced absolutely sane, yet possessed with an irresistible desire to kill, causelessly and unprovoked. Any physician of a mental hospital could supply multitudes of such cases.

Material and rationalistic philosophy gives no satisfactory clue to the origin and nature of the phenomena. The Hebrews (perhaps deriving their wisdom in part from Egypt) propounded a theory, which may be briefly stated thus —

"Every event must have a cause — if not a material cause, then an immaterial one (or perhaps it would be more correct to say a cause imperceptible by human faculties). There are multitudes of such events, and all round us are beings capable of producing them. Since mankind are the special and most favoured creation of God, those beings that help mankind are pleasing to God, and those we call angels; those which hurt mankind are opposed to God and evil, and these we call demons or Qlippoth, or by other similar names. According to their observed effects on mankind, and especially on the Jewish race and nation, we divide and classify them and give them names whereby they may be known. They may be seen of some persons in trance, or dream, or vision, and may give definite information and messages, and occasionally, in the case of rarely gifted seers, may be seen openly when wide awake.

Any number of examples of the Hebrew classification can be found in the Qabala, and most forms of what we now call psychic or mental evils may be found represented. To record them would take a volume which no one would read. For one instance — I have mentioned what in séance rooms are sometimes spoken of as lying spirits, producing delusive and untrue images. In the Qabala these are the Ghogiel (or as it is sometimes written Ogiel), who attach themselves to lying and material appearances.

The Hebrew theory was firmly believed in the Middle Ages, and the classification was much further elaborated, and the cultivation of the evil spirits was the foundation of mediaeval black magic. I have in my library a MS. of the names and characteristics of over a hundred evil spirits with their seals (i.e. the geometric symbols whereby they might be invoked or commanded) taken from the Great Grimoire, from Trithemius, and other works on black magic. Also the formulas whereby they might be exorcised, or cast out.

Gross superstition, say the rationalists to-day, refusing even to consider the theory, and the Churchmen follow suit. But have they anything to put in the place? The effects are still here, as clearly as they were then, but are unaccounted for. Brain lesions, they say, degeneracy, obscure forms of insanity. Yes, no doubt. But whence do they come, and why? Following out the analogy of disease-bringing germs, we ask how do these psychic evils, the effects (if the theory be true) of malevolent and discarnate entities, gain entrance to the house of life? Is there any natural and automatic protection guarding the normal and innocent man? We know that physically, against many of the ordinary disease germs, the mucous membrane is an absolute protection. You will not get a sore throat unless the mucous membrane be torn or wounded. But let there be the smallest breach in this armour, germs will settle and enter in, and multiply. Is there any similar armour against the psychic germs?

Here Psychology, albeit a young science only just beginning to feel its way in an unknown country, gives a clue. It is, so they say, on the subconscious mind that the psychic forces and entities take effect. In the ordinary normal material man, the man in the street, according to the slang phrase, this remains subconscious. The evil is buried out of sight and never comes up into manifestation. But with certain abnormal persons the relation between the subconscious and the conscious is much more intimate. These are seers, clairvoyants, clairaudients, and are frequently found in certain races, as the Celts, the Gipsies, and many of the Eastern peoples. From their legends, and from the stories they will tell to-day to those who can win their confidence, it is clear that they know and believe in the evil discarnate entities, and are often able to exorcise them. These natural seers seem to be protected themselves, by some form of natural psychic armour. I have known many in the Western Highlands, and especially in the Islands, and have heard many stories of their relieving or curing others, but never of a genuine seer being himself attacked,

I asked an old man once, who had the second sight, whether it would be possible to develop the gift in one who had not got it naturally.

"Possible, yes!" he replied. "But very dangerous. They would lay hold of him, and drive him mad. I would be no party to anything of the kind." I asked him what of obsession? For he had read much, and knew of the developments of modem spiritualism.

"That is what I mean," he said. "They force open the door and the evil ones enter in, and take possession, and they know not how to cast them out, or how to close the door again."

And here it seems may be the possible outline of a real psychic science. We have the classification of subhuman and superhuman entities that can affect humanity, as made by nations and races who firmly believed in them, and who had the same psychic and mental problems that we have to-day, and devised means of dealing with them. Let us say their deductions were faulty, their observations crude, their classifications unscientific and illogical. Nevertheless it was an attempt, however poor, to grapple with a problem. We have none.

We have the same problems, as shown by our natural criminals, our monomaniacs, our degenerates, and we cannot account for them. We have our natural seers who tell us something of what they see, and their accounts are at least worthy of investigation.

We speak of the universal unrest over all the world at the present day. But if one asks, Why? What causes it? — there is no answer but a shrug of the shoulders. It comes naturally. There are always periods of unrest. In extreme it brings Anarchism, Nihilism, Terrorism, insane forces wherefrom can come no good to anyone. It is a wave of madness. Does this come from some outside non-human potencies actively working with malevolent will for the harm or destruction of humanity? It is at all events a possible theory. The Qabalists recognized the phenomena, and classified the evil potencies producing it as the Gagh-Shekela or the Disturbing ones, or as Oziel, Chazariel, and Aquiel — the breakers in pieces. The name matters little. But the knowledge of the cause is as important as the knowledge of the influenza microbe, or that parasite of the spangle-winged tsetsa fly, that brings the sleeping sickness. The analogy to disease microbes suggests the need for careful investigation and tabulating of what may be called psychic diseases, and distinguishing these from actual brain lesions. And herein is field for very careful inquiry. Autopsy often proves that mental abnormalities may exist though the brain is perfectly normal. Also that what is termed psychism may in time induce a degeneracy of nerve and brain, and the work of the psychic investigator and the mental physician may often overlap. But setting this aside for the moment, the purely psychic abnormalities need exhaustive classification, in order if possible to trace them to external forces and malevolent conscious entities, if indeed they be due to such.

And here the analogy points to a very real danger. The investigators of material disease-microbes, though well equipped with all the theoretical knowledge available, the best apparatus, and though being themselves thoroughly trained, scientific inquirers were well aware of the risks they voluntarily took in the interests of science, and for the good and protection of humanity, and many of the earlier explorers in this field gave their lives for the cause.

Unfortunately we have few such competent observers of psychic diseases and abnormalities. Men like Sir Arthur Conan Doyle and Sir Oliver Lodge have been mainly concerned in investigating the possibilities of communication with those who have passed over, as in the last generation men like Sir William Crookes and many others were concerned with the investigation of physical phenomena. But psychic diseases have received little scientific attention, while on the other hand there have been a multitude of irresponsible and untrained investigators intent mainly on getting phenomena of some sort, without any knowledge of the meaning of what they get, or of the dangers they are incurring.

If the psychological theories are correct, there exists a type of more or less abnormal individuals, in whom the communication between the conscious and the subconscious mind is comparatively open and easy. They perceive the powers and forces, and it may be the beings, that are imperceptible to ordinary humanity, and these are looked on as rarely gifted psychics, from whom great revelations may be expected. And it has been found that by sitting in circle with these, and by the methods well known to spiritualists, the subconscious mind may be opened in others. Natural curiosity, and the attraction of the unknown and uncanny, draw many adherents, and so many little groups and circles are formed, trying for wonders.

All this is much as though ignorant amateurs were to go to fever-haunted marshes, to see what resulted from the sting of the spangle-wing. That the danger is not imaginary most of our mental hospitals can testify. In my own experience have occurred several very painful cases of nerve and brain diseases, of physical breakdowns, and of lives ruined by persistent attendance at these circles. A man or woman who deliberately for the sake of knowledge, or to benefit humanity, or to learn how to help others, takes the risks, may be considered a martyr to science. But surely a very grave responsibility rests on those who induce the young and ignorant from curiosity, or by specious promises, to join such circles, and, as they say, develop psychic gifts. No doubt they can be developed in many cases. No doubt a young and innocent person may be formed into a medium, but at what a cost! The normal and natural protection to which I have alluded, that keeps the subconscious mind subconscious, is by artificial means withdrawn. The psychic leader of the circle may obtain knowledge of the psychic or astral plane, but he (or more frequently she) is really a vivisector exploring the unknown by means of experiments on the living human body, but a vivisector with no anatomical knowledge, no surgical training. Results may be obtained unquestionably, and they may be valuable to those who can understand and apply them. But open wounds are left on which septic germs may settle. Or in the language of Scripture, the unclean spirit may take unto himself seven other spirits more wicked than himself, and enter in and dwell there. It is but a theory, it is true, but it is one once widely held; and whether true or not it seems to account for some otherwise unaccountable facts. One more example shall close this already too long article. In many spirit circles, notably in America, but not wholly unknown in this country, we read glowing and ecstatic accounts of spirit lovers, most captivating to hysterical girls. No new thing is this. Ancient Egypt was well aware of it, M. Mauchamp in his diary records many instances in Morocco, where such have been invoked by witches for their clients for centuries past. In the classification of the Qabalists they were ascribed to the influence of the Gamaliel — the obscene — a gross misnomer, one would say, from reading the beautiful, flowery, poetical accounts given in spirit circles. Yet I have myself seen private writings from spirit sources, communicated through well-known mediums, that have been Rabelaisian in their frankness, and would certainly draw attention from the police if they came to be known. Septic germs undoubtedly; information useful to alienists, and mental physicians. But what of the victims? Is it not time that occultists seriously took up this question of obsessions? There are trained observers capable of recording and tabulating facts, and deducing conclusions, capable too of detecting and exposing fraud, and of eliminating the delusions produced by suggestion and auto-suggestion, and from the remainder arriving at some definite information about the entities, beings, intelligences, whatever they be, angels or demons, of the superhuman or subhuman planes.

[Reprinted from *The Occult Review*, Vol. 35, No. 2, February 1922, pp. 77-89.]

5. The Cloud upon the Sanctuary – Preface

I have gladly agreed, at the request of my friend Madame de Steiger, to say a few words of introduction to her admirable translation of Councillor Eckartshausen's *Cloud upon the Sanctuary*; feeling as I do that the appearance in an English dress of this work is one of the greatest boons that has been conferred upon English occult students since the publication of *The Perfect Way*. It will probably be long before Eckartshausen's work is fully appreciated, yet it is not too much to say that every sentence of this little work deserves to be most carefully read and re-read, and studied over and over again, and even then gone back upon by the student who has the capacity, with clairvoyant, psychic, and spiritual analysis, in order that the great and valuable truths embodied therein may be completely realised and brought home to mind.

There are two classes of minds which unfortunately divide between them the bilk of thinking humanity in our age and country, whose prejudices and fixed ideals must form a barrier to their conception of the scheme therein so clearly expounded. For to the ordinary materialistic and intellectual man the conception of a Church is merely that of a human society, formed for the purpose of developing and carrying out of altruistic ideas by purely human methods, which, according to his bias, he either approves or disapproves of, or regards with indifference, but in no case looks upon as anything more than human; to such an one the idea of an interior Church, the soul or invisible guiding principle of that which is outwardly manifested, is not only fantastic in the extreme, but actually mischievous as importing a sanction which has no correspondence in reason or justice.

To the Churchman, on the other hand, who is familiar with the idea of an invisible Church, Eckartshausen's philosophy does not accurately correspond to the theological conceptions of the Church Waiting or of the Church Triumphant. He is unfamiliar with the Eastern doctrine of the Seven Principles, and he knows not that these, which he can find within himself, and by the aid of trained intuition can examine and distinguish, and reason about, can by analogy be postulated of every created thing from the grain of dust to the mighty planet, and even to the Kosmos itself; and that by the application of this key it is possible to perceive, and even to prove, that the Interior Church of Eckartshausen may co-exist with the Church Triumphant and the Church Waiting, and, indeed, not only is no contradiction, but an actual proof of the reality of these theological teachings.

Prejudice and preconception, however, will for a long time keep both these classes of minds from giving a fair and unbiased study to the masterly exposition of the great German Mystic. The small but steadily increasing class of occult students who are also Christians and Churchmen, will welcome these pages at once, and will see without difficulty the wonderful analogies opened out of the Church – the Mystic body of Christ to the human body – and consequently the necessity for the existence of various interior and invisible counterparts whereunto that Body is perpetually striving to re-unite itself, even as the Man is for ever striving to unite himself to his higher and divine genius. He will see how that his own body, as well as the Mystic Body of Christ, is in very deed the Temple of the Holy Ghost, and how in each case there must rest a cloud on the Sanctuary until the Body, which is the Church Militant, be re-united with the original astral body, whose particles were drawn not only from our human ancestors, not only from this planet, but from the justified and glorious souls of all God's sentient creation throughout the Kosmos, whereof the Church, both visible and invisible, is the material and outward expression, just as in the Hebrew or Kabalistic system, Nephesh is the expression of Ruach, as Ruach is of Neshamah, and Malkuth is the vehicle which outwardly manifests them all.

Seers and Clairvoyants, Prophets and Holy men of all ages, have been able to attain to actual certainty of these things, and to them the Communion of Saints is an open book. To such these ideas will offer no difficulty, but there are few to whom, in the same degree as Councillor Eckartshausen, has been given the power of expounding them clearly to ordinary men; and the English-speaking student is to be congratulated that Eckartshausen has found a translator at once so learned, both occultly and exoterically, an so sympathetic as the authoress of the following pages.

[This Preface was published in 1896 in the first edition of Isabelle de Steiger's translated and annotated edition of *The Cloud upon the Sanctuary*, by Councillor Karl von Eckartshausen. Reprints of the basic text of the book are currently available from several publishers.]

Witchcraft and Folklore

6. Some Celtic Memories

Many years ago it was my good fortune, thanks to the kindness of a grand-uncle, to wander over a great part of the western islands, and pick up many experiences and traditions now fast fading into oblivion. Little more than a boy at the time, I readily made friends with all whom I met of the kindly and courteous islanders. Strangers were infrequent then, and the occultism and fairy lore of the west were much more freely spoken of. Moreover, among the peasants of the islands were many of my own kin, and possibly they spoke more openly to me than they would to many others. Now the islands have largely become a playground for the wealthy Southerner, and the Board schools have overlaid the old traditional Celtic wisdom with a thin veneer of superficial and sterile facts (so-called) in the name of education, and have taught the children to speak a clipped Cockney tongue, interlarded with some vulgar Americanisms, instead of the sweet pure English uttered with the lingering musical intonation of the western Highlanders. Altogether the foot of the Saxon has been heavy on the west, and the old occultism and the old fairy lore have retreated out of sight, and largely I fear out of mind.

Therefore I have tried to string together a few rambling memories, in the hope of preserving some traditions which the present generation is in danger of losing altogether. Others more capable must judge of their value; I can only vouch for truth as personal experiences of a time when the occultism of the Celtic west was not only a very real thing, but was looked on as utterly natural.

I knew nothing of folk lore, and the idea of collecting and comparing legends and myths never occurred to me. But I had all a boy's keen relish for a fairy tale, especially when told as an obvious truth by people who really believed it. Sooth to say I was rather wearied of the superior folk who told me that there were really no such things as fairies. So it was with great joy that I wandered about among the crofters, and got the old people to tell me stories of the 'little people', and the seal men and women, and the water folk, and the Riders of the Sidhe,[1] and of

---
1. Pronounced 'Shee'.

their own experiences. Here it was that I met with a girl who had more knowledge of elementals than any one I have since met. Half-witted she was, so the schoolmaster told me; it had been utterly impossible to teach her anything at school; he doubted whether she could even read or write intelligibly, but he was a Lowlander from the Border country, and rather fancied himself on a certain intellectual agnosticism. Anyhow this girl had a certain sweet wisdom of her own, which was perhaps beyond anything that was taught in the school. She told me that whenever any of the Kings of the Elements came across the island, anyone who knew could see their footprints, and know what was coming.

One day she showed me a mark in the soft ground at the edge of a peat moss. 'That's the foot of the Sea King,' she said 'He is going up to the heights of the Coolins. There will be a rain storm tonight.' The mark, whatever it was, was perfectly distinct, six crescents arranged round a circle, quite unlike the track of any beast I am acquainted with. It was a blue and cloudless day with never a hint of rain, but sure enough at sunset ominous black lurid clouds piled themselves on the peaks of the Coolins, and before midnight there came such a deluge of rain as I have seldom seen.

'The crofters certainly get a wonderful weather knowledge,' said the schoolmaster. 'They beat any barometer.' But neither he nor any one else ever explained that track in the soft black mud.

Another time she showed me a mark on the sands near by the Kyle of Loch Alsh. It was like a little spiral, such as a tiny whirl of air might make. 'The King of the Air is on foot today,' she said. 'I must warn the fishers.' Wiser than the schoolmaster, the fisher-boys heeded her, and no boats put out, though the weather looked ideal for fishing, and it was well they did not, for one of the sudden storms to which the western islands are subject blew up without any premonitory symptoms, and the loss of life might have been terrible. The schoolmaster naturally had his explanation ready. 'Of course,' he said, 'that little whirl in the sand was the first puff of the storm. These people who are always watching the weather get to know these trifling signs, that would escape the notice of town folk.'

But once she told me a sign of which the schoolmaster could give no explanation. On the bare high road was a dark mark which I can scarcely describe. It was like a little cluster of the Hebrew letter yod, and was several times repeated at distances of some two or three yards. I saw this first and called her attention to it. She seemed distressed — 'That is the Fire King,' she said, 'he is going west. There will be a blaze tonight, I trust it may not be the town.' She was thinking of Broadford. But it was not there. Far away to the west a farm was burnt down that night. The schoolmaster could only suggest coincidence, and certainly farm-fires were not infrequent. Still the fact remains that her prophecies nearly invariably came off, and the crofters and fisher folk believed implicitly in her warnings. Sometimes too she would look down into the water on a day of bright sunshine when the white limestone of the sea floor gleamed green through the little waves that made fleeting shadows, and swung gently the red-brown seaweed that floated like a girl's hair in the clear water, and would describe with a wealth of imagery that many poets might have envied how the sea maids swam past, and how she heard their songs. I inquired if they had fish tails, but she repudiated the suggestion indignantly. 'What would they be doing with fish tails anyway? No, of course not, they are made like ourselves, only beautiful. More beautiful than we ever are.'

They are natural instinctive poets, these Celtic islanders of the west. I stood once with an old boatman on the western shore of Mull, looking out over the sea to the sunset, on one of those evenings when a faint mist lies over the water, and the eye fails to catch the line of the horizon. At one moment it looks at the breaking wavelets, or the tiny islets glowing in the golden light, the next with no perceptible break it is scanning the bright cloudlets that seem like islands in the sky. The old man gazed silently for a minute or two, then extending his arm he said, 'Do you see! The gates are down tonight. We might just take a boat and sail on and on into Tir-nan-Oge,' then after a pause, 'My lassie's there waiting for me.' I knew how the bride of the old man's youth had died some fifty years before, after a short year of married life. But he had never forgotten.

Among the old people of the islands — a race, I fear, now fast vanishing, but of which a few yet survive — money was a thing of no account. The traditional Scottish thrift and saving habit had no place. If money came their way, from a shooting tenant or otherwise, they would spend it, probably wildly, but took little pains to get it, and none to keep it. I remember once how, with a boy's presumption, I criticized that same old boatman for his carelessness over money.

'Money!' he said, and there was some scorn in his tone. 'What's the use of money? All the best things of life you get for nothing.' I suppose I looked a little incredulous, for he went on, 'Why, don't you see — there's the sunshine, and the sea, and the sweet air, and the music, and the love of woman, and what more would you want?'

In those days and among the old people the music entered into their lives in a way that the strangers from the south could never realize. The lore of the fairies and elementals, that defied the colder vehicle of words, was expressed in music on the pipes. Often as the strains of the pipes came from some lonely shieling a listener would say, 'That's a fairy tune.' They said that the old pipers would sometimes fall asleep on some fairy knoll, and in their dreams would hear strange music underground, and on waking would set the tune on the pipes. But no man could ever compose the fairy music. It was handed on from piper to piper, and was at once recognizable by anyone who knew the Celtic music.

My old friend Dr Keith Norman Macdonald picked up many of these fairy tunes by ear, and scored them for the first time; some of the best known are included in his Gesto Collection. And most of them have legends connected with them. Many of these were told to me over peat fires, when one or two pipers met and played against each other. Thus it was that I heard the legend of Crodh Challein, Colin's Cattle, a typical fairy story of the west. Colin was betrothed to a beautiful girl, but one day she was carried off by the Riders of the Sidhe, who are fairy knight-adventurers, and bold gallant lovers, so 'tis said. But Colin, who had fairy blood himself, and was a person of influence, sought the fairy queen and begged for the restoration of his sweetheart. This, however, could not be immediately granted by fairy law, but it was permitted that every evening she should come and milk his cattle, and that he should hear her milking song, and at the end of a year she should be restored to him, and this milking song was heard also in dream by a piper, who set the tune on his pipes and so it was handed down, and a bard composed words which are still sung in the islands, and have been translated and included in Malcolm Lawson's *Songs of the North*.

Even in those days the islanders were very loth to speak about the fairies unless they were certain of a sympathetic and believing audience, and at the present day, though the fairy-faith is still strong, the islanders will often affect a cynical scepticism in talking to strangers. My friend

Mr W.B. Yeats accuses the Scots of taking away all the joyousness of fairy-life. But I think he knows not the fairies of the western islands. Different regions of the astral world are familiar to different branches of the Celtic race. One must go to Brittany for the cult of the dead, and certainly any one who wishes to find fairy-lore as a real and vital faith should go to the western islands, and should go with a comprehension of, and love for, the Celtic music. Neil Munro has told the story of The Lost Pibroch as few others could tell it, and there were variants of the legend current in the islands in my boyhood, but it was generally said then that the tune was forgotten, and the last piper who could play it was dead. I was told, however, that in the recruiting days, some three years ago, the strains of the Lost Pibroch came booming over the islands, and many of the boys who were hesitating went straight off to the recruiting stations and enlisted, but none knew who played it, and the old man who told me said solemnly, 'It was no living piper who set that tune on the great pipes.'

Many strange stories too I have heard when sitting by the shore, and watching the gambols of the seals in the offing, for to the Celt of the islands the seal is at least half human, and is capable of taking human form. But woe to the man or woman who is beguiled by one of the seal people, 'the form of a god with the heart of a beast,' they say. It was in the north of Skye, not far from Portree, that a young fisherman took me once to see a seal that had got stranded in a rock pool. 'Many's the one she has killed,' he said. 'Look ye only at the eyes of her now.' Anyone who has looked into the eyes of a seal may be pardoned for believing all the wild tales that are told of them, the human beauty, and pathos, and yearning in those eyes, seem to hold an infinity of romance behind them. 'She nearly killed me,' he went on, 'and she took my foster brother. A beautiful girl she was, and none knew where she came from. We were both in love with her, and we who had never had a wry word, fought each other with knives for her, but he was the better man, and she went away with him. He came back alone, and would say nothing of where he had been or what had chanced, but the gloom had settled on him, and he went away to the fishing alone, and she capsized his boat and killed him.' The fairy-faith of the island is very strong and real. To my young fisher lad the strange fair girl who came out of nowhere was clearly the same as the stranded seal in the rock pool. He would as soon have doubted the identity of any of the village folk, and the old feelings of love for her struggled hard with the desire to avenge his brother's death, which he has certainly laid, at her door. As he talked he took his chanter from his pocket and dreamily fingered the old air — 'There is snow on the mountains of Jura'; and there it was that I first heard the story of that tune, which I wish I could give in his own picturesque poetic language. In bald Saxon it was thus — 'Malveen was the prettiest girl in the village, and all the boys were in love with her, but she would have none of them. And one day there came a boat rowed by a solitary oarsman who sang as he rowed, in time to the beat of his oars, "Tha Sneacht Air nam Beannaibh Diurach." Beautiful he was as a god, with a curious, swaying turn from the hips as he walked, and his eyes were deep and dark, fierce with the wild gleam of elemental passions, but again melting with the glamour that would lure a babe from its mother's breast. None other had a chance with Malveen. One stalwart boatman in hot wrath met and fought Angus, for so he called himself. He was found in the morning horribly mauled, with his throat and shoulders torn and bitten. Many of her old lovers warned her, but she would not listen. They knew he was one of the sea-folk. As the summer waned Angus said he was called away, and little Malveen went white to the lips with the anguish of losing him — "Sweetheart," he said, as his lips rested long on hers, and the dark curly head lay on his arm — "I shall come back when the snow is on the mountains of Jura." One long kiss and he was gone.

And the royal robes of heather clad the grand old mountains, and their ermine tippets of snow were laid on their mighty shoulders, and then the snow melted and the gold of the broom and the whin clothed the hill-sides, and again autumn grew to winter, and still he came not, and little Malveen grew pale and wan with watching, but always she sang as she waulked the cloth — "There is snow on the mountains of Jura." And at last one early winter was heard again the click of the oars in the rowlocks, and the wonderful voice singing his rowing song — "There is snow on the mountains of Jura." And little Malveen heard it, and with a glad answering cry of "Angus", she ran, light as a fawn, down the brae to the shore, and the boys saw her join her lover, who wound his arm round her waist, and that was the last they saw, till in the pale morning light they came on her body, drowned in the wash of the waves, and the harsh barking laugh of a seal was heard far out in the offing.

But the old men say in Skye, when the tide rises through the hollow caves, and the boom of the winds and the waves makes wild music, that through the uproar they can hear the old rowing song — "There is snow on the mountains of Jura," — and they know that Angus the Seal is still mourning for his little love.'

That fisher lad was full of strange stories. He was more communicative than most of the islanders, and to him the fairy folk and the sea-people were as real and familiar as the birds and beasts, and so he told me stories of their nature, as simply and naively as he told of the habits of the gulls or the fish, and it was strange how the stories seemed to be illustrations of the learned treatises of Paracelsus on the nature of the Elementals. 'They are human,' he said, 'but they don't come from Adam, as we do. They never fell. But they are like us, whether they live in the land or in the water. Some of them are very tiny. Oh, yes! I've seen them often, little people about as big as small birds may be. But there are others as big as we are, but their bodies are like mist you understand, or like a cloud in the water, so you can't see them unless your eyes are used to them. But they can make themselves solid like us; I don't know how, but they can. And then it happens that one of them will sometimes marry one of us, and the old men say the fairy gets a human soul then.'

All the time he was talking he was fingering his chanter at intervals, as if helping out the ideas that he could not put into words, and as he spoke of the marriages between the fairies and mankind he played the plaintive notes of 'Oran an Teach,'[2] the 'Lament of the Water Kelpie', and told me the story that Matthew Arnold has rendered immortal in his *Forsaken Merman*, a story by the way that is as familiar in Norway as in the western isles, only there the Merman is a fierce and cruel god of the sea, but in Skye he is gentle and kindly.

Out on the mountain side, as the shades of evening descended, there were strange dancing lights, bog-fires I suppose we should call them and have a scientific explanation ready. But to my fisher-lad they were corpse-lights, and told of a death, either one that had just taken place, or that might be expected within a few hours. 'And it makes no difference,' he said. 'You may call it marsh gas, or what you will, but it is the soul that's going out to meet its Maker. And you may say there's life in the body yet, and the doctor may be doing what he will, but the soul has gone

---

2. Pronounced *Thek*.

out when ye see those lights, and there's no skill o' man can lure it back again. Aye! though there's breath yet left in the body. And ye may tell sometimes whose death it will be. Now what manner of colour will those lights be looking to you.'

To me they always looked white, and I said so. 'Aye!' he said. 'They will be white tonight, but not always. White is for a child. The soul is pure, you see. It will be the baby up at the hill- croft, I doubt. It's been sick. Now do ye see aught coming down the hill-side?' I saw a little mist wreath clinging to the ground, just over a rough path. 'That's not a mist,' he said rather impatiently; 'it's a little procession. There's a man carrying a wee bit coffin on his shoulder. I doubt they would not get a cart up there, and there's twelve men, and three women following. But why will they be going the other side of the burn, 'tis a mile round by the stone bridge. Well! it will two days from now; come ye here and ye shall see that funeral, and then go and talk about your marsh gas if ye like. Marsh gas indeed!' 'He walked off rather contemptuously. But there is no question that on the second day from that I saw the baby's funeral as he had described, and the reason they went round by the far side of the burn was that a flood in the meantime had washed away the wooden bridge by which they usually crossed.

Many were the tales I heard of the corpse-lights, and of the Toille, or phantom funerals, and of the death-wright who might be heard hammering at a spectral coffin. But this is the solitary instance in which I myself saw the funeral that had been described to me before, and can testify that the description was absolutely accurate even to the number of the followers, and the man carrying the rough little coffin on his shoulder. Whether it be the second-sight that thus interprets and reads into the common phenomenon of the bog-fire the death warning, I cannot say. The island men assert with absolute conviction that the parting souls are thus physically visible, but in the remote glens the second-sight is so usual as to attract no wonder. Mostly it is associated with death, the winding sheet is seen around the person whose death is foreseen. If it is around his knees death may be some distance off, but as it rises the time draws near, and when it covers his mouth it is within a few days, or hours it may be. The death of the eighth Earl of Seafield was thus foretold to me by an old shepherd, fully two years before it occurred, the winding sheet being seen about his feet, and gradually rising. So far as my own experience goes this is an unusually long time. Mostly it is a matter of days, or weeks at most, and seen round a person notoriously in feeble health, wherein we may perhaps infer some suggestion aiding the sight. But this cannot explain the vision seen about a man in the prime of vigorous youth, and persisting for two years against all material evidence. But not always is the second-sight concerned with death. It may relate to utterly trivial and ordinary affairs. Thus a minister in West Ross, not long ago, told his housekeeper to set out tea for a dozen persons in half an hour. The manse was in a lonely glen, and there had been no word of any guests expected. Nevertheless the minister persisted, and sure enough within the half hour a motor-car drew up at the manse door, with a large party. They had only stopped for a moment to greet the minister, who was a friend of the owner of the car. But he pressed them to stay, assuring them that they were expected. They replied this was impossible, as they had only thought of stopping there ten minutes before. But the ample preparations were convincing proof. The minister then asked where was the boy on the bicycle? They knew of no boy on a bicycle, but in due course the boy also turned up, having followed the car unknown to its occupants. The minister had seen the whole scene half an hour before it happened. Similar instances of prevoyance are cited by Maeterlinck in *The Unknown Guest*. In the west Highlands they hardly excite surprise.

One of the most remarkable instances of second-sight coupled with a very beautiful spiritual vision was told me half a century ago, under the walls of Dunvegan castle, in connection with the well-known and exquisite Highland air, 'Mac Crimmon's Lament', by an old, old woman, who was the grand-niece of the composer of the traditional words. The narrator was Marsaly Macdonald, she had married a Glasgow man, and had left Skye for many long years, and when I saw her she had come back in her old age to see the Isle of Skye once more. And she told me how she had nursed her grand-aunt in extreme age, till one lovely winter's day at sunset in January 1788, the old lady sat at the door of her cottage looking out over the western sea, and the second-sight was upon her, and she saw no longer the things of earth, and as nearly as I can reproduce them this was Marsaly's account of how old Shiela told the story of the famous lament. Of couse it was not as I have tried to write it, in a continuous narrative.

There were many pauses and many queries of my own. But I have endeavoured to set down Shiela's words as Marsaly remembered them.

'Cha till! Cha till!³ Dost hear the sound, Marsaly. No! Comes it then only for me? Child, 'tis now nigh on half a century since I heard that lament come booming from the pipes. Why comes it back now? when the January winds are wailing, and the fateful eighteenth century draws to its mournful close. Five and forty years ago our hearts were all a-dance with joy and hope in the western islands, the dreary time of the German domination was ending. Our Prince had landed — our Bonnie Prince Charlie was among us, and all the loyal clansmen were flocking to his standard. Only with us here in Skye there was grief and trouble. For our Chief (shame that it should be said of a Macleod of Dunvegan) looked on his own interests, and forgot his loyalty, gave his adherence to the German usurper and the cruel redcoats, and what could we of the clan do.

'See, Marsaly! how dark stand the gloomy walls of Dunvegan over yonder. Often from the turret have I sung to my harp the greeting to the returning Chief, or wailed the coronach when one of the race was carried to the grave. For, ever in Dunvegan the bards were honoured, and I was one of the chief of the bards, and my sweetheart was Donald Bain Mac Crimmon, the finest piper the west had ever known, whose fathers had been the pipers of the Macleods for generations, and he was the best of them all.

'Ah, my bonnie boy! True man! True poet! best dancer in the glens! Loyal was his heart to the race of our ancient kings, and how we both rejoiced when from Moidart came the tidings that our Prince had landed, and down in the cave by the sea Donald played the great Pibroch, that was to hail Charles Stuart king of his lawful heritage, with none but me, and the gulls, and the waves to hear. Ah me! only in heaven will that Pibroch be heard now I fear me. But then how light were our hearts, till like a black cloud, the news came to us that our Chief was mustering his men, not for our country, and our king, but to help the base German crew and the redcoats.

'But what help was there! For ever a piper must follow his lord, whatever his lord may do.

---

3. Pronounced *Ha Cheel*.

"We sail tomorrow, my lass!" he said. "The galleys are all ready, and I must play a Pibroch. No, no! not that one, that is all our own, yours and mine, lass! But I pray that I may die, for I cannot wish our Chief defeat, and I dare not wish him success, for his cause is evil, and I must play his march. But I shall die before either my Chief or my rightful King gain the victory, and I shall see my Shiela no more. But cherish the memory of my Pibroch; some day perhaps it will sound in your ears again." And as he spoke there was the winding sheet around his breast.

'And early next morning was great commotion, for the clansmen were all embarking, and the chief stood in the prow of the foremost boat, and beside him was my lover, with the great pipes under his arm, the streamers flaunting in the breeze, and the sun glinting on his shoulder brooch, and he sent a full man's wind into his bag, and started bravely into the Macleod's war-march. But as he played the time and the notes changed in spite of himself as I think, and the glorious, racing, fighting tune wailed away into a low lament, and still the spectral winding sheet clung around him.

'Never was such a strange starting from Dunvegan, with a Chief gloomy and depressed, with downcast head, to the music of a wild lament, leading an unwilling clan to fight against one they loved better than life, in the cause of the Germans whom they loathed. So over the waters floated that weird lament, as the galleys lessened in the distance, and ever the burden sang to me the words — "Macleod shall return, but Mac Crimmon shall never." And I seized my harp and poured out all my soul in answer, for I knew it was my last farewell, and I should see my bonnie boy no more, and my harp wafted a message to him that somewhere in the world to come he should play our Pibroch, when the royal race should come to its own again.

'They were dreary days in Dunvegan then, when all our men were gone, and never a skirl of the pipes, nor the lilt of a dance in the hall, or on the hill-side broke the monotony for us women left behind, and weary were the days while we waited for news.

'And at last came tidings of what they called the "Rout of Moy", when the whole army of Lord Loudoun fled in confusion from half a score of highlanders, and it was my own cousin told me, who had taken part in it; and how they grappled in the dark and the rain while the lightning flashes scarcely showed them each other's faces, and the pipes wailed the lament with no pretence at a war march, and he knew it was Mac Crimmon's piping, for there was no piper like him, and how it ended in a sudden skirl, for my boy was shot through the lungs, the only one who was hurt in that mad fight, yet he gathered all his last strength, and blew all that remained of his breath into the bag, and over the struggling host of the frightened Whigs, and over the great burst of laughter of Simon Fraser and his comrades, there pealed a great Pibroch, only the opening bars, and my cousin whistled it for me, and I knew it was our Pibroch, and that my boy as he died had played the welcome of the royal race.'

She stopped then, Marsaly said, and rested long, thinking over the days that had been. Then she said—

'Since then, Marsaly, I have been as you have known me, a broken old woman living in this little cottage, watching the sunrise over the Coolins, watching the green water swirl and surge over the white stones, and the green and red seaweed float upwards, and the lashing of the waves in winter.

'And I have heard how our hopes were broken, and the Germans were victorious, and our Prince was a hunted fugitive, with a heavy price on his head, but though hundreds of our people knew where he was, not one would betray him, though they were starving. No! we leave treachery to the Germans and the House of Hanover, and cruelty and oppression to the butcher Cumberland. But for all the wealth of mighty England I would not be with their souls.'

Again she fell silent for a space, and then the second-sight came back to her and she spoke as if in a dream.

'Cha till! Cha till! I hear it again. Marsaly, what is this I see? The mountains grow dim, the landscape fades. Child where are you? The sight comes on me once more. A bare room, a girl, a priest in cardinal's robes. One lies dying. Ah! It is our Prince. Squalor and desolation, forsaken by his friends, only those two dear ones watching, faithful to the last by the bedside of the Lord's anointed.

'Cha till! Cha till! I hear the lament wailing through the mean room, recalling how it wailed when the galleys sailed from Dunvegan. The room melts away; up in the sky I catch the gleam of tartan, and I see him at last — my boy — beautiful and brave as I saw him last, and now comes swelling the grand cadence of our Pibroch. There is a great white light that issues from the Eternal Throne, and falls on the Soul of our Prince, lighting up the serried ranks of the loyal clans, waiting there to welcome him, and to breathe down on Scotland the gracious promise: The night shall pass, and the royal race shall yet return.'

So did old Marsaly tell me the story of the famous lament, and of the composer of the words. But before the end of my holidays she had left Skye, and I never saw or heard of her again.

One may fancy that even now, from the world of souls, Shiela and her Donald Bain may watch with rejoicing how the call of the 'Lost Pibroch' has roused the men of Skye to go forth once more to fight against the Germans. But with a very different spirit, and different ending now, we trust, than in the 'Forty-five.' Ghostly Pibrochs have been heard pealing over the trenches in France and Flanders, leading the highland lads to victory. May we not dream that Donald Bain himself may be playing his great Pibroch, in the joy of knowing that all those who died fighting against the Germans more than a century and a half ago, did not die in vain, and their cause and their deaths are amply avenged now.

[Reprinted from *The Occult Review*, Vol XXVI, No. 4 (October 1917), pp 197-208.]

7. Witchcraft

Familiarly as we speak of witches and witchcraft, few perhaps realize that the word witch probably means no more than a wise woman, as wizard means a wise man; or (if we take Grimm's derivation from veihan) one who consecrates. The word has gone far from its original meaning, especially in popular usage. We wonder vaguely how people ever came to believe in such things, they seem so far removed from the practical everyday life of modern times. A witch, so most people think, was a poor woman, ugly and ill-favoured, solitary, probably soured and ill-tempered, possibly mad. How could sane people take her seriously enough to be afraid of her, above all to torture and burn her. We say: 'Gross ignorant superstition', and think we have accounted for the whole problem, forgetting that some of the acutest intellects in a very intellectual age — men moreover who were decidedly sceptical in their views — such as the Scottish Lord Advocate MacKenzie, to name only one example, gave much time and thought to the investigation of the subject, and declared their conviction that there was something genuine, and not mere madness in the pretensions of the witches.

If we will but for a moment lay aside prejudice, and look at the subject dispassionately, we shall become convinced that the cult of the witch is as old as humanity, it is as old as the world, and as flourishing today as it was in the fifteenth or sixteenth centuries, and as firmly believed. Once realize this and we get a clue to comprehending one of the problems of former ages that has most perplexed historians and antiquarians.

If we try to throw ourselves into past ages, not dropping any of our modern ideas, but rather trying to find their expression among our forefathers, it is possible that in the light of common human nature we may find real living people behind the mists of the ages.

Many will doubtless question the statement that witchcraft is as rife today as ever. But it is fact that there is scarcely a witchcraft legend of the Middle Ages that cannot be paralleled by some well-known case now, and finding as ready a belief. Think one moment of all the tribe of palmists, clairvoyants, crystal gazers, sand-diviners, etc., rank impostors, some will say, and so doubtless a number of them are, but unless they were very largely believed in they could not exist, and unless there were a measure of something that was not imposture behind them they could not find this belief. And between the old spaewife and the modern clairvoyant there is but slight difference.

Well but, you will say, what of the old-time witches, who mounted on broomsticks and rode through the air to carouse on the good wine in some nobleman's cellars. Here again we have only to look over the files of *Light,* or the *Transactions of the Psychical Research Society* on the phenomena of levitation, and you will find many parallel cases. We call these things by learned names now. I have met grave and learned men, whose veracity was unimpeachable, who solemnly declared that they had witnessed levitation, some even who had experienced it in their own proper persons. I do not say the stories are true, but I know that they are very widely believed. And as for the tales of witches who became hares and wolves, I have myself seen in the Salpetrière Hospital in Paris epileptic and hysteric patients who were fully convinced that they were animals, and imitated animal cries and motions with curious exactness, to say nothing of the curious disease known as lycanthropy.

True we do not burn witches nowadays, even if we do more or less believe in them. The manners of today are less brutal. But in England they are sorely harried by the police, though the statute is only directed against fraud and imposture.

A witch then, being the derivation of the word a wise woman, who used formulae of consecration, or as we should say ceremonial magic, might obviously use it for good or for evil; we see that there may be black or white witches, using black or white magic. Within the latter category would come the bulk of psychic-healers who would unquestionably have been classed as witches in the sixteenth and seventeenth centuries. Many women were burned in the persecution days against whom the only proved charges were that they healed sick persons by some ceremonial. A study of a good collection of witchcraft trials, such as may be found for example in Pitcairn's *Criminal Trials,* will leave no doubt that most of the Christian Scientists today would have stood a very poor chance two or three hundred years ago.

The confessions of witches of those days contain lurid and graphic accounts of the worship of the Devil, and there are certain Jesuit writers today who would persuade us that all Freemasons are Devil worshippers. But without going this length it is well known that societies of Satanists do exist in Italy, and in Paris, and are not wholly unknown even in London.

We may imagine then that if we could project ourselves backwards some two or three hundred years we should find much the same phenomena that we are familiar with now, only more universally believed in, and persecuted with very great brutality. And if we ask for the reason of the persecution, there is little doubt that we may sum it all up in the one word 'fear'. There were unknown dangers that seemed to strike in the dark, and a panic-stricken public opinion called for dire and brutal vengeance.

But to work out all the modern analogies to the old world witchcraft would be far too big an undertaking. I propose to confine myself to the phenomena coming more or less within the popular meaning of the word, and try to show by definite authentic instances that the same thing exists today, in almost precisely the same form as in the Middle Ages and much earlier, and that the cult of the witch varies little from age to age.

A great mass of well authenticated stories have come within my own knowledge. But naturally in many cases I am unable to give the authorities. Most people are unwilling to have their names mixed up with anything of the kind, and an account of the experiences of Mr H. of what happened in the town of W., is singularly unconvincing. I shall therefore for the most part confine myself to cases that I can personally vouch for, and of these the most interesting to the student are those which show the survival of forms current in the Middle Ages, or in remote classical times. Naturally the greatest number occur in the West of England and Scotland among the Celtic population. But witchcraft is far from being unknown even among the Saxons of the east coast. In the Channel Islands it is rife to this day, also in Brittany; and in Morocco (as described in M, Jules Bois' *Sorcellerie au Maroc*) every Medieval incident, including the Witches' Sabbath, is familiar ground, and universally believed in.

One of the oldest of known incantations is that connected with the casting of the black thread. It was undoubtedly Scandinavian and pre-Christian, referring to some legend of a ride of Odin and Baldur in which Baldur's horse slipped and sprained or dislocated a leg. This was healed by binding round the injured leg a black thread with seven knots.

The formula accordingly narrated the event.

> Baldur rade. The foal slade slipped
> Set bone to bone, sinew to sinew,
> Heal in Odin's name.

The words are given in various forms, but the substance is the same. This spell is to be found in nearly every book on Scandinavian folklore. Afterwards it was Christianized, and referred to an accident in Christ's ride to Jerusalem, 'The Lord rade, and the foal slade', etc., 'Heal in the Holy Ghaist's name', I have been told that this spell has been practised in Orkney within living memory, but I had not actually met with it until three years ago, when being in Penzance and driving out to see some Druidic remains, I fell into conversation with the driver. At first, with true Celtic caution, he denied that any witchcraft remained in Cornwall. But after I had told him some experiences of my own in the West Highlands he told me that once he had a poisoned thumb that defied all the doctors to cure. He was told that his thumb must be amputated, but before agreeing to this he consulted a 'wise woman'. She anointed the thumb with a special salve of which she had the secret, and solemnly tied seven knots in a black thread, which she bound round the thumb, chanting something under her breath. I asked him if he could remember the words, but these he had barely heard, only he knew it was something about our Lord riding. Anyhow, the thumb got perfectly well in a very short time. Here then was a well authenticated case of a witch formula, handed down from practically unknown antiquity and practised today. Encouraged by my ready acquiescence in the probability of his cure, he told me other stories of cures by the same 'wise woman' who seems to have been a white witch, devoting her powers entirely to curing, and taking no fee for so doing.

But the evil witch who does harm is by no means unknown. One such I met with many years ago now, in what was the then little fishing village of Lossiemouth. I was told how she over-looked cattle and they died, how the sheep brought forth no lambs, and the cows gave no milk. With much difficulty and many vows of secrecy I was shown the witch's cottage, and made her acquaintance. However, when after some little conversation on things in general I asked her if she would 'spae' my fortune, either by my hand, or the cards, or in any other way, she stoutly denied having any power in that way, and it looked as though we had come to a deadlock, till fortunately I remembered a few words of Romani, picked up when haunting round the gipsy tents at Norwood and Epping Forest years before. These worked the spell, for my witch had a good deal of gipsy blood mixed with a dash of tinker, and she burst into a stream of voluble Romani, most of which was wholly unintelligible to me, though I tried to look as if I were taking it all in, and in the end she laid down the cards, and looked in my hand, made various conjurations, and told me a most elaborate fortune, some of which at all events came off. We got so friendly that I ventured to ask her about the cattle that had died, and the misfortunes that had befallen sundry folk. She said they were rightly served, being cruel unfeeling people, and that God would never allow such to prosper. I hinted that I had heard among the Romani of certain spells that brought ill-luck on man and beast, whereon she smiled, and said it was useless to tell anything to a person who knew so much. This was a clear evasion, but it came pretty near to an admission. On another interview I asked her whether a cow's milk could be drawn off without touching the cow, and she said of course it could, it only needed a rope plaited backwards, laid between the cow's hind legs and out at the byre door. You could then milk the end of the rope. Only it must be done in the Devil's name. This was, as students of Pitcairn will recognize, one of Isabel Goudie's spells, and it was very interesting to find it still in active use. Many of the farmers used to pay a regular subsidy to this witch to secure immunity from her spells, and overlooking, and I was assured that no misfortune ever came to those who thus bought her favour. In Young's *History of Elgin* a case is mentioned of an honest farmer who was advised to offer a burnt offering to the Devil for protection against the ill fortune that beset him and his stock, and, having done so, his ill-luck ceased, but his conscience troubled him sorely all his life.

A case of a very old formula was told me by the minister of Urquhart. An old man came to him one day who was a notorious unbeliever, and never troubled kirk or minister save to sneer or blaspheme. The minister was pleased at the call, and thought the old man was coming to a better mind. After some irrelevant conversation he came to his errand, which was to ask the minister for an old cock, the minister having a breed of white poultry which he took pride in. Thinking the old man wanted some chicken broth he readily promised the cock, and casually inquired what was he going to do with it, and then it came out that he had been overlooked by a neighbour, and had had terrible trouble, but that if he buried a white cock at his doorstep the evil wishes would have no power. Thought went back to the white cock of Aesculapius, and farther back into the dim past to the witches of Thessaly, and various old classic stories.

Another witchcraft story was told me by the late Sir Archibald Dunbar which was within his own knowledge. When it was proposed to demolish the old castle of Blervie the contractor employed had thrown down half of the castle, when he was warned to desist. He paid no attention, however, till one day he saw a most evil-looking old woman sitting on a stone dyke and grinning at him. She cursed him volubly, whereupon he went with a stick to drive her away, but a black dog with flaming red eyes snarled at him, and would have bitten him, but when he looked again the old woman sat on the dyke as before. Whereupon he was so frightened that he vowed he would never touch a stone of the accursed building again. Certain it is that a man was employed to destroy the tower, that he did destroy only half of it, leaving the part which is still standing, and that in consequence he did not get his agreed pay.

Sir Archibald Dunbar told me also of a tradition of his boyhood of witches holding orgies within the old Druid circle at the farm of Templestones, whereat the illumination was given by candles made of hares' fat, the effect of which was said to be that it constrained the women present to cast off their clothes and never cease dancing till the candles had burnt themselves out: There is little but vague tradition of this formula, but it is interesting that Baptista Porta mentions a similar effect as coming from a lamp filled with hares' fat, and Reginald Scott in his *Discovery of Witchcraft* has some instances of a like character.

From earliest times, and in all countries, stones have been set up for blessing or cursing. But the old rituals have been mostly lost, and modern instances are rare. One such, however, I met with on a farm in one of the wildest districts of West Ross many years ago. About a stone's throw from the farmhouse was a small circle of black stones, about twelve yards in diameter it may be. Thirteen stones there were in all. The number struck me as peculiar, and I asked the farmer if it was a

Druidic monument. 'No,' he said, 'my grandfather set those up there. Cursing stones they are. He was tenant of this farm'. I asked for more details, and somewhat hesitatingly he told the story which apparently was well known in the district, but seldom spoken of. The old man, the farmer's grandfather, it seems was betrothed to a beautiful girl, but another man carried her off. Whereupon the original lover had solemnly cursed the man who had taken her. I inquired how he had done it, and the details seemed to have been well preserved. It was once a month in the dark of the moon that he set up each stone walking round thrice widdershins and crying to the Devil to curse and blast the man's life. He also baptized the stone in the Devil's name with water from a certain spring, said to be the haunt of evil spirits. Where he got the ritual from no one knows. I believe there are some spells somewhat similar in the Grimoire. I asked whether the curses had taken effect. The man I was told had fallen off a roof and broken his neck, and the girl had died with her first child. The curser married soon after this, but he was a miserable man all his life, haunted with gloomy forebodings, and died more or less insane. I know not whether the stones still stand. Probably not. The family have long ago left the district, and I have never been able to trace them.

The curious student may find many traces of ceremonial magic both black and white in the west, both in England and Scotland, but there is naturally a great reluctance to speak of such matters.

In fact the western Celt in very many cases is at heart a pure pagan. Outwardly he may be an elder of the Free Kirk, or a Wesleyan Methodist, but if trouble comes to him he steals away at night, when no one knows, to the stone circle, or the fairy well, and seeks help from some ritual half as old as the world it may be. I once asked an old man, after many stories of witchcraft and faerie lore had been exchanged, what the minister would say, and how these things agreed with the Kirk. 'Weel, ye ken," he said, 'a man must have a religion of sorts, for the sake o' the neighbours, just as he must have a pair o' breeks — but it's no himsel'. Perhaps as good an account of the matter as many profound treatises.

Going beyond the British Islands we find all the old witchcraft legends, I will not say more firmly believed, but certainly more openly acknowledged, than is usual with us. Barbey d'Aureville's remarkable novel *L'Ensorcelée*, gives a vivid picture of witchcraft as it is, and of the life and nature of the Normandy peasants, among whom the author passed the greater part of his life.

But it is in neighbouring Brittany that we find the hold of the past is strongest. Surrounded by the Druidic relics in the wildest scenes of nature, and cut off from the modern materialism and ignorant scepticism that calls itself progress, the Breton peasant has now the faith and much of the knowledge and power of three hundred years ago. In the Morbihan the 'Mait' Jeans' or 'Espirits Follets' are the congeners of the Scottish Brownies, doing work for those they love, playing malicious tricks on those they dislike, guarding buried treasure, and the like.

In nearly every Breton village there is a witch, but not shy as in the British Islands; she is well known, and to be freely consulted by all who please. One celebrated witch, Annaic of the Morbihan, even had her photograph taken, and articles were written about her in local journals. The tap of her crooked stick on the pavement was some dozen years ago a familiar sound in the village streets, and perhaps may be so still. Any true bred son of the Morbihan would tell you tales of Annaic and her wonderful doings by the hour. She was more of a white than a black witch, curing sickness and troubles of all kinds, and helping lovers to a happy union. Yet at times Annaic could lay a deadly powder at the door of an enemy, on whom unlooked for misfortune fell suddenly and irresistibly.

The student of witchcraft who desires to understand its rationale must seek far and wide. Gathering traces in many different countries he will find his examples in as many different stages of development, and will be able to trace the same spirit in all.

The spells in vogue in Scotland or in England three hundred years ago, and of which we find perhaps only a few obscure traces existing today, may be much more clear and definite in Brittany or the Channel Islands. Others again still farther afield. When I was writing *The Devil's Mistress* I found in the Confession of Isabel Goudie distinct traces, but no more, of the 'moon paste', But what it was, and how prepared, no testimony in this country gave the smallest clue. Hints in Hesiod, and other classical authors, showed that the formula was used in Thessaly, and Medieval Italians spoke of bringing the moon down from Heaven. Still they eluded me, till at last I ran it to earth in Morocco, as recorded in the notes of Emile Mauchamp and others. The key fitted exactly: not only Isabel Goudie but the Thessalian witches were justified by the experience of a modern scientific traveller.

But great patience is needed to compare the tales of one country with another, to sift out imposture, and to bring out the residuum of real occult knowledge and power. Yet from my own experience I can say it is well worth while. It is a branch of occultism well defined, on which there is an enormous mass of evidence, and which has existed probably as long as mankind has been on the earth, and will continue to exist with little change when most other material institutions pass and decay. The cult of the witch will still flourish, openly or secretly, it matters little which, the old formulae will be practised and believed, to all future time.

[Reprinted from *The Occult Review,* Vol. XXV, No. 5 (May 1917), pp. 264-71.]

8. Witchcraft Rituals

To the student of medieval witchcraft the question continually presents itself — what precisely did the witches do? what means did they employ to produce the effects attributed to their conjurations? and again, what was their own outlook on the world? Putting out of account the charlatans and impostors, of whom I fancy the Middle Ages could show quite as plentiful a crop as the modern world, how did the genuine witch or wizard, or those who believed themselves to be such, regard themselves and their art and powers? — what were in short their experiences?

The accounts of their victims are given in ample enough detail in the trials. The Rituals may to a large extent be recovered. Some are fully expounded in the Great Grimoire, and recorded by Trithemius and others. The Confessions of known witches, notably that of Isabel Goudie, which is perhaps the most fertile storehouse of later medieval formulae, prove that the older Rituals were still practised in the seventeenth century. But the corruptions and omissions indicate that they must have been handed down orally, and were repeated parrot-wise with little understanding of their meaning. But before we can realize the witch as a vital living person we must know, not only what she said and did, but what she thought of it. How in fact, her witchcraft appeared to herself, and what it was that induced her to do it. Here the experiences of those who have made experiments in ceremonial magic today, if only one can get them, are of extreme value. But as a rule they are difficult to get. I have talked with many who profess to have occult powers, or to know those who have, but generally they are vague and magniloquent — 'I could, an I would.' There are half hints of wonderful things, but nothing tangible. The serious student wants more than this. Weird tales and strange experiences may be multiplied *ad nauseam,* but as a rule they take one no farther in the scientific investigation.

It is, of course, open to any one now to try any of the old Rituals that have been preserved, but it is rather like ignorant experimenting with poisons without knowing their nature or the antidotes. Either the results are entirely negative, which proves nothing, or there is considerable danger. In illustration of this I may perhaps be permitted to record a personal experience when, as a boy, with the rash confidence and inquisitiveness of boyhood, I determined to try a black magical formula, out of an old book picked up, Heaven only knows where, but which certainly I ought not to have had access to. The details of that experiment and its result are fresh in my memory now, after the lapse of over fifty years. Where the formula came from I know not, probably it was corrupted or 'faked' — but I took it literally. The key name was *Asmodeus Szathan*. This was to be written on virgin parchment, with a new quill pen, with the blood of a crow, and my own name beneath with the blood of a pigeon. I knew not what virgin parchment might be, but I got a new and clean piece and bribed a keeper to procure a pigeon and a crow, and the parchment was duly inscribed. It was then to be placed in some close and dark receptacle. I chose a bottle and corked it tight. I was then to walk round it widdershins seven times, repeating the names, and adjuring them to come and enter the receptacle. A familiar Spirit would thereupon appear, and would be my slave to do whatever I commanded.

With a mind full of the Arabian Nights, and Effrits and Genii, I was prepared to demand all the wonders of Aladdin, but nothing happened. Somewhat disappointed, but not discouraged, I put the precious bottle under my pillow. But no sooner was I asleep than some dark form seemed pressing upon me, and long tentacles were round my throat. I woke gasping and absolutely unable to breathe, struggle as I would. With a frantic effort I contrived to make the sign of the cross, and to commence the Lord's Prayer, and the pressure began to relax, and I was able to draw a struggling breath. But the sensation was one of extreme pain. It was as though I had swallowed a ball of horsehair, which were being slowly dragged out hair by hair through lacerated nerves. The bottle was broken. I contrived to throw it out of the window, and kept my own counsel as to the formula, burning the tell-tale parchment. My family diagnosed a vivid nightmare, and the doctor spoke learnedly about overwrought nerves, *globus hystericus*, and other slang of his profession, and administered sedatives. Of course he knew nothing of the formula. But I suspect, even if he had, his opinion would have remained the same. Naturally, I was properly scared, and left black magic severely alone for some time. Years after meeting with a psychometrist, whom I was asked to test, I wrote the same names in ordinary ink on a piece of paper, put them in a sealed envelope and handed it to the psychometrist, who at once spoke of being strangled, and threw the paper away, refusing to proceed any farther. Hence perhaps there might have been more in it than the doctor could fathom. But there is no doubt that if even a tiny modicum of success had attended this experiment I should have tried again, and gone on farther. And something like this seems to have been the beginning of the practices of many witches. The confessions show almost invariably a strong desire for power, sometimes coupled with insatiable curiosity and ordinarily utter boredom with dull and colourless lives.

Assuming that definite physical effects follow the recitation of a ritual with appropriate action by a witch, it may be questioned how far the ritual itself has any effect, beyond exciting and intensifying the will and imagination of the witch. Several of the witches of Isabel Goudie's period assert that the spells are of no efficacy unless taught by the Devil, and unless the witch have authority to use his name. But, on the other hand, it is recorded by independent witnesses that the spell of 'Horse and Hattock' might be used by any one. A tutor gravely records that as some boys were playing beside a church one of them cried, 'Horse and Hattock with my top', whereupon his top was carried up in the air and dropped the other side of the church.

That the same applies also to names, any one who pleases can test for himself. Many books on ceremonial magic give the names of Angels or Demons governing certain moods and emotions, as anger, revenge, jealousy, love, etc. When the particular emotion is rising, or stirred up, repeat the name emphatically, try to visualize a figure intensifying and carrying out that emotion. After a while the name will involuntarily rouse the emotion, and in some cases the name, even silently uttered, will rouse the emotion in another. This may, of course, be accounted for in various ways. Association, brain-waves, or what you will. But the result follows too often to be questioned. And we can well imagine that a prospective witch, being taught this simple formula, and finding it work, would become intoxicated with the idea of power, and would go on from one formula to another. One of the witches in the Crook of Devon in Kinross-shire records in her confession that having once practised the invocation of names, it became so fascinating that, whatever their resolves might be, they could not help trying the formula as sure as a certain hour came round. The excitement of being able to arouse the particular mood in themselves at will, and to see the same mood awaking in another person roused and held by their will, gave a sensation of power that was irresistible, though they knew full well that ere long they were certain to be caught and to pay dearly for their pranks. One of them records the savage glee with which she set the neighbours quarrelling, and watched from her window a free fight in the village street.

In most cases it seems to have been a small success at first that led to further experiments. This I have been told is often the case with spiritual healers today. There comes an earnest desire to heal some one who is sick, and a conviction of being able to do so, a hand laid upon the sick person, and a speedy recovery. Another experiment also succeeds, and therewith grows confidence. Simple rituals are learned, which intensify the will and concentrate the desire to do good, appropriate names come to be used, it may be of saints perhaps, and results seemingly almost miraculous follow. And this power which may be used for good, is potent for evil also, given the evil will. The confessions of many of the medieval witches leave no doubt that something like this was the origin of much of the old world witchcraft, and it is to be noted that in nearly every case where we get anything like a full confession, it was the discovery of the power to affect another person that gave the first impetus, the learning of spells and rituals came after. This is the reverse of the popular belief that the would-be witch was taught formulae by the Devil, or by some more advanced student of the mysteries, and forthwith began to play with bogles. I once asked a friend who had very considerable psychic powers whether there were any rules for the attainment of these, and he replied: 'The first and most essential is complete confidence. If you doubt your power to succeed you will fail. Take the very simple case — you are walking behind a friend in the street, on a sudden impulse you think you will make him turn round and look at you. He does so. Perhaps you are astonished and think you will try again. This time you fail. Why? Because you are doing it for an experiment, and not sure that you will succeed. Your mind is two ways. Yet it is a very simple matter which any one can do, and no more really occult than starting a petrol engine if you have a strong enough spark. Therefore it follows that until you are well practised you should never tell any one what you are going to do. This at once gives the counter suggestion of an experiment, and the possibility of failure. The spark is not strong enough. No result follows.' The extreme caution as to secrecy inculcated on witches in old times as to their designs and methods is usually attributed to fear of persecution. Probably it was far older than persecution days, and much more occult than generally supposed. The silence so strongly insisted on by the Old Templars, the Freemasons, and by students of ceremonial magic was an essential of occult working, and necessary to successful witchcraft.

But how, we ask, did the witches themselves regard their own operations when successful? Here we must distinguish. The ordinary uneducated peasant woman who had become a witch, as I have tried to indicate, seems to have had very little thought or care for the consequences of her actions. She found a certain fierce excitement in the putting out of strange powers, and this fascinated her, to the exclusion of all other considerations. Some of the exercises involved acute physical pain.

One of the Salem witches tells that she was directed to crouch with one leg bent under her in a cramped position every evening at sunset. All day she dreaded the exercise, which was very painful, and firmly resolved to have no more to do with it. But towards evening came a certain looking forward to the time — 'Just a moment or two tonight for the last time, and then never again,' she said. And at sunset there was an exhilaration in getting out the iron stirrup that held her foot in the crouching position, a growing excitement and beating of the heart with the first twinge of pain. Then a wonder how long she could keep it up, a resolve to count by hundreds, and she vowed to herself if she passed one hundred she must complete the next, and so on. Psychologically I fancy that a sense of power came with the mental conquest of the body, and that herein lay the fascination. Of this witch it is recorded that she had great power of evil, and did much harm to all who offended her. But the initial exercises, according to her own account, were not undertaken with any ulterior object, but had a fascination of their own. The strongly developed will power that had dominated her own body was directed to ill by a venomous jealousy of a neighbour. A successful experiment of cursing led to others. Formulae and Rituals came in her way, seemingly accidentally at first, then were greedily sought for, and so the fully equipped black witch emerged from training. This account, which is very illuminating in its way, was written by Mr Robert Calef, a merchant of Boston, U.S.A., in 1695, and published in London in 1700 and Salem in 1797. I believe that Mr Cotton Mather professed to have been an eye-witness of the powers of this witch, but so far I have not been able to meet with his verification. This seems to answer the question why, if witches had these powers, they should have remained in squalid poverty and obscurity. It was not wealth or luxury that they sought. The nerve excitement caused by the practices of witchcraft in its early stages had a fascination that was an end in itself, and, afterwards, the gratification of moods of hatred, or revenge, or love, or jealousy, was a sufficient end, or, in the case of the white witch, the pure desire of doing good.

There still remain bewildering portions of those old confessions relating to the experiences of witches who saw the result of their spells and formulae, who witnessed events that seemingly transcended all natural laws, and which we are apt to set down as delusion, or stark lying. Some of these may in fact have been accidental operations of unknown natural laws such as we meet with occasionally today. Many others besides myself have seen things moved about without human hands at a spiritualistic séance, in apparent contravention of the laws of gravitation. But assuming all fraud eliminated, and test conditions perfect, the natural conclusion is that one is confronted with some material force, capable of doing material work, of whose nature we are ignorant, but which is as open to scientific examination and explanation as any other material force. Many of the experiences recorded in the confessions seem to refer to levitation pure and simple. As when one of the North Berwick circle speaks of being bodily lifted up in her chair, and carried into another room. It is true that another of the same circle speaks of seeing the Devil carrying her and others. But at the spiritualistic séances today, we are told how 'the Spirits' have moved chairs and other articles for no apparent reason except to demonstrate that 'They' are there. It seems easier, both in the case of the witch covens, and of the séances, to assume some as yet unknown force accidentally set in motion. But the visions, which seem really to have occult value, as throwing light on the mental outlook of the period, occurred so far as one can make out between waking and sleeping; and we find the dream and the reality so closely blended that it is impossible to disentangle them. Thus a white witch charged with healing, and condemned to be burnt, while lying in prison awaiting execution, dreams of a beautiful youth who appears and gives her a rose, with the assurance that she shall suffer no pain. On awaking, the rose is physically there, and she goes to the stake without a tremor, 'being assisted of her Master the Devil', says the chronicle. Had it been in medieval Catholic Italy, instead of Presbyterian Scotland, she would have been canonized, and the story been widely published, instead of being relegated to an obscure MS volume and well nigh or quite forgotten.

Then, again the witches of Isabel Goudie's coven went wild rides, and made expeditions far and wide, always, however, waking in their beds, but subsequent testimony showed that, in some cases at least, the things that they fancied they had done only in fancy, had been materially accomplished. These things also are paralleled today in the experience of those who have dreamed of visiting friends or relatives on some of the fields of battle, and have afterwards heard that they were veritably seen there, in dream or vision, the notable point in such experiences being that they appeared utterly natural. And it was at these times between waking and sleeping that apparently the greatest number of the witch visions occurred, and formulae were taught. Then it was that most of the communications with the Devil took place, and then the witch on the appropriate day and hour was able to journey to the Witch-Sabbath. Was this all a dream? Clearly, from the descriptions left us in various confessions, the witches did not think so. In the ordinary practices there was the fascination, the intoxication of a mad excitement. Probably the effect on the brain was not far removed from the effect of the intoxication of alcohol, or perhaps we might rather say of hashish, but simply and easily procured, and accompanied by ecstatic visions. The physical presence of the Devil (whatever this might actually be) enormously increased the delight of the intoxication, and the culmination was in the revels of the Sabbath. Much might be said of this. The undoubted traces have been summarized in brilliant descriptions by Goethe in Germany, by Merejkowski in Italy of the Renaissance, by Max Hueffer in this country, partially too by Harrison Ainsworth in his Lancashire Witches, but none of these are really very convincing. They hardly caught the witches' own thoughts, and leave but the impression of a vivid nightmare. Yet there are actual descriptions by witches who profess to have been there, and possibly it might be done.

Returning for a moment to the question of the Rituals. There is little doubt of the antiquity of very many of them. We find them in the Grimoire, and in Trithemius; we search back through the pages of Virgil and Hesiod, and we seem to see the origins of the same formulae. We look at the Book of the Dead, and the same meet us again in ancient Egypt. In the Confessions of Isabel Goudie and other witches of her circle appear mutilated and corrupt forms of the same, still recognizable; and so with the Kinross circle, and the North Berwick circle, and many others. And today among the Gipsies many of the old formulae are still current, if only we are lucky enough to find them communicative on the subject, which is very rare. Charles Godfrey Leland got some, and preserved them. But the very corruption of them indicates a notable point, namely, that the precise ceremony is not essential, nor the comprehension of it. There are certain things they do. They make wax images, or they tie knots in black thread, or they wet a clout and beat it, or lay it out to dry, and they recite certain words that have in many cases become mere meaningless gibberish (but always, be it said, with a certain rhyme and rhythm). In many cases these can be traced back to actual invocations and prayers to gods believed in when the world was young. A large volume might be filled with the history of witchcraft rituals and invocations, but it would bring us no nearer to understanding the witch. It would remain a curious study in folk-lore. The one outstanding and relevant fact is that the Rituals, mutilated and corrupt as they are, yet work, or at least the practitioners believe they do. And so we practically arrive at this. A man or woman — but more often a woman — who is a natural magician, is led to try some simple experiments, and succeeding by means of a power which probably is latent in all of us, is moved to go on, loving the excitement, and loving the success and the power till the excitement grows like dram drinking. And we have to admit on the evidence that there must be some power in the Rituals themselves. They not merely inflame the imagination of the practitioner. They do this, but they do something more, and the Ritual and its user mutually act and react, creating a wild intoxication of ecstasy. It becomes impossible to resist, impossible to stop; fame, fortune, reputation, life itself may be thrown into the gulf, to secure more and more the delights of that mad dream.

And to the outer world the effects are manifest. People incurred the ill-will of witches and were cursed, ill-luck dogged their footsteps. There was an unknown secret power threatening them. Waves of panic set in. The ministers of religion improved the occasion to rouse a fear of Satan and all his works in the interests of religion, and so tales were told from mouth to mouth till no story was too fantastic to find credence, and a clamorous demand arose for the cruellest and most drastic persecution, and among all this welter it is hard enough to find and follow the shining thread of truth. Yet truth is there, and witchcraft is a very real thing, the materials for the study are accessible, and a rich harvest awaits the patient investigator.

I have perforce omitted many most interesting phases of the subject, such for example as the transformation of witches into animal forms, and the curious effect of what is termed repercussion. That is to say the idea that when a witch in animal form is wounded, say by a blow or a shot, the actual wound will appear on the human body when the witch returns to her own person. Of this there is much evidence, and several ingenious theories have been formed to account for it. Or again, the power of witches to see and have intercourse with elemental spirits, and for this also there are appropriate rituals. One very old MS in the Ashmole Collection at Oxford was discovered and copied by Bishop Percy. It is entitled 'An Excellent Waye to get a Faerie', and is full of interest, throwing a flood of light on other rituals and traditions. This form of magic is practised to this day in the Western Islands, and I have myself been shown what was declared to be the spoor or track of elemental spirits, and have heard predictions of weather and other coming events based thereon.

The student should make up his mind definitely whether it is witchcraft or folklore that he intends to study: both are profoundly interesting, but essentially different, though they overlap at many points. Perhaps we may say that folklore is the archaeology, and witchcraft the biology, of this phase of human history. We study folklore from outside, curious only as to its external aspects, the legend is a legend and no more, its form and its variants are the important points. But we study witchcraft from within; the nature and psychology of the witch, what she did and why she did it, her own view of herself and her powers and doings, what in fact it feels like to be a witch, are the essentials of the study, and the truth of the stories becomes of paramount importance.

If we can but succeed in making the witch human, we have gone a long way towards understanding one of the most complex problems of medieval, and indeed modern, history. And this we shall not do by talking glibly of ignorant superstitions, and relegating all the stories we have to the domain of folklore. It is a field of occultism well defined, and illustrated by a wealth of example, not difficult of access, and very well worth the working.

[Reprinted from *The Occult Review*, Vol. XXV, No. 6 (June 1917), pp. 328-36.]

9. On Witchcraft in Scotland

[In his 'Notes of the Month', for September 1915, Ralph Shirley, editor of *The Occult Review*, printed this extended comment on Brodie-Innes's newly published novel, *The Devil's Mistress*, prefacing it with these words: 'As to what use Mr. Brodie Innes has made of [the sources from which he has drawn his story] from the point of view of the writer of romance, I think he can best tell us in his own words, and I am therefore subjoining the statement on the subject which he has been kind enough to send me for the special benefit of readers of this Magazine'.]

It is a little strange that among all the diligent investigation of occult phenomena, one of the most instructive and fertile fields has been almost entirely neglected, namely, the so-called witchcraft of the sixteenth and seventeenth centuries. In the records of this subject we find nearly every class of phenomena that attracts inquirers to-day, and examined by the keenest judicial intellects of the time. This was the case in Scotland, where we find a man like Lord Advocate Mackenzie, brilliant, sceptical, and trained in the most exact sifting of evidence, devoting much time and thought to the study of the subject, and convincing himself at first hand and against his will of the reality of many of the alleged phenomena. We find not merely the vulgar spells familiar to every one's mind, but all the range of telepathy, clairvoyance, psychometry, prediction, trance-mediumship, levitation, in fact all the subjects that are the field of occult students to-day, recorded in exact detail, and submitted to careful and thorough judicial investigation. And it is safe to say that there is not a single type of occult phenomena that may not be found in these remarkable records. The accounts are very voluminous, some of them very difficult of access, they are full of much that is purely trivial, yet to the patient student they yield a rich harvest.

Perhaps one of the most interesting of all, and the key to nearly all the occult phenomena of the time, is to be found in the confession of Isabel Goudie, the witch of Aulderne, the manuscript of which is preserved in the archives of the Court of Justiciary, in Edinburgh, and considerable parts of which are printed in an Appendix to Pitcairne's

Criminal Trials. The occult powers and knowledges at that time were ascribed to the direct agency of the Devil. But, be it said in passing, this was not the Devil of theologians, or of the Bible, but rather a species of Pan, the personification of the Powers of Nature. The very same powers which the brethren of the Rosy Cross claimed to possess seem to have been exercised by many of the witches, and proved by very complete evidence, and in these witchcraft records the modus operandi may be traced in full detail.

To Isabel Goudie the Devil came in the guise of a man, who became her lover, and here we may note a remarkable circumstance. At the identically same date in various parts of Scotland, and also in America, there are accounts of the appearance of the Devil in human form, and every one is precisely similar. I have in my library two somewhat rare little books. One is entitled, W*itchcraft in Kinross-shire — being Full Details of Criminal Trials for Witchcraft and Sorcery at Crook of Devon;* the other *Wonders of the Invisible World, or Salem Witchcraft,* published at Boston, and consisting largely of letters [131] addressed to the well-known Mr. Cotton Mather in the latter half of the seventeenth century. It is practically impossible to imagine a common origin for these accounts. Yet in every one the personal appearance of the Devil is the same, the grave scholarly aspect, the neat grey clothes, knee breeches and grey stockings, the buckled shoes, the blue Scotch bonnet. How then did Isabel Goudie, in the lonely farmhouse in Aulderne, at the very same time give the same description to the minutest details? She alone, however, gives the account of the Devil as a lover, and from other confessions of the same place and time we gather that she was the prime favourite — the queen of the coven.

The great value of her confession lies in her obvious desire to tell everything, all that the witches did, and how they did it. Much was of the nature of what is now called "Sympathetic Magic"— and Isabel's spells may be usefully compared with the voluminous accounts of the same formulae collected by Frazer in *The Golden Bough*, from all countries, and all ages. It is impossible that these could have been known to the farmer's wife in a remote country district in Scotland. Yet she was taught the very same means to attain similar results. In her accounts of how she was taught and the things she was shown, either in words or in pictures, we see a great resemblance to what is now called in modern occult slang "The Subliminal Consciousness." At that time it was ascribed to intercourse with a personal Devil. The theory, perhaps, matters little, the results are very similar. Isabel Goudie records how she drew the moon down from heaven. Now, whatever this means precisely, the very same thing, and the very same process are stated to be used in Morocco to this day, as is told by Dr. Emile Mauchamp, whose remarkable posthumous work, *La Sorcellerie au Maroc,* has been ably edited by M. Jules Bois, and these again are precisely the same spells as were used ages ago in Thessaly, as told by the ancient Greek writers, and recounted by Virgil in the sixth Book of the Aeneid. How then came Isabel Goudie to use the same ceremonies, and practically the same words, which, it is safe to say, were unknown, even to scholars of her day? The Devil, the Etheric Double, the Higher Self, the Subliminal Consciousness, all are theories, more or less plausible; the one thing certain is that these phenomena do occur.

Another remarkable point is her visit to Fairyland, as told in her confession, and how she got there. There is a manuscript in the Ashmole collection at Oxford, which was copied by Bishop Percy, and of which an account appeared in *The Queen* for May 14, 1881, entitled, "An Excellent Way to Gett a Fayrie," and this same excellent way did Isabel adventure on, with success as she avers.

It is also to be noted that the things which Isabel says she did by magic art are recorded in absolutely independent documents of the time to have occurred, such as sicknesses, deaths, and other catastrophes. It is, of course, possible here that she may have heard of all these events, and claimed to have caused them. But the coincidences are too many to make this probable. Isabel Goudie was the wife of a farmer living in a lonely farm on the edge of Lochloy, which was a dreary mere some two miles from the town of Nairn. She was of superior station to her husband, who seems to have been a dull, heavy man, and in the neighbouring ruins of the Castle of Inshoch she met with the grey-clad scholar whom contemporary records describe and term the Devil.

In the Kirk of Aulderne, some two miles off, she was baptized by him, renouncing her Christian Baptism, and the old Castle of Inshoch became their rendezvous, transformed as her imagination pictured it, or diabolical glamour caused her to see it, to a magnificent feudal hall. Here, under the guidance of her demon-lover, she learned the spells that would make a floating straw into a splendid horse, how to make the wax images so famous in all witchlore, how to use the flint arrow heads to this day called "fairy arrows" in Devon and Cornwall, and in the West Highlands; how to make the Moon Paste, which also is a formula current in Morocco and in Brittany to-day, and derived from ancient Thessaly. She made the acquaintance of Sir Robert Gordon, of Gordonstown, the famous wizard, who had been a privy councillor of King Charles I. He also, according to tradition, had made his own pact with the Devil, and in Gordonstown House to-day are many letters from the "wizard laird"; his portrait hangs in the drawing-room, and the remains of his alchemic furnaces may still be seen.

In the local folk lore of Morayshire are still many traces of the witchcraft of Isabel Goudie, many customs not to be understood without reference to the confession. The spell of "horse and hattock," whereby the weird riders got their horses, and hunted not merely deer, but men, was long known and it is said, practised by the boys of Forres, for pure mischief. It would take far too long to follow out all the curious lines of investigation suggested in this wonderful document. But the diligent student of occultism will be richly rewarded if he will take the confession and carefully verify every point. Where, for instance, Isabel records how the minister of Aulderne was cursed by the witches; turn up the Presbytery records and see how that curse bore fruit. Above all, compare the ceremonies, and the words of the Spells, with those directed to the same end in other ages and other countries, and notice particularly that Isabel was both a black and a white witch. She could ban or bless, kill or heal, but her healing was in the name of the Holy Trinity, and the cursing was in the name of the Devil.

Altogether in this confession and in the various documents and records suggested by its study, lies a mine of occult information hitherto practically unexplored and promising the richest results.

10. An Egyptian Ritual Against Apophi and its Relation to Modern Witchcraft

Some years ago a learned and famous Egyptologist said to me that the most striking characteristic of ancient Egypt was its modernity. The whole life of the people, their ideas, their social and domestic customs, the very children's toys, seemed more familiar to us than, say, the Tudor period in our own country. And this is notably the case with their occultism, with only this exception, that with them it was far more precise and scientific than it ever was in this country, or in modern times, and for that reason intensely valuable to the student of today. The Kings and Priests of Egypt were the elect of those who had studied with success in the 'School of Wisdom', a philosophical aristocracy, chosen because they were not only wise, but could use their wisdom. The staff of the king-initiate was of so mighty a potency that, with it in his hand, the leader of armies was as mighty as Pharaoh himself.

Dr Wynn Westcott writes: 'In studying Egyptian magic one has at once a thoroughly scientific satisfaction. One is troubled with no vague theories; but receives precise practical details; we observe that every square inch of the Upper and Under Worlds is mapped out.'

Wherever, therefore, we can find an Egyptian prototype of modern witchcraft formulae, we are likely to find in the former a complete and reasoned scientific system, of which the latter give only vague and halting traces, much corrupted by oral transmission from the ignorant to the more ignorant. The root-formula of ancient Egypt was that the evolution of what is material follows the type and symbol of the emanation of the spiritual; that spirit and matter are opposite faces of the same mystery. Hence we have an elaborate system of correspondences, according to which the conceptions of the mind, the words of the mouth, and the functions of the body possess analogies from which a complete system of the rules of life and death can be constructed.

I will here allude to one phase only of witchcraft, that to which the mind most readily recurs in considering the question, namely the formulae of cursing, often thought to be the sole manifestation of the evil powers of witches and wizards, and which is the dark reverse of the powers of healing and blessing.

In Egyptian mythology the great bad god was Typhon Apophis. He it was who obstructed and destroyed the benefits bestowed on man by Ra the Sun. The rationale, therefore, of the Rituals for banishing evil things was to devote them to Typhon Apophis, from whom they came, and then to expel and banish him and them bag and baggage, in order that the power of Ra to bless the earth and the dwellers thereon might be re-established, and this power belonged to the priest-initiates of the Temples.

For the casting out of evil, then, the rituals were devised, and this seems a long way from the witch's cursings. But we have to remember that in ancient Egypt, as in medieval Europe, evil was a term of very varying significance, and one thinks perhaps the hierophant's conception of evil might sometimes have been merely that which was personally annoying to himself. After all, this is but human nature, and we can readily imagine that if a farmer on old Nile should withhold his temple dues, and attempt to cheat the priests, as without doubt they occasionally did, it might be a short and simple solution to devote him to Typhon Apophis, even as we may bid a man who has defrauded us go to the devil. Only in ancient Egypt we are told they did it with effect.

An instance of the survival of this old idea was told me by a London doctor. A man came to see him from the Basque, reputed to be a great magus and healer, a man of strange knowledges, desirous to learn something of bacteriology. Among other things he was shown under a powerful microscope a typhus germ. At this he looked very intently, returning again and again to this particular specimen. At last he said, 'I have long wished to know exactly what Typhon was like. Now that I know, I can cure the disease. I have a patient.' Some days after he returned with a clay model fashioned exactly like the germ, some two or three inches in diameter, and asked the doctor to accompany him to the patient, a fellow-countryman, lying in a sordid bedroom in a miserable slum, and undoubtedly suffering from typhus fever, devotedly nursed by his wife. No idea of calling in a doctor seemed to have occurred to them. They trusted implicitly to the Basque 'wise man'. He placed one hand on the patient's head, and with the other drew from his pocket his clay model, chanting under his breath some strange formula. Then he threw the model on the ground, and in a seeming access of fury stamped upon it, breaking it to pieces, reviled it, spat upon it, and cursed it volubly, in a quaint mixture of French and Basque.

An Egyuptian Ritual Against Apophi 115

Finally he said, 'Now I know Typhon. He is gone. He will not come back.' My friend, the doctor, naturally insisted on proper notification of the case, and the taking of the usual prescribed measures. But before any steps could be taken, the fever was abating, and the man on the road to recovery. Being a scientific sceptic, he ascribed the recovery to the excellent nursing of his wife, and to a vigorous constitution. But in any case it was curious to find the old Egyptian banishing of Typhon Apophis practised by a Basque in London, in the twentieth century. This was a work of healing, and one fancies was much on the lines of the work of the old priest-initiates. But it is easy also to imagine that instead of a sick man it might be some one who had offended the exorciser; such a one would of course, in his opinion, be inspired or possessed by evil spirits, would be a servant or an instrument of Typhon Apophis, and the exorcism a right and proper thing. Whatever injures or offends us is evil in our eyes, and the ritual would readily come to be used for private vengeance.

We ask naturally what was the old formula of Egypt, devised in the days when ceremonial magic was an exact science, whose inherent strength has enabled the system to survive for many thousand years, long after all knowledge or belief in its rationale had been lost to its practitioners. With this key the student can interpret many of the recorded practices of witches and wizards, of which themselves were utterly ignorant.

In the British Museum is such a formula contained in the Papyrus of Nesi Amsu, a Scribe of Amen Ra (No. 10188), dated in the twelfth year of Pharaoh Alexander, the son of Alexander (i.e. Alexander II), about 312 BC, almost every detail of which may be paralleled from the witchcraft trials. It must be recited over the name of Apophi, written in green ink on new papyrus, and over a wax figure of Apophi inscribed with his name in green ink. This green ink was for some time a puzzle to me, for the black magic rituals mostly prescribe the writing of names in blood, usually the blood of a crow, but occasionally of other birds or beasts. But an old minister from the western islands, a great Gaelic scholar, knowing that I was curious in such matters, showed me an ancient Gaelic MS of fairy lore, wherein it was said that one may perhaps be afflicted by ill-disposed fairies, and for remedy thereof a certain fairy name should be written in green, the same being the fairy colour, and if this were buried by the doorstep of the afflicted person the fairies would be unable to attack him. The wax image of course appears constantly in all the literature of black magic. In the first of the witchcraft trials in Scotland Buchanan relates that the witches roasted upon a wooden spit the image of King Duffus, made of wax. The Clavicula Salomonis has particulars for making and consecrating the wax. Other materials, however, were sometimes used. The details of the making of Isabel Goudie's moon-paste I have recorded in *The Devil's Mistress,* the lacunae in the Scottish accounts being supplied from Morocco, the processes being obviously identical. In the trial of Lady Monro of Fowlis, June 22, 1590, the material was clay. Whereof also the Basque before noted made his image of Typhon. In this case the indictment bears: "In the fyrst, thow art accusit of making twa picturis of clay, in companie with Christiane Roiss and Marjorie Neyne McAllister, alias Loskie Loncart, in the said Christiane Roissis Westir Chalmer in Canorth, the ane made for the destructioune and consumptioune of the young laird of Fowlis, and the uthir for the young Ladie Balnagown, to the effect that the ane should be put at the brig end of Fowlis, and the uthir at Ard moir, for the destructioune of the saidis young Laird and Ladie. Quhilkis twa picturis being sett on the North syde of the Chalmer, the said Loskie Loncart tuik twa elf arrows and delyuerit ane to ye said Katherine, and the uther ye said Christiane Roiss Malcumsone held in her awin hand, and thow shott twa shottis with the said arrow heid att ye said Ladie Balnagoun, and Loskie Loncart shott thrie Shottis at ye said young Laird of Fowlis."

In this trial it is also recorded that certain images were made of butter, which is a curious parallel to certain ceremonies recorded by Abbe Huc of the Tibetans.

A distinction strikes one at once in comparing these modern rituals with that against Apophi. The wax image in the latter case was that of the great bad god himself, and it was his name that was written in green ink. But the witches never, so far as is recorded, made an image of the Devil. The reason of this becomes evident at once when we reflect that to the mediaeval witch the Devil was not the bad god, but on the contrary he was to her the bountiful bestower of all delights, the good god whom she delighted to honour. According to Isabel Goudie and her circle the Devil was a lover more delightful than any man. And though some of them do say in their confessions "The Lord forgive me for speaking of him as a man," this interpolation belonged to their penitence, and perhaps was inserted by the scribe who took down their words more or less imperfectly. The image, according to this ritual, of whatever material formed, was to be destroyed, and its destruction to involve that which was represented, or at least its banishment, therefore it must be something inimical to, and deemed evil by, the exorciser. And certainly the Devil was not deemed evil by the witches practising black witchcraft (for here I say nothing of white witches).

A parallel may be found in the old custom which lingered to comparatively modern times of burning Judas Iscariot, a sort of medieval Guy Fawkes celebration, wherein apparently, in its origin, all the sins of the parish in the preceding year were laid upon the figure, which was then solemnly burnt, amid considerable jubilation.

I have seen a record of a certain parish in England where Judas was burnt almost to the time of living memory, the rector whereof, probably more of a folklorist than a divine, laid upon the head of Judas sundry misfortunes that had happened to the parish, including a bad harvest, explaining that these arose from the misdoings of the parishioners. The following year the harvest was excellent, and the people's churchwarden, who was the chief farmer in the district, was so impressed by this circumstance, that he took his turn, and laid on the head of Judas some of his own private grievances, including the conduct of a neighbour who had got the better of him in a bargain. This was deemed so superstitious that the burning of Judas was prohibited. I regret that I am not permitted to give the name of the village, some of the descendants of the chief actors still living there. The story, however, curiously repeats the old Egyptian ritual against Apophi, and shows how easily an attempt to exercise occult powers for good may pass into black magic.

Recurring now to the papyrus of Nesi Amsu, the exorciser being ceremonially purified, and having made the wax figure according to directions, shall burn it in a fire of dried grass, when melted shall mix it with excrement, at the 6th hour of the night of the 15th day, and throw it into the fire at daybreak of the 16th day. Spit upon it many times at the beginning of every hour of the day, until the shadow comes round again. Defile him with the left foot. The instructions here specially relate to the control of weather, the exorciser is directed to perform the ceremony when tempest was raging in the East, and when Ra sets red and threatening, then will the ritual prevent rainstorms and thunder destroying the crops. But not only for this purpose; the chapter of the papyrus concludes, 'It is good for a man on earth or in heaven to do this. He will attain dignities which are above him, and be delivered from all evil.'

Here then we see Ra in the character that in modern mystical phrase would be called the central spiritual sun, manifested materially as the physical sun in the sky, when it was weather conditions that had to be modified (as necessarily was frequently the case in Egypt). But manifested also as a bringer of good to the exorciser himself, both on the material and on the spiritual plane. Hence he is directed to use the formula often, as a Christian of today might be directed to be regular and diligent in his devotions.

I would here caution the student to beware of the very common error of assuming that old mythologies are nothing but weather myths, and the old ceremonial magic no more than an attempt to control the weather, in fact a sort of glorified prayer for rain or fine weather, a matter wherein an African witch-doctor can usually give many points to the parson. Ancient Egypt gives us the key. The old wisdom-religions go right to the heart of things, to the inner spiritual causes of outward material phenomena, and operating there by means of ceremonial formulae the outward effect followed. Weather was one of the commonest examples, and, it was said, one of the easiest.

The second chapter of the papyrus relates to the method of dealing with enemies, called there the enemies of Ra-Hamarchis; and Ra being that power that brings good (or what he deems to be good) to the exorciser, the enemies of Ra-Hamarchis will be usually his own enemies. Wax figures must be made of these, and not only of themselves, but of their father, and mother, and children, and their names also inscribed in green on papyrus. These are then devoted to Apophi and tied round with dark hair. Then the exorciser shall curse them, spit upon them, defile them with the left foot, and pierce them with a stone knife, after which they are to be put into a flaming fire, and burnt with the Xessan plant (I have not been able to identify this) at sunrise, noon, or the first hour of the night. The figure of Apophi as before directed should then be burnt at the festival of the new moon. For the use of hair in the cursing rituals reference may be made to Isabel Goudie's confession. I have among my treasures a Jewish phylactery; the parchment scroll inside the tiny box is tied round with a single long black hair. A learned Rabbi told me the purpose was probably to invoke a blessing on some dearly beloved. The same formula being used according to the intention either for blessing or cursing. The piercing with a stone knife is paralleled by Lady Monro's elf arrows; these being, of course, the flint arrow heads, believed in Celtic Scotland to have been made by Satanic agency. In Egypt flint weapons which are found in great abundance were considered as relics of the earlier gods, the One Supreme, the All-Father, Neter, whose worship was pre-dynastic, being symbolized by an axe, whose head in the tomb paintings is bound to the shaft by thongs, proving that it was a flint head. The later symbol had the shaft wedged into a socket in the head, showing that metal had superseded flint.

The next book of the papyrus directs the exorciser to write down the names of all the male and female demons of which his heart is afraid, and to wrap these in a coverlid, together with a figure of Apophi, to tie them round tightly and put in a fire, to spit four times, and stamp with the left foot. 'The doing of this,' says the papyrus, 'hath great effect on earth, and in the nether world.'

The nether world here clearly means that which we call the astral, and is a recognition of the fact, well known to occultists, though for the most part only empirically known, that to control the manifestation of many potent forces it is necessary to employ both material and astral means.

The expression 'the demons of which his heart is afraid' is unfamiliar to us now. But a study of the minor evil gods of Egypt show that their manifestation in the human body is in bodily weaknesses, such as the craving, chronic and uncontrollable, for alcohol or hypnotic drugs such as hashish, or such a weakness as fear, violent anger, jealousy, or the like, the attacks of which are sudden and involuntary. These weaknesses are often unaccountable, and practically incurable by modern official methods. The Egyptian ascribed them to possession by some of the minor bad gods, and dealt with them accordingly. So if an initiate, or one who had power, found himself assailed by uncontrollable fear, let us say, he recognized that the god, or demon, having charge of this mood, had somehow found entrance to his house of life, and he promptly wrote the demon's name, devoted him to Apophi, and exorcised them both. So we find in medieval Europe the thaumaturgist-saints would recognize obsession, where we with the superior knowledge and wisdom of the twentieth century see only 'an obscure nervous condition' which we can neither explain, nor account for, nor cure, and they devoted the obsessing demon to Satan, and cast him out. The black magicians of the Middle Ages sometimes not only cast him out, but caused him to go in, and this also by the power of the name. I have been shown over a hundred names and seals of demons from medieval books of magic, and many instances are recorded from the times of the Pharaohs till within a couple of hundred years of this present time, of magicians who in time of war, have cast fear into the hearts of the enemies of their country. Froissart records the work of magicians who accompanied the German armies in his day, causing fogs to cover a retreat, and the like.

Many of the troubles anciently ascribed to obsession are now sometimes dealt with, and it is said successfully, by hypnotism, and a new vocabulary has grown up, and we hear much of suggestion, and autosuggestion, of the subliminal, and superliminal consciousness, and of unconscious cerebration, none of which seems to take us very much further than the old theory of obsession, but enables the scientist to evade the use of a much-dreaded term, and to present a demi-semi-materialistic theory, even if it be an unaccountable one. There seems some reason to believe that the ancient Egyptians were well acquainted with hypnotism, as a means of exorcizing demons.

This part of the papyrus of Nesi Amsu concludes with a long list of the titles and offices of the scribe, but whether these are intended to be recited for the terrorizing of Apophi, or are simply given as warrant for the ritual which he sets forth, is not clear. Probably the latter, but possibly also it may be a hint to any exorciser to state during the performance of the ritual his own qualifications and titles to command the spirits. The next chapters contain the words of exorcism. This is the 'Book of the Overthrowing of Apophi, the Enemy of Unnefer, Life, Strength, Health, Triumphant'. To be recited in a Temple of Amen Ra, Lord of the Thrones of the two Lands (i.e. of Upper and Lower Egypt typified by the dual crown of the Pharaohs) at the Head of the Apis Bull, in the course of each day. The hymns mainly consist of a beautiful and poetic celebration of the glories and the victory of Ra.

In an old Rituale Romanum, which is one of the treasures in my library, is a formula of exorcism which opens with the recitation of the psalm "Lift up your heads, O ye gates! and be ye lift up, ye everlasting doors! and the King of Glory shall come in." It seems almost like an echo across the centuries of the old Egyptian formula.

In the Temple of Amen Ra the same ceremonies were gone through, but with more elaboration. The officiating priest spat four times on the image of Apophi, he degraded it with his left foot, taking on himself the form of Horus, he made a steel lance (this was a later addition to the ritual, which in its origin dated from the time when only flint weapons were known), with this he pierces the heads of the demons whom the heart fears, saying, 'Therefore shalt thou be exalted, Ra, for thy fiendish enemies are pierced, Apophi is slaughtered, and fiends of the devil have been cast down' (Compare 'Be thou exalted, Lord, in thine own strength. So will we sing and praise Thy power,' as recited in the exorcism.) He then puts fetters on Apophi. Ra, and Horus the son of Ra, declare that Apophi shall be bound and fettered, that he do no more mischief on the earth, for justice has come upon him.

The priest then smites Apophi with the stone knife. This seems to be the continuation of the older ritual. The image is then with appropriate words put on the fire.

It would seem that this ritual should be performed just before the dawn. For the concluding rubric is 'After Ra has risen, stand facing him with arms bent (that is in the position of adoration — as figured in the tomb paintings), saying, "Ra has triumphed over thee, Apophi"'; repeat four times, "In very truth has Ra been made to triumph over thee, Apophi. Destroyed is Apophi. Therefore art thou exalted, O Ra, for thine enemies are destroyed. Shine therefore, O Ra, for thine enemies are fallen. Verily Ra hath destroyed all thine enemies, O Ra-a-a — Life, Strength, Health."' This ceremony in the Temple of Amen Ra was clearly a formula of white magic for the banishing of evils, famine, and disease, as well as moral evil and wrong, and therefore is appropriately paralleled by the Church formulae of exorcism. With this may be profitably compared the black magical formulae, as recorded in the confessions of witches. Storms might be raised, and boats wrecked in much the same manner as the beneficent rain might be invoked in time of drought in the Nile valley, and again by material actions, coupled with appropriate words. Isabel Goudie employed a wet clout beaten with a wooden beetle. And the words as quoted by the witches were often a degraded corruption of psalms and Church rituals. The evil against which the spells were directed was that which was obnoxious to the witch herself; the enemies devoted to the powers of ill, and ceremonially cursed, were those who had offended her. The good sought was the gratification of her own passions, the product of selfishness, envy, malice, spite, jealousy, or the like, often developing into the pure delight in doing harm for the pleasure of cruelty.

In the accurate and scientific system of ancient Egypt we may find the clue to much that is puzzling in the magic, white and black, of more modern times. We have but to suppose such a reversal of ideals as has produced the Satanists of our own day, and assume such a reversal as should set Typhon Apophis in the place of Ra, or should put pure and undiluted selfishness in the place of altruism. Hate sits on the throne of Love, and black and white magic are traced back to the same original.

[Reprinted from *The Occult Review,* Vol XXVI, No. 2 (August 1917), pp. 75-84.]

11. Ethnological Traces in Scottish Folklore

Is it possible by means of folklore to solve any of the problems of the various races that have swept over Scotland, whose blend now forms the bulk of the inhabitants of this country? The problem is so intricate and difficult that surely any light from any source, any clue, no matter what, deserves attention and investigation. In the course of a short paper I cannot hope to do more than indicate one or two out of very many directions in which research might be expected to yield useful results.

A word of caution is necessary to start with. We must not assume, because we find the same folk-tale in two distinct countries, that either of them came from the other, or that both came from the same source. It may have been so; but, on the other hand, they may, quite as probably, have arisen independently in two widely different places; and this is especially the case with respect to so-called nature-myths. Primitive peoples trying to personify the sun, or the wind, or the weather, will do so much in the same way, and make very similar stories. Another caution, which seems to me much needed by one class of folklorists, is not to try to force every folk-tale into a weather-myth.

But, all due allowance being made for these cautions, there seems no doubt that the folk-tales of various races, have characteristics of their own; and when we know from other evidence that certain races have lived here in this land, and we find folk-tales bearing the characteristic marks of the folklore of each race either actually current in Scotland, or recorded as having been current within memory, it seems we have a clue, at least as important and worth investigating as the shape of the skull, the flattened shin-bone, or other physical points. Not positive proof, it is true, but what a lawyer might call adminicles of evidence.

The earliest races are lost in the dim mists of antiquity. There were Neolithic men, cave-dwellers, river-drift men. They have left their flint weapons, occasionally their rough and spirited drawings on bones and horns, but probably no tales that we have now go back to an antiquity so remote.

Then we have the rearers of the serpent mounds, the builders of the stone circles, all those who are classed together and called 'Druids'; and also the makers of those subterranean structures often called 'Picts' houses' (be they houses, or storerooms, or places of defence, or places of burial), whom Mr. MacRitchie[1] considers to have been a primitive race of Mongolian pygmies, and the origin of the traditional fairies. All of these have left material traces which we can investigate; and there are, besides, traditions of Picts, Fomors (whoever they may have been), and others before the coming of the Celt. Now if we appeal to folklore here, we do find here and there stories utterly unlike the usual character of the stories of this country, dim legends of remote and inaccessible places, where in caverns underground there still are said to dwell the last remnants of the savage and diminutive race, ugly, cruel, and blood-thirsty, desiring always to catch and sacrifice a lonely wayfarer with loathsome rites. It is very difficult to find these traditions now, partly because there remain very few unexplored and inaccessible places in Scotland, and partly because, for some reason or other, there is always a considerable reticence about recounting the very old tales. Still, here and there one may yet find old shepherds or gillies who will recall that some grandfather, or remoter ancestor, in their youth used to tell of a traveller being caught, and perhaps rescued with difficulty; and perhaps, if one has rare luck, some ceremony of sacrifice may be described, or hinted. These ceremonies seem to have a remarkable similarity to what is told in Russian folk-tales, such as those collected by the late Mr. Ralston and others; and herein may possibly lie some confirmation of Mr. MacRitchie's theories, for the stories are not Scottish. In every characteristic they are utterly alien, and they are Mongolian. Some memory may be here of that primitive pygmy race; but, on the other hand, nothing can possibly be more remote from the Scottish or Celtic fairy faith, so well expounded by Mr. Wentz,[2] which is eminently kindly, graceful, and friendly to humanity (if somewhat tricksy and mischievous), than these cruel, savage, half-human, half-bestial creatures, who are yet entirely material and physical.

With the Celts, who came later, are inseparably associated the Iberi, and these possibly became a mixed race in Spain, the Celt-Iberian Peninsula. These Iberi the late Dr. Phenè traced from Asia Minor, through Greece, Southern Italy, Etruria, Spain, the Basque Country, Brittany, the

---

1. See David MacRitchie, *The Testimony of Tradition* (1890), and *Fians, Fairies, and Picts* (1893). There are modern reprints of both titles.
2. See W.Y. Evans-Wentz, *The Fairy-Faith in Celtic Countries* (1911). There are modern reprints.

south and west of England, Wales, the west coast of Scotland, and Ireland, bearing with them everywhere their skill in gold and enamel work, and the cult of the serpent. There seems a strong probability that the serpent mounds, of which a few many be found in Scotland very similar to those in the track I have mentioned, may be due to the Iberi, and the circles to the Celts. If, as Dr. Phenè thought, the name Iberi is the same as Ibri, and so connected with Hebrews – the Beni Israel, the Ibay-Erri, men of the river, or Crossers Over – we may take the curious occurrence of biblical myths in Celtic folk-tales as evidence, when conjoined with more positive proof, of this theory of origin. Many of these tales have been modernised and retold with great effect by Fiona MacLeod, Lady Cromartie, and others. As recounted at the fireside by old Highlanders, they have a simplicity and humour which is quaint and rugged, but with little of the poetry or the reverence these two writers have put into them.

Also if, as some have supposed, the Tuatha de Danann be the same as the Danai of Homer, this may perhaps be the source of the Greek element in Celtic tales which so impressed Professor Blackie.[3]

Folk-tales are apt to cluster about the serpent mounds and the stone circles, but in the case of the former usually they are obscure and difficult to get at. The mounds are avoided; the traditions are of buried treasure, but also of terrible supernatural guardians. In the stone circles, on the other hand, there are formulae and ceremonies that may yet be performed, and whoever can successfully invoke the presiding god of the circle may have whatever he desires. It is natural that these stories also should be told with bated breath, and only to those who are sympathetic and able to keep counsel, for the ministers frown on such beliefs and customs. Nevertheless they are held far more commonly than is generally supposed. An elder of the Free Kirk, and a most God-fearing man, has been known to go at the full of the moon to a stone circle, and do circumambulations and sing old fairy tunes when his wife was dying. I was told the wife got well. Also it is not uncommon in some places for the girls to go on a midsummer midnight and deposit their little trinkets – tiny brooches or what not – on the central stone, and pray for their lovers, or pray that lovers may be sent to them. This belief is akin to the offerings dropped in wishing-wells or hung on wishing-trees. Of course all this is in strict secrecy.

---

3. Prof John Stuart Blackie (1809–1895). See his *The Language and Literature of the Scottish Highlands* (1876).

Another relic of this old faith I have seen myself in the shape of 'cursing stones'. A circle of black stones set up by a crofter over a hundred years ago, one at the dark of every moon, between the old and the new; twelve stones in all there were, and they took a year to set up, each one with walking widdershins, prayers said backwards, and solemn calling on the Devil. The purpose was to curse the man who had stolen his sweetheart. The grandson of the crofter showed me the stones, and told me the story; he said the man cursed took to drink, fell from a roof, broke his back, and died a lingering death in great agony. Of course the evil magician should have come to some terrible end, but I was told he married and lived prosperously to a green old age. So this pagan faith still flourishes; not so markedly as it does in Brittany, but yet quite notably if one knows where to look for it, and how to coax the stories out of the people, which is not easy.

The principal admixture of pure Celtic folk-lore comes from the Scandinavian immigrations, and to disentangle this we need to compare the stories as told in the West Highlands and the Islands with similar stories told in the extreme west of Ireland. For, by history and tradition, where the Gael of Scotland absorbed the Norse invaders, a section of the Irish retreated before them into the wild west, and preserved the purity of their race and their legends, but lost the strength and vigour that the Scottish Gael gained from the blend.

Pure Gaelic mythology covers a wide field, ranging from the Ossianic epic, through romantic and chivalric stories, such as those belonging to Finvara and the Riders of the Sidh, the semi-religious legends of a future life in Tir nan Oge, the Celtic Paradise; the stories of Elementals, particularly the Elementals of the Waters, including all the tales of seal-men and seal-women, those curious half-human creatures who sometimes take wholly human form and intermarry with the children of men; and again, to the pure nature-myths and weather-myths, of which there are plenty.

Most of these stories are current also in Norway, but there is a notable variation which runs through them all, Among the pure Celts the Elementals are gentle, kindly creatures, very friendly to the race of Adam's breed. But with the Scandinavians they are fierce, cruel, and revengeful. In Irish bardic tradition we find the pure Celtic spirit, as shown in the stories of the Daughters of Lir, and of Mananaan Mac Lir, the old gray wizard of the sea, who advised and befriended the swans. But in Norway woe betide him who meets the Kelpie of the Waters, the fierce and terrible sea-horse, with whom may be instructively compared the white horse of O'Donnoghue, Prince of Breffni! Both these types, often blended, may be found among the local traditions of the Isle of Skye where also the blend of races is very marked. The relation of the Ash Yggdrasil of Scandinavian mythology, whose boughs stretched out into heaven, its highest point overshadowing Walhalla, and its roots reaching down to dark hell, with the rowan or mountain-ash has yet to be worked out; but there is no doubt that there is a remarkable similarity in some of the legends, and a great store of folk-tales cluster round the rowan-tree, as also they do around the *Sambucus racemosus* or red-berried elder.

The story of the Forsaken Merman, so beautifully told by Matthew Arnold, is common in Norway, Sweden, and Denmark. In the Isle of Skye, formerly colonised by Norsemen, there are three ballads on the subject. Rhythmically they are akin to the Danish ballad of 'Agnes and the Merman,' but it is noticeable that in the Norse legend the merman is the water-horse, the Rosmar, a huge, uncouth creature of the arctic waters, fierce, savage, and cruel, though he could assume any form, and, in the likeness of a man, married Morag. But in the Celtic form of the story he is gentle and lovable. There are exhaustive notes on this legend in 'Hind Etin,' Child's *English and Scottish Popular Ballads* (large edition); also R.C. Prior's *Ancient Danish Ballads* (vol.iii.), under the title 'Agnes and the Merman.'

The Celtic folklore of the Western Highlands seems to have a genius for absorbing and assimilating the stories of other races, and that not only Scandinavian; even as the Celts themselves have absorbed the races that came to conquer. A notable example of this is in the famous fairy flag of Dunvegan. It is said this flag was given to a MacLeod by a mermaid whom he loved, and who loved him and promised to come to his help, or that of any of his race, whenever the flag was waved; but, alas! MacLeod proved false to the sea-fairy, and the power was restricted to three waves only. The association of a flag, which distinctly belongs to air or fire spirits, with a water Elemental, is in itself curious and the story itself has somehow an exotic flavour about it. And when we look at the flag itself closely, there is little doubt that it is a piece of Saracen embroidery. With this clue, we study the Moorish, Saracen, and Arab traditions, and we find many similar tales of enchanted flags whose waving brought the help of Elementals. There seems, then, great probability that this flag was in fact brought home by some crusading MacLeod, possibly with an Eastern bride, whom he deserted, and that the people of Skye adopted and adapted the tale, fitting it on to a mermaid, as being to them the most likely source of a fairy gift. The battle of Mille-garaidh, in Waternish, is said to have been the last occasion when the fairy flag was unfurled, with an unfortunate result for the invaders from Clan Ranald, who falling under the spell of the flag, thought they saw a vast concourse of armed men, whereas in reality there were but a handful, so that they fled in terror to their galleys, and were almost cut down before they reached the shore. This was in 1570.

There is another class of stories which are found in some form or other very widely distributed: those, namely, of mortals who are carried away by the fairies or some kind of supernatural beings, to revel for a period that appears to them like a single night, but which, in fact, varied from seven years to three hundred in the case of Ossian. These tales are found among the Arab folk-stories. The American Rip van Winkle has certainly a Teutonic origin. But it is claimed that similar traditions were current among the North American Indians. And there are legends of the same nature among the Maoris, whose folklore is among the most interesting and instructive that exists. It is impossible to say that any of these are derived from any other, and we must almost needs conclude that they rose independently. But in the Celtic variants there is a distinctly individual type, and in these stories we find a much nearer approach to the fairy-tales of our childhood than in most of the folk-stories. A noticeable legend belonging to this type is associated with the well-known Gaelic tune – Crodh Chailein, or Colin's Cattle. There are several variants of the story. In its main lines the betrothed of Colin, a wealthy young farmer, was carried off by Finvara and the Riders of the Sidh; Colin was a favourite of the Fairy Queen, and went to ask the return of his sweetheart. Now, by fairy law she must remain for a year and a day (perhaps reminiscent of the custom of handfasting); but it was allowed that she might milk his cattle every evening, and though he could not see her, he might hear her milking-song. At the end of the time she was restored to him. Here we find Finvara and the Fairy Queen at variance, and a glimpse of the laws of fairyland, which in Celtic mythology was a very definite place. Moreover, we have the association of the legend with a certain tune, which is classed by Dr. Keith Norman Macdonald as one of the fairy-tunes. In these fairy-tunes, again, there is material for careful and systematic investigation. According to tradition they were heard by pipers when sleeping on the fairy-knolls, and played over when they woke. For the most part they were never scored, but passed on by ear from one piper to another, and may be of very remote antiquity. Dr. Macdonald finds in the fairy-tunes special qualities which are not found in the Gaelic folk-tunes, and these very qualities have by other musicians been thought to be similar to Egyptian music. There is an old legend telling of the Egyptian immigration of a band of refuges under Galethus, an Achaian, and Scodra, the daughter of Pharaoh, with a following of Egyptians. Possibly the folk-music, as exemplified in the fairy-tunes, might form one clue to this ethnological problem.

Another may be found perhaps in folk-dances. These have hitherto been too little studied in connection with folklore. There is no doubt that they open a very wide field for research. In all countries there have been two leading classes of folk-dances – the war-dance and the temple or religious dance. The primitive dances of North American Indians, Maoris, and others may well be taken as examples, for the special character is strongly marked and the purpose of the dance unmistakable. They will not perform a war-dance for social amusement. A broad distinction seems to emerge from the accounts of all these dances. A couple dancing opposite to each other, as in the Irish jig or the contra-dance – miscalled country-dance – is a social amusement usually symbolic of courtship; the crossing figures, combined with setting movements, recall the charge in battle, stir the warlike passions, and are characteristic of the war-dance. The circular dances, in which the performers either move in a circle or wind in and out in circles going opposite ways, are distinctly religious, belonging to the circle temples, and probably connected with serpentine movements and the serpent cult. With this clue we may, with some probability, conjecture that of the characteristic Celtic dances the reel was a war-dance; the Skye eightsome a religious dance, in which possibly the number the number eight had a special significance; and the so-called schottische merely a social amusement. The sword-dance is a display of skill, and has, with some probability, been ascribed to the triumphant dance of the victor after a fight, when his foeman's captured claymore was crossed with his own on the turf. The study and comparison of the dances of those races which have combined in our Celtic population might yield valuable hints.

When we come to the eastern side of Scotland, and the so-called Lowland peoples, the character of the folklore is entirely changed. In the Lowlands it is Teutonic. The Folk-tales are mainly concerned with ghosts and hauntings. If we meet with Elementals at all, they are neither the gentle, kindly folk of the Celts, nor the fierce and revengeful type of the Scandinavian, but rather gruesome and horrible. Also on this side of Scotland, and among the Teutonic races, we get the witch legends very prominent; and in some districts the cult of the witch persists to the present day. The hauntings generally deal with crime or are entirely unexplained, possibly unexplainable, as in the well-known case of Glamis. The Banshee bears a Celtic name, but as a death-warning spirit I have personally known very many more Banshee traditions attached to certain families and properties in the Lowlands than among Celts.

All these stories follow much the same lines. We hear of ghosts that haunt certain places, and are seen by animals. Horses shy at particular places for no obvious cause; dogs are terrified, though nothing can be physically seen or heard; men occasionally see dim figures. Ghosts are seen about certain houses; tragedies are continually re-enacted. Usually these are revenants of murderers or murdered persons. There is a striking similarity between these tales and the native folklore legends of Germany, which point to their Teutonic origin. I say advisedly 'native,' for the graceful fairy-stories of Germany nearly always, on investigation, prove to be either French or Celtic in their inception.

Of the witchcraft stories there is, naturally, a very abundant crop, and this is a branch of the subject well worth very careful investigation, for in Scotland we have probably material for the most complete classification of witch-lore of any country in Europe. The confessions of the witches preserved in the records of the Court of Justiciary give us not only the doings of the witches, but in some cases the actual witch rituals, the ceremonies and words for the invocation of the Devil, and the methods of obtaining power and knowledge; and these are for the most part native to the soil, and not derived from any foreign source. I have taken the trouble to compare some of these rituals with the Great Grimoire of Pope Honorius and the rituals of Continental Satanism, and am convinced that Scottish witchcraft is quite individual. Moreover, some of the witchcraft beliefs are still current.

It is sometimes said that these folklore traditions of hauntings and of witchcraft in the Lowlands are wholly lost since the spread of education and the board schools. Education has doubtless produced a certain shyness in speaking about the old-world faith, a certain pose of superiority, and the idea that it is clever not to believe; but if we can only win the confidence of the people enough to penetrate below the crust, the old beliefs and the old lore are found to be as vital as ever.

A story may be mentioned here which is very interesting in this connection, as an example of transference, being originally Scandinavian, afterwards Christianised, appearing as a charm in Orkney, and also current in Lowland Scotland. In Grimm's *Teutonic Mythology* (vol, iii.) it is told that when Balder and Wodan were riding, Balder's colt dislocated a fetlock. Woden the wizard cured it with an incantation. The memory of the incantation remained as a conjuring charm in Thuringia, Afterwards the same legend was told of Christ when riding into Jerusalem. In this form the spell survives to this day in Norway and Sweden for a horse's ailment. In the *New Statistical Account of Shetland* (p. 141) the same spell is mentioned, and an Orkney variant in *The Old Lore Miscellany* (vol. i., p. 400). Also in Chambers's *Fireside Stories* (Edinburgh, 1842, p. 37): 'When a person has received a sprain it is customary to apply to an individual practised in casting the "wresting thread."' This is a thread spun from black wool, on which are cast nine knots, and tied round a sprained leg, or arm. During the time the operator is putting the thread round the affected limb he says, but in such a tone of voice as not to be heard by the bystanders, or even by the person operated upon, the following verse:

> The lord rade   Set joint to joint
> And the foal slade   Bone to bone
> He lighted   And sinew to sinew
> And he righted   Heal in the Holy Ghost's
>   name.

The development of his legend is worth noting. Originally a Norse tale of the healing of a foal, it becomes a Christian charm for sprains of the human body. The whole lore relating to spells and their connection with the Mantra of the East, as preserved in the nonsense burdens of folk-songs, is most interesting, and has been very little explored.

If it were asked in what part of Scotland the ethnological traces of folklore might be studied with the greatest advantages, I think I should be inclined to put the province of Moray first, on account of the great variety of folk-tales and legends to be met with there, and the number of different races that have swept over it and left their mark. Cave men, Neolithic men, have been there, and have left quantities of flint implements, of which a large collection is now in the Royal Scottish Museum. Fire and serpent worshippers have passed, and their trace is found in the burning of the Clavie at Burghead — possibly one of the very last remains of fire-worship in the kingdom, and still observed with due reverence on old New Year's Day. Burghead itself was a Norse colony, and is mentioned in more than one saga. Druids, too, must have been very strong at one time, judging by the number of stone circles, many of which have local traditions, either still current or recorded in old books. These mostly bear evident traces of having been originated, or garbled, by ecclesiastical editing. For the purport mostly is of heathen rites, still carried on, and of the circles being the haunt of various breeds of devils. Over the province of Moray, at an early date, the great Somerled brought an army of Celts from the Islands, claiming to be the Mormaer of Moray, and thence the Righ na h'Alba, or king of Scotland; many of his followers must have settled in the fertile plains, and hence, probably, the many distinctly Celtic legends which are found in the province and the Gaelic place-names. But shortly after there occurred a great deportation of the turbulent inhabitants of Moray, of whom it is said that some went south into Perthshire, where they were still called Moray men, and were the progenitors of the Murrays of Atholl, and other great Perthshire families; and others crossed the Firth and were known as Sutherlanders, or men from the south. While in their place came a Teutonic plantation, from Flanders and the Low Countries, and also, as in the case of the Leslies, from Hungary. These all probably brought their folklore and folk-traditions with them, and hence we get a distinct blend of Celtic tales in Moray, quite different from the West Highland mixture.

For the preservation of all these stories we are probably largely indebted to the ecclesiastical influences, and therefore we expect them to be coloured by Church prejudices and traditions. These, however, are usually not very difficult to dissect out.

In the witchcraft legends again Moray is supreme. There is probably no single type of witchcraft story, no single witch ritual known, that is not well exemplified in Morayshire. The most complete account of Scottish witchcraft in any single document is the remarkable confession of Isabel Goudie, the Auldearn witch. One of the most famous of Scottish warlocks was Sir Robert Gordon of Gordonstown. The first recorded burning of witches took place at Forres, and a stone still marks the spot. The meeting of Macbeth with the weird sisters is too well known for repetition, and though the place is disputed, it was certainly in the province of Moray. The murder of King Duncan was almost certainly at Bothnagown, now Pitgaveny, on the Loch of Spynie. Probably there are witches sill extant in the province. Within living memory there were several, and of the good old-fashioned type, who overlooked cattle, and prevented the cows giving their milk, and to whom the farmers paid tribute to secure immunity from their spells.

We must not dismiss the province of Moray without allusion to a strange and inexplicable piece of folklore, prevalent there and along the shores of the Moray Firth – namely, a secret society for some magical practices among farm hands, known as the 'Horseman's Word.' It is alleged that there was a traditional spell, handed down from one to another among the members, whereby the wildest horse could be tamed at once; there were weird and solemn rituals of initiation, and dire oaths of secrecy. These have been exceedingly well kept, if indeed there were anything to keep. It is said to exist still, but some who profess to belong to it assert that there is now nothing but foolery and horse-play, whatever may have once been the case. It is possible that there may have been some connection with some such spell as that which I have mentioned of Balder and Woden, but it seems impossible to obtain any reliable information.

I hope these few rambling and rather desultory remarks may have the effect of leading some far more capable than I am to investigate this subject of folklore in connection with ethnology, and may, at all events, suggest that some clues worth following may be found in this direction.

[Reprinted from *Chambers' Journal*, Vol. 14, March 8 and March 15, 1924; pp. 237-240 & 253-254.]

12. Bluebeard and the Maid of Orleans: A Study in Fifteenth Century Sorcery

A strange conjunction of ideas truly. One rubs one's eyes and wonders what possible connection there could be between the bogie of our childhood, pictured as a huge savage-featured man with a monstrous turban, a cerulian-hued beard, and a gory scimitar, and the pure and saintly Maid of Orleans, figured in her silver armour with the white banner and white charger. Yet the historic connection is undoubted.

When Perrault wrote the story of Bluebeard, in his *Mother Goose Tales*, the original was the Baron Gilles de Rais, or Retz, Maréchal de France, one of the wealthiest of the Grand Seigneurs of the fifteenth century, whose chief estates were in Brittany, and who in early life was a devoted follower and adherent of Joan of Arc. He is described as having a beard of such exceeding blackness that it was actually blue-black, and there is evidence that before the time of Perrault he had been popularly known by the soubriquet of Barbe-Bleu. In Breton legend and folklore the castles of the Maréchal de Rais, of which the ruins may still be explored, have always been identified with the story of Bluebeard. But the curious dual personality which associated him with Joan of Arc has puzzled historians and folklorists alike.

Abbé Charpentiére, in *Une Page de l'Histoire du XV Siècle*, says that the life of the Maréchal may be divided into two epochs, not only distinct but absolutely at variance one with the other. This theory, however, scarcely accords with the known facts, and moreover itself needs explanation. Assuming (as seems fairly certain) that Gilles de Rais was the original of Perrault's story, we have as historical fact that Gilles and Joan of Arc were contemporaries, that they were both Bretons, that no comrade of hers was more respectful and loyal than he was, and up to his death she was the object of his devoted worship, and that they were both burned for alleged sorcery. The reports of both trials are extant, and are in extraordinarily full detail. Here, then, we may look for some clue in the practice of sorcery and magic in the fifteenth century, and the way in which it was generally regarded, and herein we may perhaps find a clue to some obscure happenings to-day. For human nature does not vary greatly from age to age.

One point, however, must always be kept in view — the fifteenth century did not recognize the distinction, which we are apt to draw pretty sharply, between black and white magic. The test then was whether any presumed occult or supernatural powers were or were not under the aegis of the Church. If so they were manifestations of divine grace, if not they were from the Devil, no matter how pure and holy they might be. All Europe in fact was strongly tainted with Manichaeism. There were two great Gods, one good, the other evil, continually fighting, and only the Church could discriminate. Meanwhile the belief in sorcery and magic was practically universal, and its practice pretty general.

Let us see then what manner of man was this Gilles de Rais when he first emerges into the light of history in 1425 at the age of about twenty. He was of noble family, and one of the wealthiest in France, good-looking, talented and fascinating. His portrait at Versailles is purely imaginary, but that in Vol. 3 of the *Monuments de la Monarchie Française,* taken from a sumptuously illustrated MS. presented to Charles VII by the Berry King at Arms, and known as the most famous portrait, is probably genuine. He was a poet and an artist of no small capacity, ardent and generous. Withal, we find him recklessly extravagant, and devoted to sumptuous entertainments and theatrical display, a designer of prodigal masques, and a great ritualist — loving ornate and costly ceremonial, whether of Church rituals, or popular masquerades, and utterly careless of the cost. He was a gallant soldier, but craved to be always in the limelight. From the first he seems to have been a diligent student of occult learning. There is extant a treatise said to have been composed by him about the age of seventeen on the "Art of raising the Devil" Then as now the Celtic inhabitants of Brittany were firm believers in the supernatural, and their faith a strange mixture of Paganism with a devout Catholicism. Even to-day a Church may be seen dedicated to St. Venus, with an image of the old Roman goddess carefully preserved. Gilles was Breton to the finger tips. Enthusiastic, perfervid, and superstitious, the type is common enough in Ireland and in the Highlands to-day. It needs little imagination to fancy how keenly interested must have been the young Breton noble in the stories that were beginning to be told in whispers of the gifted peasant girl of Domremy, in whose ears breathed angelic voices, bidding her go forth for the salvation of France. The story would appeal to every side of his complex nature. The supernatural, in which like a true Celt he fervently believed, was clearly and indubitably manifested for all to see. The mystic and romantic elements glowed like a halo round the form of the Missioned Maid. Her wonderful passage across France, right through the enemies' lines, and triumphant arrival at Chinon, must have stirred the imagination of the keen young soldier. And if anything were wanting, her instant recognition of the Dauphin, whom she had never seen before, among a crowd of others, was proof positive of her occult powers. Here indeed was a leader worthy the ecstatic devotion of a knight errant — a saint, an amazon, and a champion of the cause to which himself was pledged. The lady of his dreams had materialized, and thence forth became the ruling star of his life, and for the time the raising of the Devil and other questionable arts were in abeyance. Everything we know of Gilles proves that he was all his life a Manichaean, God and the Devil were to him opposing powers, and he strove to serve both, never quite certain which was the most powerful. But under Joan's influence the good was always predominant. While with her, he was the chivalrous Christian knight.

In Joan herself also the Pagan elements were strong. We read of her in childhood, with the other children of the village dancing round the Fairy-tree — *l'arbre fée de Bourlemont* — and invoking the fairies with the same absolute and unquestioning faith as that with which she knelt at Mass, and saw visions of saints and angels. And when her voices came, guiding and instructing her, they were more real and authoritative than the words of the priest, and we find that witchcraft was often whispered, though for obvious reasons not openly at that time. The Celtic nature does not vary, and those who understand the Irish or the Western Highlander to-day will find little difficulty in comprehending Joan of Arc and Gilles de Rais.

The times for France were very critical. Without going at all into the tangled history of the period, which is too well known for repetition, it was a question of France for the French, or France under the thumb of the Teutonic Anglo-Saxon. Brittany itself, which stood for the freedom of the Celtic race, was divided and distracted. We have seen similar Celtic failures in our own country, from similar causes. In this welter Joan and her noble devoted knight stand out like pure figures of chivalry.

Gilles was fabulously wealthy, and he obtained from Charles VII a commission to be Captain in her escort, and thenceforth his chief delight seems to have been to pour out his wealth with reckless prodigality in her service, or in her honour. He lived as in a dream. It was a supernatural adventure they were engaged on, and, if we may judge his psychology from that of the Celt to-day, he was probably convinced that as the cause was divine so the means to carry it on would be miraculously provided. Alchemy, of which we know he was a student, could bring gold in any quantity desired, but what need for Alchemy? one word or prayer from his wondrous lady, and showers of gold would replace all that was spent. So triumphantly they went to Orleans, and Gilles maintained practically an army at his own expense, and was royally cheated by every one who came near him. Estate after estate was mortgaged to provide funds for his vast expenditure. Of this time a characteristic story is told, which is little known. Once Joan, being nearly worn out, dismounted and went to sleep in a wheat field in the plains of La Beauce; the enemy endeavoured to surprise the passage of the Loire, which was defended by the French troops. Unwilling to wake her, Gilles de Rais seized her banner and lance, and mounting her horse led the charge which repulsed the enemy. His vizor was down and her followers believed it was the Maid herself. When Joan awoke she searched in vain for her standard, lance and steed, and called equally in vain for La Hire, La Tremouille, and Xamtrailles. Gilles de Rais suddenly appeared with what she sought for. But he had been wounded in the forehead, and the blood had stained the white banner.

The details of this march on Orleans, and the historic siege are fully recounted in the Mystery play known as the "Mystery of Orleans," the historic value of which, though disputed by Quicherat, has since been fully recognized by the most eminent scholars. Whether the libretto was written by Gilles de Rais must remain uncertain, but there seems no doubt that it was composed under his direct inspiration, probably by one of his literary retainers. Much of it is pure doggerel, some has evidently been added by later hands, but here and there are perfect gems of lyrics, such as that which closes the scene of Joan's interview with the Archangel Michael, and these may with probability be ascribed to Gilles. Such Mysteries were in the fashion of the time, originally religious, but afterwards setting forth some historic event. This professes to give fully all the events leading up to and including the raising of the siege of Orleans. A prominent part is assigned to the Marechal de Rais, who played it himself and at his own cost produced the Mystery in the town of Orleans five years after the events portrayed on May 8, 1435, the anniversary of the raising of the siege in 1430. Whoever was the author of the libretto or whenever it was written, there seems little doubt that the details of the march must have been supplied from the daily journals and notes taken at the time, and the scenes depicting Joan's childhood, her visions, her voices, and interviews with saints and angels, must have been given by herself. The Marshal's fondness for theatrical entertainments is well known. He had designed and produced several Mysteries before this of Orleans, and it seems most natural to suppose that the design and construction of this famous historic representation was the joint work of the Maid and her devoted knight, and that it represented faithfully their ideas of the adventure to which they were jointly pledged. The cost must have been enormous, for at all these entertainments it was Gilles himself who provided all the actors, numbering in this case 140 principals, besides innumerable supers, citizens, soldiers, trumpeters, etc., all of whose costumes were made afresh for the purpose, and nothing was imitation, it was real cloth of gold and silver, and the finest silk and velvet. But what matter the cost? It was a divine adventure, and all would be restored in the Millennium they, were bringing about. It was no earthly quest. This intense faith breathes in all the Mystery, from the miraculous childhood of Joan, her memorable interview with Charles VII, and the saints and angels who attended her, the wondrous bringing to her of her true knight and faithful follower, to the rush upon Orleans, the relief of the city by the two young magicians, and the triumphant return after the victory of Patay. The occult forces were everywhere successful, and Eldorado was well in sight. What matter though gold were poured out like water? All were to be rich and prosperous immediately — God was victorious and the Devil finally vanquished.

But having some inkling of his strange nature, one asks whether even at this time Gilles had absolutely abandoned the practice of sorcery. From his confession some ten years later it seems that when in the company of the Maid, and under her influence, his trust was entirely in her divine mission; but when away from her he still retained an interest in Alchemy, and in the magical formulae he had studied.

As we know the tide of fortune turned. But as they marched upon Paris there is no doubt that the Maid of the Armagnacs was regarded by the French as a divine angelic figure, a talisman ensuring victory to the Kingdom of the Lilies, but by the Saxon English as a veritable witch, whose black magic frustrated their best efforts, and all records show that Gilles de Rais looked on himself as the chosen and divinely appointed guardian of this most precious possession. The check before Paris must have shaken his faith badly. Could it then be possible that the divine magic was to fail them, after all the manifestations of success? But the loyalty of the Celt never swerved. Though she was wounded, and as we read lay for hours in a ditch unheeded, her devoted knight never quitted her side. Even when she was taken prisoner at Compiègne, and transferred from dungeon to dungeon, and finally carried to Rouen about the end of 1430, it is known that during all the earlier proceedings against her she evinced the greatest confidence in her final liberation, and the triumph of her cause; and during all this time we find Gilles with a considerable force at Louviers only sixteen miles distant and making several attempts, whose object could only have been her deliverance. True to his Celtic character, though the magic had failed the loyalty was undimmed. But ecclesiastical sentiment had changed. In the tide of success she was a divine figure; but in failure, and in the hands of the enemy, the questionable nature of her visions, which had been set above the directions of the priests, were remembered, and so was the Paganism of her intercourse with the fairies at Domremy, and many other circumstances which pointed clearly to witchcraft. Moreover the Anglo-Saxon invaders clamoured loudly for her execution. They were impatient of the formalities of the trial. A witch was a witch, and should be burned out of hand, they said. It is, however, some satisfaction to know that it was not by the Church that she was actually condemned, but by the hypocritical and apostate traitor Cauchon, Bishop of Beauvais, who we are glad to read was excommunicated by the Pope for this very deed, and his ashes scattered to the winds.

Even after she was condemned and burnt Gilles was never able entirely to believe that his lady and comrade was actually dead. He seems, from his confession and other documents, to have always cherished the idea that she had but disappeared for a short season, and would return and lead her faithful followers to victory. It was a pathetic faith, and one entirely consonant with his character, leading him in later years to be deceived by the pseudo Maid, the dissolute Clare des Armoises. Much of the story has to be picked out with difficulty from the contemporary records. Gilles de Rais died a death of infamy, universally detested for his unspeakable crimes, while his lady and comrade, the pure and pious Maid of Orleans, after being burned for sorcery, was solemnly rehabilitated at a future trial, and became continuously more and more the national heroine. No wonder men shrank from associating his name with hers. Some historians even went so far as to assert that he had no share in her exploits, and that the Maréchal who assisted her was one Rieux, a nonentity not undeservedly suspected of cowardice. But this theory, which has appeared even in comparatively modern historians, has been entirely disproved, notably by the careful work of Abbé Bossard, and there is now no doubt whatsoever that Gilles de Rais was a gallant and skilful soldier, a brave defender of France, and a true comrade and devoted follower of the heroic Maid; and that a large portion at all events of his vast fortune was given to the help of his country, and of his lady.

But now had come a time of crisis. The cause, for the time at any rate, had failed; the magic that was to restore all his prodigally wasted wealth had proved futile. The Maid was gone, whether dead or not, his estates were all either sold or heavily mortgaged. We find him trying, and often without success, to raise comparatively small loans for immediate needs, and the other side of the Manichaean nature asserts itself. Alchemy must restore fallen fortunes, it is always possible to make gold. True, his experiments in that direction had been hitherto unsuccessful, but they had not been very vigorously prosecuted, and the formulae required the assistance of spiritual forces, the invocation of elementals. This must now be tried. Things had got serious; success was an imperative necessity. It is clear that to get anything like an adequate perspective we must take into account the sorcery and occult arts of the fifteenth century. Modem writers, as M. Anatole France, Mr. Vizetelly, the American Dr. Wilson, and others, endeavour to minimize this side, and treat Joan's visions and voices as entirely subjective, the echo of her own pure and ardent thoughts, and all the horrors and crimes of Gilles de Rais as natural depravity and brutality. But it is certain that not thus did they regard themselves, and the figures so built up are not living or vital. If, however, we remember that they were Celts, with the fullest conviction that they were living amidst supernatural happenings, and taking all their surroundings very much as a Celt of to-day would take them, and moreover that the occult happenings which they believed in have their counterparts and find their credence in modern times also, then this marvellous old fifteenth century romance starts to vivid life, and Bluebeard and the Maid become living persons, whom we might almost have known. Unexpected clues occur sometimes in Scottish family history. It has happened to myself occasionally in searching through the muniments of some old Highland family to hear the casual remark "Yes, that ancestor fought with Joan of Arc." There was a Scottish Guard in the time of Charles VII, many of whose records are still available, and the names of old Highland families are frequent, and so it chances that letters and diaries sometimes contain brief but priceless clues: a mine for the working of future historians.

In all the details we know of the life of Gilles de Rais, we find, as we should expect from his race and nature, violent reactions. We find him with the most ecstatic devotion, singing himself in his own choir at a sumptuous High Mass, and immediately afterwards in scenes of prodigal debauchery. We find him again, after attempts at sorcery and black magic, humbly praying for forgiveness from an offended God. The two attitudes are both characteristic, and lead to the strong probability that the recourse to sorcery, after the failure of the quest and the capture of the Maid, was no sudden change of character, as Abbé Charpentière would have us believe, but the development of the nature that was there from the beginning, and that even while he was following Joan there were reactions to the cultus of the powers of evil.

In 1432 there came over a district of France, including Southern Brittany, parts of Maine and Poitou, a vague and undefined feeling of apprehension, a terror of some brooding astral evil. Michelet, in his *Histoire de France,* describes it forcibly as that of an invisible supernatural beast of extermination, possessed of diabolic powers, which many deemed to be a physical manifestation of the Evil One, appearing here and there without warning, and leaving traces of fear and mourning, of insanity and death. What was certain was the constant disappearance of children of tender age, without trace, and as though by enchantment. The clue appears in the story and confession of

Gilles, and in the fifteenth century processes of sorcery. We have the details of Gilles's effort to restore his fortunes by alchemy. The remains of his laboratories and furnaces may even yet be traced. But this was at the outset scientific, a genuine attempt to effect the transmutation of metals, which many scientists to-day regard as feasible. But the occultists of the fifteenth century held that for success it was essential to obtain the help of elemental spirits, and of demons. Despite the thunders of the Church Italy at that time swarmed with sorcerers, who professed themselves able to invoke and compel these powers of darkness. It was popularly said that even some of the Popes themselves practised sorcery in secret. So we find Gilles sending emissaries into Italy to procure magicians, who should instruct him in these forbidden arts. Many of their names are preserved, but he himself said in his confession that the whole number was so vast that he could not remember them all. Certain it is that most of them robbed and deceived him to the top of their bent, as we may well imagine. We have plenty of parallel cases to-day. His confession records nothing but continual failure, and continually growing desperation, also continually more extravagant demands from his sorcerers and assistants generally. The blackest side of all sorcery has always been the practice of necromancy, a word little understood and constantly used in a wrong sense as meaning any kind of magic. (It was recently used by a learned divine to apply to Spiritualism, and the glimpses of the world beyond the grave.) Necromancy properly means the working of magic by means of dead bodies or portions thereof. The theory is briefly set forth in a quaint little black-letter volume of the fourteenth century, shown to me by a private collector. The body of man or beast was apparently regarded as a magical implement, wielded by the spirit, and was compared to the rods of Moses and Aaron, Joseph's divining cup, the High Priest's ephod and breastplate, and the like. Every organ had its special part in the great magical implement, and any one taken out and informed by the spirit of the magician enabled him to obtain information, to do works of magic proper to that part, and to control certain spirits. This type of magic was greatly in favour with the augurs of ancient Rome, who used parts of the bodies of sacrificial victims in divination. Tiberius at Capreae, amid his unmentionable debaucheries, is said to have used the bodies of slaves, and to have tortured and killed living victims for magical ceremonies. All the necromantic formulae agree that though much may be done with animal bodies, far more certain results can be obtained from human bodies, especially those of children. And this belief has persisted for unknown centuries, and is not dead yet. We meet it in the witchcraft trials of the Middle Ages, and prominently in the well-known formula of "The Hand of Glory." Some years ago I was speaking with a Russian nobleman on the alleged Ritual Murders said to be committed by Jews at Easter. While not himself professing to believe the stories, he showed me a Hebrew MS. with an interleaved Latin translation, giving a formula for the making of a Teraphim, whereby with a consecrated knife the head of a child must be cut off and placed instantly on a gold plate engraved with Cabalistic signs, and the names of seventy-two great angels of the Name must be invoked, whereupon the head would speak, and being properly interrogated would disclose any secret asked of it. I am told that this document was from internal evidence a forgery, and made up to justify a pogrom. But it proved the wide existence of a belief. Almost all the instructions that I have come across on necromancy contain a most strongly expressed caution, that if one shall by these means be able to invoke spirits which he is unable to control, it is probable that they will enter into him and dwell there, producing especially the madness of Saevitia, and the lust of rapine and cruelty, the peculiar form of mania which is now known as Sadism. Certainly the ghastly and horrible records of necromancy seem to bear out this caution. When all London was startled with horror at the crimes of Jack the Ripper, the late Mr. Bernard Quaritch showed me a MS. he was then wishing to buy of black magical formulae. It was not the Grimoire, though containing much of the same matter, and, *inter alia,* the very formula on which Jack the Ripper seemed to have been working, the very mutilations, were minutely described, and the desecration of Christian emblems. It was not remarked at the time that if the sites of the murders be marked on a map of London, they form, viewed from the west, an inverted cross, and the latest and most atrocious, the Mitre Square murder, was probably exactly on the site of the High Altar of Holy Trinity Church, Whitechapel. This may have been an accidental coincidence, if so it was remarkably exact. A man trying to work the formula in that old MS. could not have done it with more painstaking accuracy. And if the evil spirits invoked did verily obsess the murderer it would account for many things. And this case does not stand alone. Scotland Yard has the details of many attempted works of necromancy, judiciously kept very private, and veiled even so far as they are known under the convenient covering of homicidal mania. Baring Gould, in the *Broom Squire*, and the late Monseigneur Benson, in his story of 'The Blood Eagle', record necromantic practices in the West of England.

Such then was the last alternative that his Italian sorcerers suggested to Gilles de Rais, and such was the meaning of that strange cloud of apprehension that overhung the land. Prelati the Italian supplied the formulae, and worked many of the invocations; at first it would seem with sacrifice of animals, then a child was demanded and procured, still no tangible result followed. Prelati avers that he saw and conferred with the evil spirit, Barron by name, whose seal is well-known to students, and reports more demands for more and more sacrifices, fuller necromantic invocations. All the money that Gilles could by any means lay hands on went to his innumerable emissaries, employed in kidnapping for him. The tradition of obsession by the evil spirits whom he invoked and failed to control, seems to have been borne out in actual fact, and the vague haunting terror that had spread over the land of a brooding astral evil, ascribed to a physical manifestation of the Prince of Darkness, may well have had more truth in it than materialistic historians would be willing to admit.

Was his nature then entirely changed since the death of the Maid? By no means. We find still the same Manichaean duality. After the worst debaucheries of crime we see him earnestly, almost frantically, imploring forgiveness of his sins and professing a sure confidence in his ultimate salvation. It was in 1435, five years after the martyrdom of the Maid, that he caused to be presented at Orleans the Mystery of the siege, and himself took his own part, representing the time of his chivalrous devotion to her cause, and at the very same time he devoted a great part of his remaining possessions to the "Foundation of the Holy Innocents" in order, as the deed of gift recites, that the souls of children might intercede for him at the Throne of Grace, for then surely he would be forgiven and saved. Looking at his character as depicted in the Mystery one might wonder why he stood in such great need of forgiveness. The dungeons and oubliettes of Machecoul, of Champtoce, and Tiffauges, and all the ghastly discoveries there of the bodies of scores, nay possibly hundreds, of innocent victims give the answer. We see the same violent reactions, only now the evil obsession was ever more and more the normal nature, and the service of God the reaction, bred often of fear of the consequences, and dread of the powers of hell. Yet even in the worst excesses the memory of the Maid held him, and the confident hope that somehow and sometime she would return. One little story, seldom told, indicates this. A woman whose child had been kidnapped came to the castle of Champtoce in despair, seeking for the little one; the guardian of the gate was about to drive her away as his orders were, when he recognized his niece. So he advised her to go on the terrace where de Rais was promenading with his greyhound, to caress the dog, and say suddenly to de Rais without preamble, "I have seen Jeanne." She did so, and he was startled, and asked how she looked and what she said. The woman replied, "She was shining with light, but looked sad and wept for my child. She told me to come here to seek for him, he had been seized in the Bois des Ingraudes." Gilles at once sent for the child, fortunately still alive, and restored him to the mother.

No need here to go into the story of his apprehension and trial and conviction. These can be read in many books, and his confession, recounting his crimes in fullest detail, remains one of the most remarkable documents in all the long history of occultism and magic. We read that after his conviction, on the way to the scaffold, he prayed continually to God, the Blessed Virgin, and the Saints, and professed the most sure hope of salvation. He was executed at Nantes, on the other side of the Loire opposite to his castle, and his body was afterwards rescued from the flames by his family, and buried in the Eglise des Carmes at Nantes. An expiatory monument was erected by his daughter to his memory. It stood on the side of the *Hotel de Dieu*, but no portion now remains; a rough lithograph in Verger's *Archives Curieuses de Nantes* shows what it was like, and a fragment is preserved in the archaeological museum. At one time miraculous powers were ascribed to the statuette of the Virgin that surmounted it, which was known as "La Bonne Vierge de Cree-Lait," the milk-giver, and many were the pilgrimages of nursing mothers to the shrine marking the place of execution of Bluebeard.

Thus then these two young Bretons, who had so gallantly set forth from Chinon in 1429, believing themselves under occult guidance, a belief almost justified by a practically miraculous success, on an expedition that we may well deem saved the Kingdom of the Lilies for her own sons, both suffered a shameful death on the scaffold for sorcery. It was a strange *camaraderie*, the wealthiest and most powerful noble in France following with devoted loyalty the humble peasant girl of Domremy, a strange end in which France, at the instigation of her English enemies, sacrificed the two comrades who had done more than any others for her liberation. Strangest of all, perhaps, that while the high placed criminal de Rais suffered the extreme penalty, the instigators and abettors of his crimes went scot-free. Prelati, who taught him necromancy, and who confessed to having raised and conversed and bargained with the Devil, LaMeffraye, the villainous old woman who prowled through the country kidnapping children for the horrible rites, and many others, gave their testimony and disappeared, nor is there any record of any proceedings against them.

But though Bluebeard and the Maid suffered a similar penalty, posterity has given no hesitating judgment. From age to age the love and veneration for Joan of Arc has grown, and she has become the national Saint and heroine of France, while the name of de Rais has been consigned to the lowest depths of execration. Bluebeard (the name given him it was said in his lifetime by a lady who greatly admired the soft silky blue-black beard of the handsome young noble) became in Brittany a name of fear, a haunting demon, who though dead might at any time reappear. And, as is often the case, many gruesome stories which had long been current in the countryside were fathered on him.

Gilles himself had one wife, and a daughter who survived him. But the folk tales of the dark inhuman monster who put to death his wives in varying numbers of three, seven, and in one case twelve, have been told in all countries. J. F. Campbell, in the *Popular Tales of the West Highlands*, has preserved one with curious points in common with the Bluebeard stories. The idea appears in Grimm's *Marchen,* and in the *Arabian Nights*. The fatal curiosity, the blood-stained key, the dramatic watch of Sister Anne from the topmost tower, and the rescue just in time. Abbé Bossard quotes a story current in La Vendée, giving the Sister Anne episode almost exactly as told by Perrault. There were also the stories of an earlier ruffian of Brittany known as Comorre the Cursed, many of which have become mixed with the Bluebeard tales in the course of years. Undoubtedly by the time of Perrault a Bluebeard legend had grown up in Brittany, but how far the story as he tells it was current there before his time, and how far he elaborated his folk-tale from other sources, must at present remain a mystery, the materials for the solution of which have still to be unearthed. The popular figure of Bluebeard as an Eastern in a monstrous turban suggests a connection with Oriental legend. No such representation would be accepted in Brittany. The Bluebeard story is told there to-day as it is told in our nurseries, and the sites are pointed out. The window from which Sister Anne watched for the three brothers, the chamber where the corpses of the headless wives were found are shown as confidently as the laboratory of de Rais' alchemical experiments, the dungeons where the children were confined, and the pit where the bodies were discovered. Truth and fiction are inextricably blended, and who shall now disentangle them? Certain it is that the reality, which is proved to the hilt, is more horrible and ghastly than any invention of Perrault or any other.

And with this we may set the last recorded words of Gilles de Rais after his condemnation, "Fathers and Mothers, and all that hear me. Keep yourselves, I entreat you, from all lax rearing of your children. For my part, if I have committed so many and great crimes, the reason is that in my youth I was always allowed to do as I listed, and to follow the bent of my desires."

As Mr. Vizetelly well says, these are words for every age, and may well be applied to our own. They may perhaps help us, with other strange matter, to comprehend the marvellously complex character of Gilles de Rais, Maréchal de France, Barbebleu.

[Reprinted from *The Occult Review,* Vol. 27, No. 1, January 1918, pp. 19 - 32.]

Occultism and Divination

13. The Hermetic System

This system is not to be found in any book. A knowledge of the system is acquired much in the same way that George Smith read the inscribed bricks that came from Babylon and Nineveh; the bricks were all broken to pieces, but he was lucky enough to find out that the same words, the same inscriptions, were written on a great many of these tablets; and so when a bit of the inscription was wanting in one, he was able to supply it, or partially supply it from another. So, putting one with another, he managed to read out complete inscriptions in various places. Thus we have to trace out the Hermetic philosophy. Here and there we gather traces of it, from all the philosophies of the West. We can find, it is true, what is said to be the *first* origin of it: there are pretty reliable transcripts of what is called the Emerald Tablet of Hermes, on which the first principles of the philosophy are written — unintelligible without a key. We have also in the 'Virgin of the World' and 'Divine Pymander' scattered sentences containing great wisdom, but almost unintelligible. If we want to interpret them, we must look to Egypt for a clue, which we find in the hieroglyphics — as, for example, in illustrating the passage of the soul after death; and in connection with that, one cannot but be struck with the similarity of the teachings of these hieroglyphics and the great doctrines of Christianity, a similarity so evident as to seem to indicate prophetic foresight.

Long before the time of Moses, these Egyptians had as clearly as possible the idea of the fall of man, of the redemption of man, of the atonement by sacrifice, and of an incarnation. Besides hieroglyphics, we have the 'Book of the Dead', the great ritual which was buried with every mummy of note, and which might be taken as the guide-book of the deceased in his adventures in the world of death, the picture of what would happen to the soul.

Not only from ancient Egypt, but from the pupils of ancient Egypt, we can get light. Every one of the nations which came into contact with Egypt in her glory took away something — altered it may be and modified, with omissions and additions — still everywhere is traced the wisdom of Egypt. First of all of these we must take the tribes of Beni-Israel, the Hebrews.

Moses was learned in the wisdom of the Egyptians, and he taught exoterically and esoterically. Exoterically he taught it in the Pentateuch. Moses, of course, had divine revelation himself, but when did Moses get that revelation? After he had been trained in all the wisdom of the Egyptians, after he had become a trained occultist, an initiate, an adept. It was that training which rendered him a fit vessel for the revelation. The esoteric teaching of Moses is contained in the Kabala. Any one who wishes to understand all the difficulties of the Pentateuch, must understand the Kabala. The Kabala was the key that was taught to the priests, and the priests alone, whereby they were able to expound as much as they thought desirable, or were allowed to teach, to the people. But the Kabala was an absolute secret until after the coming of Christ. It was only in the second or third century that the Kabala was compiled and made accessible: before that it was purely esoteric and secret.

Among the nations contacting with Egypt were the Phrygians, the Romans, and the old Hittites. There was a close connection between the Hittites and the early Egyptians. At one time the Egyptian kings were proud to intermarry with the daughters of the kings of the Hittites: and Phrygia was the centre of the Hittite kingdom. There the wisdom of Egypt took root, and there in the original Mysteries was the great mystery of revelation gradually expounded to the neophytes as they were able to learn it. As with many another nation, these Mysteries became absolutely corrupt in later times.

Arabia came into close contact with Egypt, and learned of the wisdom of Egypt. There again the hieroglyphics help us considerably; for we know that the Queen of Punt, in that line of country, was an honoured guest in the courts of Egypt at the time of Thotmes II or III.

In medieval times we find the Arabians the great teachers of science to Europe. What was their science? The remains of the ancient mystic learning of Egypt: only the remains it is true, and these were corrupt it may be, materialised certainly — grammarie become grammar, alchemy turned to chemistry, astrology merging into astronomy, but still it was the old science; and even in the forms of the figures the Arabians gave us, there is a world of wealth of occult learning, and the key to many of the Egyptian mysteries.

Alchemy was not a search after making gold; it was a search after the secrets of nature and the Divine wisdom, the secrets and the knowledge of nature as leading to, and being the key to, the knowledge of God. Astrology was not, and is not, fortune-telling at all. The Zodiac shows the whole history of man, past, present, and future — not the history of any individual man or woman during one short lifetime; it is the destiny of our planet itself through myriads of years that we read in the Zodiac. The Book of Revelation is one of the greatest astrological books that ever was written.

The Jews, Phoenicians, and the Phrygians, all just about the time of Christ's coming went strangely back to Egypt; this was outwardly caused by the power and the policy of Alexander the Great. The pupils went back to their old master, and so we have the great Neoplatonic school founded in Alexandria, — we get the Hermetic doctrine in its then state. The result of this concurrence is exceeding instructive in working out this Hermetic philosophy.

These concurrent streams passed on through the Middle Ages; and through these times of darkness and of materialism the philosophy was kept alive in occult schools — as has always been the case throughout all history; whenever a race or people get materialistic, philosophy is kept alive secretly in private schools. When the people grow fit to understand these parables and dark sayings, then again they are told openly. There were many of these occult schools, and many exist to this day. An enormous amount of learning exists in them, an amount those outside do not credit. The Rosicrucian body is a solid fact, and not the sub-section of Freemasonry which goes by that name; it is absolutely an esoteric school, possessing extraordinary wisdom.

A large amount of wisdom has also been preserved among the Freemasons, although they have lost a great deal of what they ought to have; they have a large quantity of exoteric symbology, but, sad to say, they have in great part lost the key to it in the meantime.

The Knights Templars in the Middle Ages again, handed down a great deal of wisdom and knowledge. They are gone; but there are schools of occultism descended from them still existing, and from time to time these schools allow certain portions of their knowledge to be proclaimed generally. To such allowance we owe the foundation of the Theosophical Society in the West. And the East has taught us much — for example, the seven principles. No one knew anything about the seven principles till it was taught from the East — or about Karma.

According to the Hermetic doctrine, there are always certain persons specially illuminated, to whom special revelations are given, these individuals not being connected with any school. The Roman Church accepts this fully, as it is bound to do; and it is to be hoped that Protestants ere long will also do so, for it is certainly a fact that there are seers and prophets among us still. Here there is a special danger, however, viz., that divine revelation may be given to the prophet, but unless he is perfectly selfless, and casts his personality aside altogether, he will not be able to give out the teachings he has received in all their purity. Such teaching was the foundation of Dr Anna Kingsford's book *The Perfect Way*, but it is coloured, and largely coloured, with the personality of the seer, and therefore there are mistakes in it. The errors, however, are close to the surface.

That brings the Hermetic school in the West down to the present day. Look at the result. These two great schools of philosophy have gone on side by side, one in the East and the other in the West, and with hardly any communication whatsoever until this present time. Now there is a very remarkable change, for this is a time of special concurrence of various schools, a most important time in the history of the world — signalised by several important things, one being that England, the greatest Christian power in the West, now dominates India, the greatest Buddhistic centre in the East. And this domination is not merely physical, for we are teaching the Indians their religion. The teaching of the pure Buddhistic faith in India, and the establishment and maintenance of Buddhistic schools in Ceylon, have been largely due to the energy of English and American theosophists. We should not try to get Buddhists converted to Christianity, but first endeavour to make them good Buddhists. The Buddhist has developed himself as far as Manas, but he has not developed the principle of Buddhi. To make him a Christian before he has developed the principle of Buddhi would be to make him a hypocrite. That principle must be called into action. If we read the most esoteric of the Eastern writings, we find that the mysteries of Buddhi are only communicated to pledged chelas under the strictest pledges. The Easterns must progress, or become extinct: that has always been the experience of the past. If they are to progress, it is the influence of the West that will do it. If proof is wanted of that, look at the way they regard Parabrahm — it is essentially the same as the Hebrew concept of negative existence — the three veils of negative existence of the Kabala — unthinkable, unapproachable. Between Parabrahm and humanity there can be no intercourse whatsoever: the one is totally incomprehensible to the other, therefore prayer is an absurdity. The Buddhist says that he invokes his higher self, and he is quite right; that is the highest he knows, and he is quite right to invoke the highest he can reach. Buddhi, the vehicle of the Ineffable Supreme, is undeveloped and unknown; therefore the intellectual abstraction which the Buddhist calls his higher self is the only thing which he can recognise above himself. Buddhi, the Christ soul, is undeveloped. Now the Hermetist, the Western, on the other hand, has developed that principle, and by means of the vehicle he can comprehend. 'I am the way, the path, and the light.' This idea runs through the whole of the Bible, and refers to the Christ soul. There, in a nut-shell, is the difference between the two. It is only a difference of one step, and the Buddhist does not require to be deprived of one single iota of his faith, so far as it is pure that is to say; but, on the same lines, he can be led on by the Hermetic philosophy to take another step. And seeing that the Buddhist is more highly developed in both the higher and lower Manas than we in the West, he can give us valuable assistance there.

Consider also the way in which both systems look at the body. The Buddhist merely gets to an intellectual abstraction; therefore to him the body is a hindrance. So the good Buddhist is nothing but an ascetic; he must deny his body in every possible way, he must prevent it functionising. But for the Hermetist who understands the whole of the seven principles, the body is a vehicle; and therefore, as a vehicle, to be raised, to be cherished; to be subordinated to the central will. And therefore, where the Western raises the body by his meditations, prayer, raja yoga exercises, raises it to union with the divine, the Eastern has nothing to do but to cast it aside as a hindrance imposed upon him by his Karma in some previous incarnation. This is a most important key to the difference between the two systems.

[Substance of a paper read on 22 October 1892. Reprinted from *Transactions of the Scottish Lodge of the Theosophical Society*, Vol. I, Part VI (1892), pp. 84-7.]

14. Occult Symbology in Relation to Occult Science

Every science has its symbology, and consequently there must be an occult symbology, with this distinction that as occult science is the synthesis of all sciences, — the algebra, so to speak, of their arithmetic, — so the symbology of occult science must be the root of all symbology of all sciences. Further, every symbol of occult science is absolutely appropriate; it is the geometrical expression of a physical truth, and also of a psychic and of a spiritual truth; for that which is a truth on one plane, is a truth on every plane, if only we read the correspondences aright.

The propositions of Euclid are abstract truths; and no man ever could draw the ideally perfect figures necessary for their complete demonstration, yet the physical truths which those ideal figures represent are the basis of all physical science.

It will only be possible to illustrate this tonight by taking a few of the simplest of the occult symbols, and indicating a few out of their many interpretations, with one or two examples, to show how the great glyphs are written on the face of objective nature for those who have the eyes to see.

Beginning at the very beginning with the first postulate with which I started in my introductory lecture 'The Universal All', we have to see how this conception was represented in symbol. It is clearly undifferentiated and infinite. Imagine yourself alone in such a state — the world, the sun, the whole starry vault of the sky gone; you can picture it only as a hollow sphere, any other form would imply differentiation; also, considering yourself as a point of consciousness in the midst of the void, straight lines of infinite length might be drawn from you in every direction, — all being infinite, all are equal, therefore you are in the centre of an infinite sphere. This, on the flat, can only be represented by a circle, the inside of which is blank because undifferentiated, the bounding circle forming a good symbol of infinite duration because it has no point at which you can say it begins or ends (fig. 1).

The contents, so to say, of this infinite sphere, are what is called in Sanscrit Mulaprakriti, or the root of matter, homogeneous world-stuff. So soon as the first flutter of manifestation begins, the first differentiated point may fitly be represented by a dot in the centre of the circle (fig. 2). The most elementary form of manifested matter is revolution in the form of a vortex-ring, as shewn in an experiment in the lecture on 'The Borderland of Physics'. If we rotate a transparent homogeneous sphere rapidly, and look at the axis of revolution, it appears like a point; but turn it to one side, and the axis appears like a line forming the diameter of the circle. In old times the origin of matter was often symbolized by an egg, thus we hear of the cosmic egg, the world egg, etc.; and we see the appropriateness of the symbol, if we look at the egg as a hollow sphere, representing dormant but complete vitality; as soon as incubation commences there appears a germinal spot, soon separable into three layers (for we cannot get away from the mystic three). And thus the first point in physical life is the establishment of a three in one.

The first beginning of differentiation is clearly dual (this comes before the manifestation of life), it is positive and negative, energising and receptive, or whatever you like to call them. No names are precisely accurate, and the appellation male and female sometimes used is open to serious misconception; really it is the objective energy which does something, and the subject-matter to which that something is done. The most obvious symbol for the receptive matter is water, whose characteristic, when lying at rest, is to repose in a horizontal plane; so, as the point in the circle symbolises the first manifestation, the horizontal line symbolises the first division into receptive and energising, and gives us fig. 3.

The circle representing infinity, and the diameter manifested matter which is finite, we should naturally expect to find that there was no discoverable relation between them — 'the finite cannot comprehend the infinite.' And so in fact it is; this relation, the despair of mathematicians, is usually symbolised by the Greek letter π— in itself a meaningless symbol, but to those who know that it is really a corruption of the Hebrew letter ה which symbolises the female or receptive principle, it at once becomes full of meaning; and we see that the great π problem, as it is called, or squaring the circle, will only be accomplished when the finite is re-absorbed into the infinite. It is to be noticed also, that this symbol (fig. 3) is the alchemical symbol for salt, which signifies the union of two natures, a correspondence which will be of use to us later on in this course.

The energising and vitalising principle is fitly symbolised by fire, whose nature ever aspiring is represented by the vertical straight line, and these two form the cross in the circle (fig. 4), which therefore represents matter in manifestation or matter vitalised by spirit, and on this cross of matter must every infinite spirit cast into matter suffer until its reunion with the infinite. This is the key to all the symbology of the pre-Christian cross. Constantly appearing as the glyph of some divine or semi-divine being who suffered for humanity in human shape, also as the symbol of many nature myths, as the passage of the sun over the equator at the equinox (and other passings over), also the symbol of the renewing of mere physical life. Every one will interpret the symbol according to the extent of his own development; to the purely material man it will be phallic, and nothing more. The most highly spiritual will see in it the glyph of the whole divine plan regarding the cosmos, its genesis, progress, and destiny.

Looking on revolution as the first manifestation of matter, if we cause the cross (fig. 4) to revolve rapidly, the ends will bend away from the direction of rotation, and thus the form known as the swastica (fig. 5)[1] becomes the natural glyph of matter in revolution — that is, in manifestation. This is one of its meanings, for it has many.

But now, since all matter in manifestation must have three elements, — namely, spirit, matter, and 'that' which unites them, which we for the present call 'Fohat' — clearly a simple line is incomplete as a symbol; therefore on this earth plane we require a figure which shall typify three in one, and this the triangle does better than any other figure. The triangle apex upwards (fig. 6) symbolising the aspiring nature of fire, that with the apex down (fig. 7) the unstable quality of water, and also by its base upwards the horizontal extension.

As these elements become more material still, their base lines are doubled; thus air partakes of the aspiring quality of fire, but in a more material and earthy state, and accordingly the symbol of air is (fig. 8). Similarly earth is matter in a still more gross state than water, and its symbol is (fig. 9); and thus we get the four elements of the ancients. In

---

1. The arms of the swastica are sometimes turned the other way; the interpretation varies according to the direction, a point to be afterwards explained. Much curious learning on this old symbol may be found in Schliemann's *Troas* [*i.e. Troy and its Remains* (1875). There is a modern reprint, Cambridge UP, 2010.]

regard to these I should like to say to men of science, that if it be true that there is one primordial substance, then every substance we see around us, or which we can find, must be a mode or condition of this one, and the ancient classification which postulated four typical modes only, viz. the solid, liquid, gaseous, and igneous, is worth consideration. Take water, for instance, its solid form is ice, its liquid form we are all familiar with, its gaseous is steam, and its igneous form we were shewn in the lecture on 'The Borderland of Physics', when fire was applied to the two gases into which the decomposed water had been resolved. The normal condition of water at present is liquid, that of gold solid; but there was a time when the normal condition of gold was liquid, and that of water gaseous or perhaps igneous. This view of the elements may lead to theories and discoveries of science undreamed of at present.

From these forms the circle, the cross, and the triangle appropriately grouped, many other symbols may be formed; thus take, for instance, the well-known symbol of the planet Venus (fig. 10). After the final and deepest fall of man into matter, his consciousness descended from the circle of infinity, his spiritual being into the cross of matter; hence passional desires, and all that is symbolised by Venus, and the cross below the circle became a most appropriate glyph for the power which was then dominant in his life, and for the part of his nature which is now subject to those desires.

Of course this is only one of the interpretations of this symbol, for, as has been said, every symbol is a door with seven locks each having seven keys, and every one must be interpreted on every plane before the full meaning is gathered.

The interpretation of the symbols of the planets and of the signs of the zodiac, however, are for the most part very complex and difficult to follow. One key may, however, be given here; it is often laid down in books on occultism that the signs of the Zodiac were originally only ten, and that Virgo and Scorpio were originally one, as the likeness of the symbols seems to indicate, Libra being added by the Egyptian priests. In this there is a certain amount of truth. Libra was introduced by the priests of Egypt, or perhaps earlier, but not as an addition but a substitution; the original sign was the altar Ara (fig. 11), sometimes called the altar of Abel, which, with the decanal signs, clearly shows the mystery of the atonement, rising above the law of Karma. The sign of Libra, or the balance of the table of Osiris, indicates the weighing of the acts of the dead, and the future state as the certain result thereof, a conception natural and obvious to a people whose ideas were bounded by the lower principles, and who had not learnt the possibility of rising above these principles and beyond the law of Karma, The substitution of Libra for Ara marks a distinct stage in the progress of religious history; many others are marked in the Zodiac, and will appear as we proceed. The symbol of Libra is simply Ara cut off at the top (fig 12).

To see one instance of how these symbols are written on the face of physical nature, and how every one of them must be in fact just as true on the physical plane as it is on the abstract metaphysical or spiritual plane, consider a ray of light. We know it is threefold; we pass it through the triangle, that is the prism, whose section is triangular, and the Unity becomes a Trinity, three prismatic colours coming from the white light and retiring into the white light again, and each one being in itself a perfect vehicle for the manifestation of light.

We thus reach the conception, that every true symbol is the material presentation of a spiritual truth, and that it is necessary that every spiritual truth should have its material manifestation occurring all round us always, in every blade of grass; occurring in history, in the steps of each man's development; occurring also in the history of the human race, in various events, for those who have eyes to see.

This idea is further illustrated in the figure of an ordinary cube called by Aristotle the most perfect of figures, and universally taken as the symbol of man. Its six sides, unfolded, form the cross, with which we commenced; and the cross arm removed consists of three squares, symbolic of the upper triad; the upright of four squares, symbolic of the lower quaternary.

[Paper read on 11 December 1891 . Reprinted from *Transactions of the Scottish Lodge of the Theosophical Society*, Vol. 1, Part II, (1891), pp. 25-8.1]

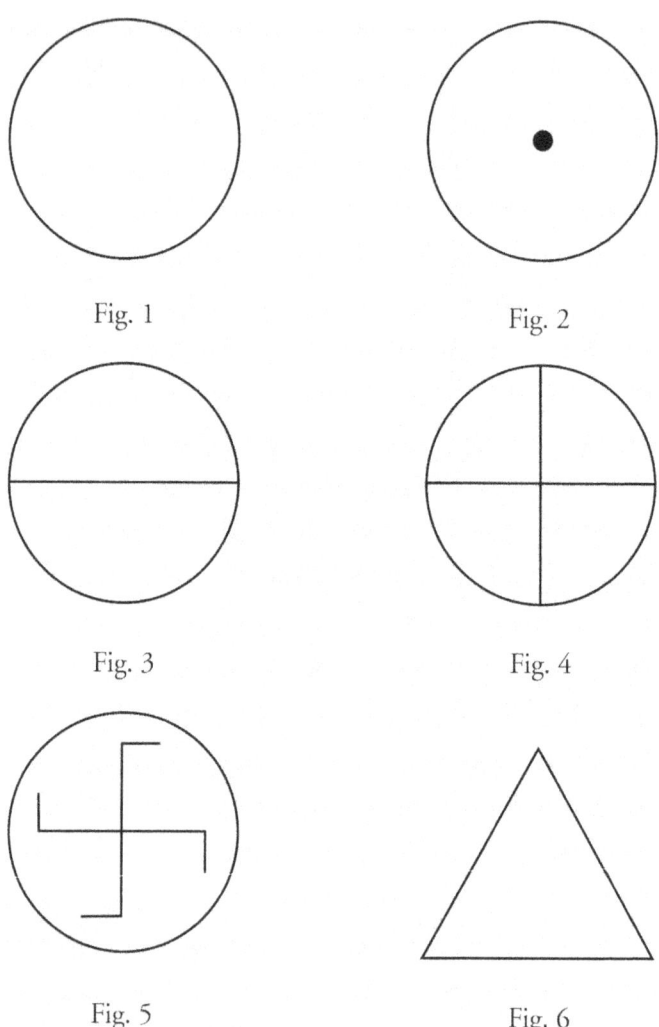

Fig. 1

Fig. 2

Fig. 3

Fig. 4

Fig. 5

Fig. 6

Occult Symbology in Relation to Occult Science 163

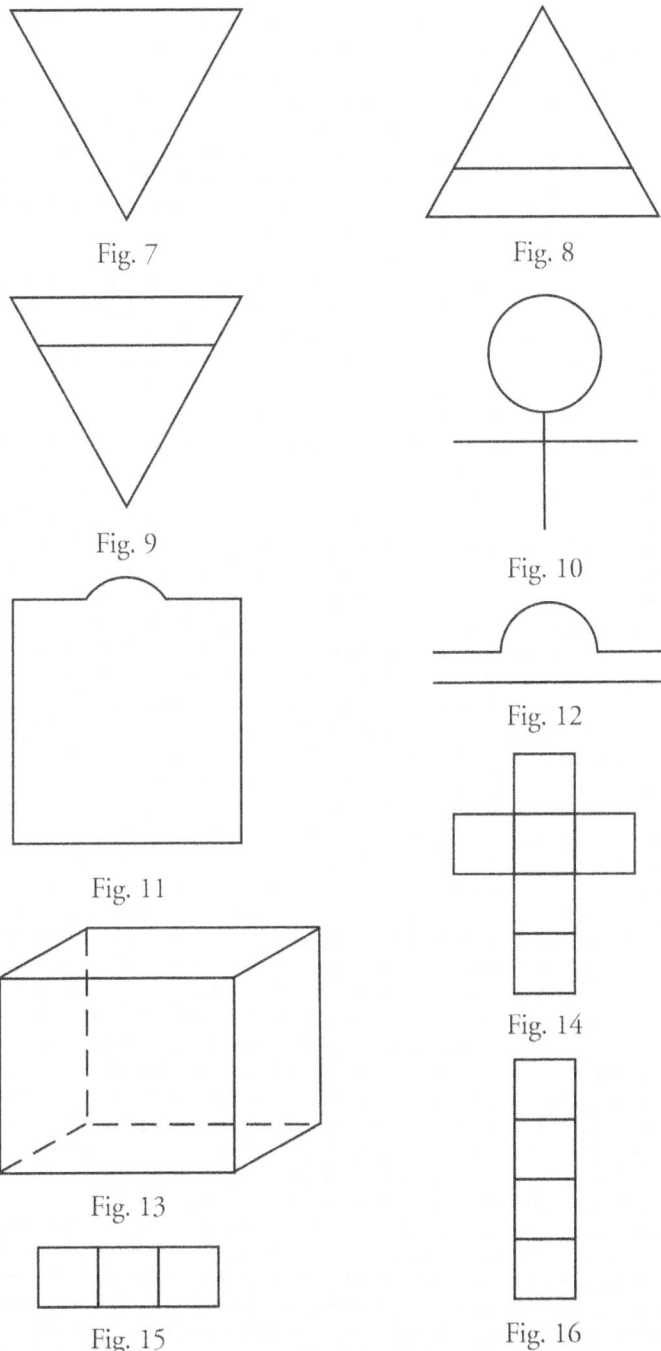

Fig. 7

Fig. 8

Fig. 9

Fig. 10

Fig. 11

Fig. 12

Fig. 13

Fig. 14

Fig. 15

Fig. 16

15. The Esoteric Teaching on the Origin and Significance of the Zodiac

At most we can expect to make but a small beginning upon this, because the teachings of the Zodiac run pretty much through the whole of the Hermetic philosophy. But, as you all know, the lecturer at our last meeting laid a very fine and solid foundation. He gave us a very good idea of what the Zodiac is, and how it is that the signs of the Zodiac are constantly changing; and he also gave us a conception of the great year, the period of 26,000 years roughly, which lies at the root of most of the teachings and calculations founded upon the Zodiac.

Now the first point beyond the ordinary physical astronomy which strikes one is, What does the Zodiac mean, and how in the world did these groups of stars, apparently chance groups of stars, ever come to have this extraordinary significance which has been attributed to them all over the world, and, as far as we can learn, in all ages? I think the answer to that may be given in one short sentence, and that is 'the periodicity of phenomena under the influence of extra mundane causes'. Sometimes we are so familiar with these phenomena that we neglect them, and cease to be surprised at them. Take only the simple case of the ebb and flow of the tide. This must have been noticed from the very earliest times that men ever lived by the sea-shore or noticed anything; and we are perfectly familiar with the fact that the tides are governed by the moon. But supposing that we did not know the theory of gravitation and the theory of lunar attraction, we should be very much puzzled to account for these phenomena of the tides, and we should probably set down anybody who spoke of the moon as influencing them as a superstitious ass. In fact, I have seen old books of the 'goody goody' type that have set down as a gross superstition the idea that the moon had anything to do with the waters of the earth. Of course you know that has been a tradition from the very earliest times, and in all the so-called Pagan mythologies: the moon, as the origin of the waters of the earth, has always been a prominent fact, but a fact which apparently was absolutely sterile until the principles of gravitation were thoroughly established. That is one example of the periodicity of earthly phenomena under the influence of supra mundane causes. Then, of course, the growth of plants and trees in spring is another. We say lightly enough that the increase of heat and the increase of light in the spring, after the sun has passed the vernal equinox, causes the flow of the sap in plants and trees, causes the germination of the seed, and so forth. Well, I would ask you to look back at some statistical table and examine the matter. Of course the days get longer after the vernal equinox, and theoretically they get warmer and lighter; but as a point of fact it frequently occurs that they do not. It frequently occurs that, in consequence of cloud or mist, or something or other, the actual register of light in England or Scotland is less after the vernal equinox than it was before, and the temperature is often actually colder. These things are all registered. Note carefully whether there is a backwardness of vegetation corresponding thereto. A backwardness of vegetation there probably is, but is there a backwardness of vegetation corresponding to the decrease or the non-increase of light and warmth? There are statistical tables which give you the materials of the problem accurately. However, even supposing that light and heat were the only causes for the rising of the sap and the germination of the seed, they are extra mundane causes. Well, then, naturally the mind of the earlier man, which was far more metaphysical than the minds of men today, tried to carry this on — the mind then was far more devout, also far more reverential, far less material. And another thing was observed, and that was the fact which is condensed into a proverb now — viz., that history repeats itself — large events tend to recur in almost precisely the same sequence after long intervals of time. And there are two theories about this. One is that men, through long ages, set themselves to tabulate all events, and to formulate theories about them. Another theory is, that the knowledge of the laws governing this tendency of history to repeat itself were divinely revealed to mankind, and handed down through successions of initiates, through occult colleges, and that therein lay the secret wisdom of the initiates in the mysteries of all countries and races. To us it matters little which of these theories is the true one — analytical or synthetical, it matters not much; but, at all events, we find that the old seers and initiates had the theory very strongly developed and very clearly marked out, and they fixed upon certain marks in the heavens as a great clock whereon these vast cycles and periods of time might be registered; and this clock was that band of constellations round the ecliptic which we now call the Zodiac; and for the hands upon it were the seven planets moving round, and never, or perhaps only at almost inconceivable spaces of time, reoccupying the same position. In order to make this clock, this great band of the Zodiac, useful, and in order to indicate what the different parts thereof might be expected to produce as an effect upon the earth, certain names and symbols were given to certain parts of it, and these had their own peculiar significance in past history and in present history, and therefore, they concluded, in future history. Therein lay the occult mystery of prophecy. Now there were all sorts of aids to the reading of these signs and symbols. It seems to me that it is almost incredible that they should have been arbitrarily chosen, because they are so exactly apposite; they have fulfilled their prescribed conditions through historic ages with such extraordinary closeness, that the races of men who could have formulated those singularly appropriate figures, if they did so by observation, and by recorded observation, must have had a considerable number of stellar years to go upon; and a stellar year being, as I said, 26,000 years, gives you some idea of the enormous periods over which observation must have extended, if these Zodiacal figures were drawn from recorded observation.

Well, one point which I mentioned at last meeting is a very notable one — the glyph of the Supreme God at any time over the face of the world being formed from that sign which the sun occupies at the Vernal equinox. And here you will remember what the lecturer told us then, that this point is continually moving backward round the Zodiac. Whatever we take as our given sign which the sun occupies at the vernal equinox, at that point of time 2,000 years later the sun will occupy the previous sign. Thus about 4,000 years before Christ the sun at the vernal equinox was in the sign of Taurus, and then we find the bull-god everywhere; and the bull was the sign which was everywhere worshipped, the bull-headed god of Assyria, of Egypt; and in the Egyptian hieroglyphics there are many examples of the bull-headed god; and I think invariably you will find that these hieroglyphics either belong to the time of the Hyksos or earlier, or else if they are of later date that they are obviously copies of earlier inscriptions. An Egyptologist can tell without any possible reasonable doubt, on seeing a set of hieroglyphics, whether they belong to the date at which they were reported to be painted, or whether they were copies from earlier hieroglyphics; for of course in ancient Egypt there was just about as much copying of earlier work as there is now. We get houses built now in the Tudor style or Gothic style, or what not. So the Egyptians at the time of Rameses, or especially in the later weak, degenerated Ramesides, copied the hieroglyphics of their great predecessors. Well, the bull symbol in the course of time, and about the period when Moses was born, gives way to the symbol before it, Aries. Moving backward through the signs, the sun at the vernal equinox occupies the sign of Aries, and then the lamb or the ram comes to be worshipped all over the world. And when I say 'worship', I do not mean literally, but that the lamb or ram symbol is taken as the glyph of the Supreme God; and the ram is also the symbol of the sun. And so, when the sun is rising at the vernal equinox in the sign of the ram, we have the Lord on His own throne, so to speak, and that is one reason for what otherwise might be a very curious fact, that from that time till now the vernal equinox has been said to take place on the first point of Aries, a conventional sign. Long ago the sun moved out of the constellation, but still astronomers kept up an imaginary Zodiac, an ecliptic with imaginary divisions, called after the old signs, and they stuck to the name of Aries. I have no doubt any astronomer could give you a dozen reasons why. The occult reason why is, that that sign — the sun on his own throne, symbolising the male principle slain, the Lamb slain before the foundation of the world, showing, too, the moon, his mate — is the glyph of the whole period, the Supreme glyph. The Lamb of God is the glyph, one Supreme glyph of the Christian Church all over the world now just as much as the Pascal lamb in the time of Moses, the ram symbol of Zeus, the ram of Phryxos Helle, and the ram of many another mythology of the same date. This is also the meaning of the horned Moses. Many people have asked, and some have asked in vain, unless from an occultist, what the horns of Moses mean? It is easy to say that we are told there was a glory on his face when he came down from the mount, so that a veil had to be placed on his face. That may be one reason, but that would be pictorially represented by a halo or by a veil to Moses. Now we very seldom see a picture of a veiled Moses, but we do frequently see a picture of a horned Moses; and the reason is simply because Moses was the earth leader at the time when the ram was the Supreme glyph in the heavens, and the symbol of the ram was transferred to Moses, and so horns were placed on his head. There is another thing to notice there with regard to our own country, and that is that the bull (although the sun at the vernal equinox has long passed out of the sign of the bull) yet remains the glyph of England. Why should we speak of England as John Bull? Very few people could give any reason at all why the Bull; and, supposing the Bull, why John? There lies an occult reason behind that. The bull is the symbol of material strength, and the name of John, the most tender, the most feminine of the names of all the Scripture is attached to it — the name of the beloved disciple taken as the intuitional form, and coupled always with the name of Mary, so showing the spiritual development linked with the earthly and corporeal strength, the highest — the potentiality, at any rate, of the highest — spiritual development linked with the potentiality of the greatest bodily and material strength, pointing out the English-speaking race as the future rulers of the whole world. And I think there is little doubt that the whole tendency of history points in that direction.

The greatest influx of spirituality seems to come now through the English-speaking race. Let us say that there is great spirituality, that there are great truths, in the Buddhistic faiths. So it is. There are lessons which all of us might learn, and lay to heart. But look to the East, and you see English-speaking people — Englishmen and Americans — teaching the Buddhists their own religion — reviving Buddhism. The Buddhistic schools in Ceylon would have been absolutely dead but for American enterprise, and their masters and mistresses today are American. The leaders and reformers of the Buddhist temples in India are of the English race again. Our energy and our spirituality is giving back to the East their own faith, and a magnificent faith it is, and a great gift. And all that seems to lie within that name of John Bull, and it seems to belong to the potency of that sign, but corrected by the sign Virgo, which symbolises the name of John.

Another point is the view the Hermetic philosophy takes of the Zodiac. That will carry us a little bit further. According to the Hermetic philosophy, the Zodiac gives us the universal and real world, the accidental, individual, or phenomenal world, as one — as above, so below, — and it teaches us to look at the Zodiacs of all nations, and to find therein the central point — the invariable and immovable central point — typifying the Divine Creator, from whom radiate all diversity; that diversity being all still Himself, teaching us the oneness of things, teaching us the Trinity in unity, and teaching us the higher pantheism, and that they are all one — three aspects of the same truth. So in the Egyptian Zodiac we find the bird-formed deity, symbol of the Supreme Creator, occupying the centre; in the Hindu Zodiac we find the man in the attitude of prayer generally, and half-hidden by clouds; but in many of them, and also in the Chinese, we find the man, or sometimes the dragon, occupying the centre. In all of these we find the one, the three, and the multiple; and radiating out from that centre we find these various signs, no matter exactly how they are represented.

Now, what does all that mean according to the Hermetic philosophy? It means that the Zodiac is the circumference of an enormous vortex ring. The vortex ring is the first word of creation, so to speak — the tiniest of things. The very best guess at the ultimate atom is that it is a vortex ring, and the band of constellations occupying the ecliptic is likewise a vortex ring. As above, so below; the infinitely great and the infinitely small — all one. And the arrangement of the stars, or component atoms, as we might perhaps call them, of this vast vortex ring may give us the thought of God in the creation of the cosmos. But why the vortex ring? There again the Hermetic philosophy gives an answer. Matter blown out, sent forth, forms a ring, a vortex ring, on account of a resisting medium, on account of meeting with some resistance to its expansion. Some resistance there must be to give it the twirl. We all know how a ring of smoke can be blown in order to make a vortex ring, and how there is always the resisting medium. We cannot blow a vortex ring in an absolute vacuum. And now comes in the Hermetic philosophy, and says, the first emergence of the word, the breath, the thought of God that blew the vortex ring, met with a resisting medium of limitation, of darkness, of sin, and of death — symbolised by the dragon, the great dragon through the sky, trailing one-third of the stars with its tail. That was the glyph of the darkness, the resistance which the thought of God met with, the abyss of evil. And from the contest between these two — the Word of God sent forth, and the darkness and the evil which it had to contend with and to overcome — was born these whirling motions which are the basis, the root, of all motions of the cosmos, and the root of all metaphysical motions — mental, psychical, and spiritual motions, as well as physical. The contest between the light and darkness, the contest between Ahura, Mazda, and Achriman of the Persians, produces the motion, the synthesis, the sphere. The Spirit of God moves upon the face of the water, and from these opposing forces comes the whirl, which means the motion within a confined space — the limitation which is the condition of creation now. In that sense the Zodiac is a vortex ring, and in that sense also the Zodiac is the western analogue of the Shakra, the great wheel of the divine law of the Eastern. For if you once grasp it, the symbology of each is practically the same; the Zodiac, the tree, the serpent, these are the great glyphs. The serpent of eternal generation, the divine serpent, the serpent of light and of wisdom, the infernal serpent of darkness and of sensuality; the tree of Eden and the tree of Calvary, the tree of death and the tree of life — that tree aspiring upwards as the tree of life towards the Shakra or the Zodiac, the great wheel of the divine law. This is the glyph as expounded both in East and West.

We need to go but a very little bit further on. First we get the fish. And at the time of Christ the sun passed out of the constellation of Aries at the vernal equinox, and came into the constellation of Pisces. And then we have the glyph of the Ιχθυς we have the Vescica Pisces, we have the mitre as the bishop's symbol — we have endless glyphs. And there we pick up again the reminiscence of the last period of the Kali Yuga — the previous Pisces' month, if I may use the expression — when the worship of Dagon first began in Phoenicia, or somewhere about there. Probably it may not have been in Phoenicia; it may have been in Atlantis. The Atlanteans were growing old at that time, but they were in existence still. Dagon was worshipped in Palestine and Phoenicia when the sun was still in the sign of Taurus. Therefore it must have been, if the theory be true, a relic of the former time — the last time when the sun at the Vernal equinox was in that sign — and as a relic, corrupt and degraded.

Now we are coming just now into the sign of Aquarius. 'There shall meet you a man bearing a pitcher of water', said Christ; and now the meeting had come, and the development of the intuition, the female power, is a noticeable fact all over the world — the enormous interest which now at the close of this century is taken by every class, and by every manner of man or woman, more or less, in all mystic or occult subjects. Every one is carried on the wave Whether he will or no. History repeats itself; and the time has come for the history to repeat itself, as marked on the great clock on the Zodiac, by that hand of the sign at the vernal equinox, which is one of the great time-markers of the stellar year.

Well now, do we seek to know what is coming hereafter? Two thousand years hence the sun will be rising in the next sign, and that next sign is Capricornus, the he-goat — the goat of Mendes, the goat of the inverse pentagram, the goat of black magic and sorcery that will be the dominant power in the world two thousand years hence, or the whole system of prophecy is wrong. And one may ask whether one does not see certain signs of it already — certain signs that the seed may even now be sown which is to produce that evil fruit two thousand five hundred years or so hence. Then look at prophecy — the prophecies that we have. Take the Book of Revelation, and there we find the sorceries and witchcraft and evil things, especially the evil of material and sensual sorcery, which is to come after the present age. Then take the Hindu prophecy. We are near the end of the first period of the Kali Yug — the black age — black with horrors and terrors; the first five thousand years black with materiality. And has not that been so? Compare our civilisations now with the civilisations of five thousand years ago — about the time when Nineveh was in its glory, and when Egypt was rising into its material glory. The civilisations were magnificent then — as great as they are now. Their scientific achievements must have been as great as ours, if not greater; their art must have been as great as ours, if not greater. But they had spirituality, where we have not. And since that time the whole course of the world has been the gradual increase of materialism in every civilisation that has been born, grown up, and perished on the face of the earth. That was prophesied long ago in the old Hindu and Chinese records. And now we are entering upon a second five thousand years of the Kali Yug, which will be, if that prophecy be right, spiritual degradation, black magic and sorcery, and every kind of abomination of that nature. We are emerging from materialism now, and the evil potencies of this planet are getting into something worse — spiritual instead of material degradation. So it looks at any rate, and so say the prophecies both of East and West. And in the same way you can go on — you can trace out the plagues in the sign Sagittarius, the plagues shot by the arrows of the sun, the arrows of Apollo, which Homer speaks of. Though put down by chroniclers to destruction of Troy, and a thousand years before Christ or so, undoubtedly that legend belongs to the last Sagittarius month in the Kali Yug, and that Sagittarius month is coming again some five thousand years hence, when the second five thousand years of the Kali Yug come to an end. That is prophesied also in the Hindu and Chinese records, and similarly in Revelation. You get then the reign of the devil upon earth in the time of Scorpio, the converse of the sign of Virgo. And I ask you to notice the similarity of the two signs — only one marked by the sign of the cross, the other marked with the sign of the devil. So the woman shall bruise the serpent's head; and thus those two signs are very similar, having only Libra between them. And above Libra lies the decanate of the altar, the sign of the altar in the decanate; and I pointed out before how the picture of the altar was the real sign of Libra. It is very difficult to make ♎ into a balance, but it is very easy to imagine it to be an altar — say the old hieroglyphic form of an altar, with the sacrificial fire in the middle. Cutting off the top of it, you have the sign of Libra. And look in the Book of Revelation, and you will see that following the reign of the devil upon earth, the Church — that is all the faithful, that is all those who understand how to use their spirituality — shall be taken away, and kept safe underneath the altar. Another important thing is, you take Scorpio, and in the upper decanate of Scorpio is the sign Aquila, and that is the eagle of St John, and the good power of which Scorpio is the evil.

Without going further into these matters, that is a sort of general idea of what is occultly meant by the Zodiac. I have just given you these as a few fragmentary examples picked up here and there. Now if history repeats itself, and will repeat itself — if that be true, then ancient wisdom has given us a clock by which we may time the periods. Is that clock true? Are these periods right, or are they not? A careful study of history will throw a good deal of light upon it; and, at all event, that belief which impressed millions of men in generations long past, of races very far diverse, and countries far remote from each other, deserves a certain amount of careful recognition. And there we want distinctly the help of physical astronomy; we want these periods calculated for us; we want to know precisely at what time the signs of the Zodiac and the planets occupy certain positions, and to compare these carefully with tradition and with hieroglyphics. Some of you probably know that the Egyptian priests told Herodotus that at one time the pole of the earth corresponded with the pole of the ecliptic. The lecturer tells me that that is false astronomy, and most probably it is in our present constitution; but looking back upon those passages in Herodotus, and looking at some of the old hieroglyphics, I rather incline to think that the Egyptian priests meant that this was the case in a wholly antecedent period of the earth's history, not in historic times at all, but in the times of some of the earlier root races; and I should like to know whether there is any reason to say that such a position of the earth's axis would be impossible at the time when the incandescent earth occupied the position of a sun to a possibly inhabited moon. That was probably a fact, as we were told in the course of astronomical lectures last winter. Supposing that it were a possible fact that Egyptian priests might have drawn a Zodiac or hieroglyphic representing such a position of the earth's axis as indicating to them that far distant time — probably, I think, if we may go by the Hindu calculations, about eight to nine millions of years ago — that is a calculation which one may leave to physical astronomers; but in the meantime, the Zodiacs which we have — the Zodiac of Dendera among others, and the Hindu and Burmese Zodiacs — present many points yet unsolved, The three Virgins — the one holding a child, another nursing a child, and the third holding an ear of corn — might seem to indicate three separate stellar years, and these three separate positions of Virgo appear in the Zodiac of Dendera. Another problem is the Esne lion, and the altered position of the lion's tail — probably pointing to some particular object, some particular star, probably indicating the position of the lion at the time that was indicated by that Zodiac. This again should be looked at with regard to the exact position of the gallery in the Great Pyramid. The gallery of the Great Pyramid was seen to point at the time of its construction to Alpha Draconis, as the hieroglyphics are said to give a particular position for Alcyone at the same time. Now I am told that although the gallery of the Great Pyramid, at the date ordinarily given for its construction, would have pointed directly to Alpha Draconis, it would not have been in the required position; therefore, that the date of the Pyramid must be two thousand six hundred years earlier than is generally given. Whether that be or not, I must leave for the calculations of physical astronomers; but in the meantime, I can only hope that I have given some little indication that there is a little occult meaning in the Zodiac.

[Paper read on 1 July 1893. Reprinted from *Transactions of the Scottish Lodge of the Theosophical Society*, Vol. 1, Part X, (1893), pp. 149-56.]

16. Remarks on the Lecture on the Zodiac

THE esoteric symbolism of the Hermetic philosophy was adduced from the Zodiacal signs from the earliest ages of Egypt. I cannot even attempt to touch upon any of the many deeply interesting occult and esoteric problems which have been suggested by the lecturer and by his illustrations, many of which were new to me, and many of which threw very great light upon the symbology of our own and of various other races and religions. But there is one point I should like to mention now, by way of showing how far this subject stretches, and that is — and I believe that it is without exception — that if you find the sign of the Zodiac which the sun occupies at the vernal equinox at any period, that sign will give you the glyph or symbol of the Supreme God at that age all over the world. If we go back to the time before the date of Moses, to the time when the Hyksos were in Egypt, we find the sun rising in the vernal equinox in the sign of Taurus, and we find there the bull-headed god of Egypt and Assyria. Not only so, but we find the bull-headed god in India; we find the bull carrying Europa across from Asia to Europe; and here I may say that we have to look, not only to Egypt, Assyria, and India, but very specially into Phrygia. Carrying it on a little bit further, to about the time of Moses, we find the sun rising in Aries at the vernal equinox; we find the ram, or the lamb-god — the ram or the lamb as the symbol of the Supreme God. We get the paschal lamb of the Jews; the ram symbol of Zeus among the Greeks, later on adopted by the Latins; we get the ram in India and in Burma, the ram which we now find in many of the Indian and Burmese and in Chinese temples; and in Phrygia we get the ram of the golden fleece, that ram whose fleece was afterwards brought home by the Argonauts. And taking the general chronology as given by the Greeks, the date of that migration must have been about simultaneous with the entering of the sun into Aries at the vernal equinox, and with the adoption of the ram or the lamb as the Supreme God among the Jews. Then carry it further on, to about the time of Christ, the beginning of the present era, and we find the sign passing out of Aries and passing into Pisces, and we find there the adoption of the fish as a symbol all over the world, as far as we know it. We find the

Ιχθυς adopted as a monogram of Christ. Of course we all know the meaning of that monogram, — but it is the fish. And we find the fish symbol in India. And here I may note a curious thing, that you will find all these Zodiacal signs on the Indian packs of cards — the circular cards. If you light on a complete pack, you will find every sign put down, and referring to the different avatars of Vishnu. One's memory naturally recurs to the fish-god, the Dagon of the Philistines, and to the whale that swallowed Jonah; and these being distinctly and clearly before our present era, must be probably 22,000 years before.

At the present time the sign is passing out of the constellation of the Fish and passing into Aquarius. With regard to that, I may mention the curious fact that that sign was given in the Bible when the Saviour was going to Jerusalem for the last time, when He sent before Him Peter the fisherman, with the direction, "Ye shall go into the city, and there shall meet you a man bearing a pitcher of water." It is useful to note there the coincidence of the time, somewhere in the eighties, when the sun passed out of Pisces at the vernal equinox and passed into Aquarius. Almost coincident with the end of the first 5,000 years of the Kali Yug, and almost coincident with a number of other cycles which I have had occasion to mention to this Lodge before, all pointing to some new access of spiritual light, if not actually to a new revelation somewhere about the present time. It is too early yet to say what this new sign may denote, — what change in symbolism, what change in our knowledge of, and in our relation to, the Supreme which we worship. But this much we know, that the water is a female sign, and that the female element in the Supreme is vastly more recognised already than ever before. An indication of that may probably be found in the promulgation by the Roman Church of the doctrine of the Immaculate Conception, the recognition of the father-motherhood of God by the Hermetists and others, and the general recognition of intuition — the female power, combined with knowledge, the male power — as giving wisdom. These are very slight indications, but we can only expect very slight indications at first.

On looking further still into the future, we can read by the light of the signs that are coming, and the symbology of these signs, something of the meaning of the great Book of Revelation. On that picture-bible of the Zodiac we can read the history of future times in almost exactly the same language as John has given us in the story of his great vision in

Patmos. We can see the plagues that are coming upon the earth; the curse and immorality that will come under Capricorn; the reign of the devil in Scorpio; then the balanced power of Libra, wherein, in the decanate of the balance occurs the altar, under which the Church is to be kept safe, as St John tells us in the Revelation, during the reign of the devil upon earth; followed by Virgo, which is the reign of the saints upon earth.

This is only a very rough indication, but it shows how very much may lie behind the Zodiac.

[Reprinted from *Transactions of the Scottish Lodge of the Theosophical Society*, Vol. 1, Part IX, (1893) pp143-144. The lecture referred to was delivered by William Peck, on the Zodiac in the context of historical astronomy.]

17. The Tatwas: Four Lectures

The Tatwas in Relation to the Human Organism, especially as regards —
  (1) Moods and Emotions
  (2) Health and Disease
  (3) Clairvoyance and the Cosmic Picture Gallery

I have taken three points as illustrative of the three notable characteristics of mankind: First of all, Moods and Emotions; secondly, Health and Disease; thirdly, Psychical.

But, first of all, it is well to see how it is that the tatwic vibrations affect human beings at all. And let me say here, to clear the ground, that this science of the tatwas is not intended either to override, or to explain, or to stand instead of, any physical science whatsoever. It does not stand instead of anatomy, or medicine, or chemistry, or biology; it accepts all these. If I may use an illustration, I would imagine a great and complex electric engine, the whole structure of which, in its various parts, our scientific men are diligently studying, measuring every wheel, every pivot, and every part of the machine, and seeing what is the characteristic motion of every part. These labours are most useful and essential; but there is something further than these labours will ever tell us, and which is another science altogether, and that is the nature of the electric force which drives that engine. Now, both these inquiries are essential, if you would have a perfect knowledge of the engine. You must know every atom; you must measure and analyse the minutest part; and therefore, to every scientist, in every possible walk of science, the philosophy of the tatwic vibrations says, 'Go on; the more you can find out the better: my science does not conflict with yours in the very slightest degree.'

The five tatwas, the five vibrations, are as follows:

	Shape	Sense	Element
Akasa	Dotted Globe	Sound	—
Vayu	Circle	Touch	Air
Taijas	Triangle	Colour	Fire
Apas	Crescent	Taste	Water
Prithivi	Square	Smell	Earth

And every one of these is dual — positive and negative, to use the phrase which has got into common use in electrical science; it is not a very accurate one, but it will pass. And those five are attributed to the five ordinary planets — I do not say with particular accuracy, but still they are so attributed; and the positive side of every vibration is said to be attributed to the sun, and the negative is said to be attributed to the moon. Now, when our world began to revolve upon its axis, and also to go round the central sun with poles inclined to the plane of its orbit at a particular angle, it generated two centres of force, one positive and the other negative; and it generated a double kind of current, a positive current and a negative current, and these currents really account for most of the physical phenomena of the globe. These currents are of different kinds. Look at any physical atlas and you can trace some of them; you can see the magnetic currents coming to a pole, not at all coincident with the geographical pole, nor coincident with the pole of extreme cold, which also again is different from the north pole or the geographical pole. You will also see traced the prevailing currents of the wind, and of the ocean, and so forth, so that the conclusion you will draw is that there is a species of circulation round the surface of our globe, arising, probably, I might say almost certainly, from it rotation on its axis, and from the inclination of that axis to the plane of its orbit; and two centres, two poles, a positive pole and a negative pole. And these poles govern the tatwic currents, or the life currents, as they pass over the globe. Well now, as in the macrocosm so in the microcosm, as above so below, as in the great so in the small; and we find precisely the same thing in the hatching of an egg. If you carefully examine eggs from day to day, from the first day of incubation up to the time of hatching, you will see the gradual formation of first one centre and then another within the yolk of the egg — a little knot apparently of the yolk matter. There is a certain difference among occult writers as to whether it is the positive or the negative pole which is formed first, or whether both come into existence together. From the philosophy of the tatwas, there should be very little doubt that it is the negative or south pole that comes into existence first. But at all events, whichever comes first, or whether they come both together or not, these two knots which form the yolk of the egg into a polar body represent the north and the south poles, represent the two centres of action, represent ultimately the heart and the brain, the vascular system and the nervous system; and from one to the other passes a line, a thread, a groove, a canal, the medullary canal. And here you have the first origin of the completed chick which is to emerge from that egg; and here too we have the germ of the two centres upon which the tatwas are to play hereafter. Now, the subsequent process is simply one of development, very similar to the development of the solar system, the development of a circulatory system. And that development produces in each of these centres a four-fold auricle and ventricle of the heart. From these issue nadis or tubes, conducting-wires or carriers of the vital force; tatwic forces — always circulatory, the sensor and the motor nerves issuing from the positive pole of the brain, arteries and veins from the heart. The circulation of the blood from artery through capillary to vein and back to the heart, is now tolerably well known. The mode by which the vital impulse leaps from the sensor to the motor nerve in the brain is, I believe, not so well known; but at all events I believe it is known that the action is circulatory, and also that the nerve system is the positive life carrier, the blood circulating through the system being the recipient of life force. Well now, on such a machine as that, very briefly as I have indicated it, which is thoroughly explored and experimentalised upon by anatomists and physicians, comes this system of tatwas working constantly, like the electric current working an electrical engine.

And now, taking my first point, the moods and emotions, every one of these tatwas has its own particular effect, and they occur in regular rotation. If you wish to know how often they recur you can find it in this way. I told you that the positive life current is said to answer to the sun and the negative to the moon. Now, the positive life current passes through the entire body once in twenty-four hours, and the phenomena are then repeated. The proportion of the revolution of the sun to the moon is roughly one to twelve; therefore, roughly speaking, the tatwas pass just twelve times to once of the solar current. Now, the first tatwa, Vayu, is the gate of motion. When that tatwa is in currency, its effect upon the human body is to produce restlessness, desire to do something, to go somewhere, or something of that kind. The following, Taijas, is warmth, colour, light. It produces anger, heat of any kind; whereas Apas produces receptivity and calm contentment; and Prithivi produces the opposite to Taijas, indifference. Now the question will naturally arise, firstly, How is it that these tatwic vibrations operate upon the body? and secondly, How is it, supposing they operate in the way indicated, that every human being is not affected with precisely the same moods at precisely the same time? The answer to that is this. To the way that they operate I can only give you there the Eastern theory — and I believe myself that it is a good one, and I know of nothing in physical science to contradict it — viz., that every nerve ganglion consists of a central nerve cell and five cells grouped round it, small microscopic, or less than microscopic, it may be, each of which is so constituted as to respond to one or other of these tatwic vibrations. A ganglion may consist of any number of such cells and cellules. Now, when Vayu is running, the vayu cellules in each ganglion are set in motion, begin to function, and the nerve restlessness pervades the entire body. Similarly when the Taijas vibration comes on. But then, why is not every human being similarly affected at the same time? In the first place, because to respond immediately and perfectly to the tatwic current requires absolutely perfect health of every nerve, every ganglion, every cell, and every cellule; and secondly, even supposing that every human being in an assembly had such perfect health, you still have to take account of the personal equation. Let an electric flash be started at one end of this room and every person here will see it at a different time, slightly different of course, but different and calculably different, as every astronomer knows, because the personal equation has to be allowed for in all astronomical observations, and each observer's has to be known, calculated, and allowed for, in order that his observation may be rectified. Therefore, when the vayu tatwa comes into play upon the world in general, every human being upon the world will respond to it at a different time, in proportion to the rapidity or slowness of the carrying power of their nerves, and the sensitiveness of the particular vayu centres; and these different centres are of different grades of sensitiveness in all different individuals. Now, that is assuming perfect health, and that no extraneous operations at all interferes with the running of these vibrations. But beyond these we have human free-will, and human free-will acts, and will always act, notwithstanding all our scientific calculations of the forces that play upon it; and not only the free-will of the individual himself, but in nearly every case the will of others as well. Take the simple case of hypnotism, which is a strong illustration. The hypnotist, by means of suggestion, is able to put out of action, so to speak, a whole group of nerve centres, rendering them mute and irresponsive, so that although the vayu tatwa may be passing over the earth, the individual is unaffected by it, because a species of suggested anaesthesia has passed over and muted the vayu centres. Then that which can be in this way permanently, strongly, and vigorously suggested by the hypnotist in the hypnotic state, can also be suggested in lesser degree by any one person to another. And so you get all the varying emotions. I have taken this division of moods and emotions — perhaps not a very scientific one; I am not sure that Professor Bain[1] would agree with me — but still it is a rough and ready classification — to call those impulses which are generated by an individual within himself independently of others as moods, and those which are the result of the action of other people upon him as emotions. Now, for instance, if there be a violent animosity between two persons, the approach one to the other, by this species of suggestion, is pretty sure to bring the taijas centres — the centres of heat, anger, and so forth — into strong action, to keep those centres functioning even after the taijas current has passed; to retain, so to speak, the taijas vibration circulating through the body, and excluding or muting the functions of the other centres. And so with all the other emotions, love, and so forth, in precisely the same way.

Well now, that gives us a certain key to the second head, viz., Health and Disease, because every species of disease is some faulty functioning of either the nerve system, or the circulation system, taking its effect and manifesting in various specialised organs. Now, how can that fault be cured, if it is curable at all? It can be cured simply by restoring the harmony of the tatwic vibrations of the nerve. Because the five tatwas constitute a perfect balance which produces in the individual perfect health. Each one as it occurs harmonises with the other; each one glides, not with any sudden change, but imperceptibly as the colours of the spectrum; each one glides into the other precisely at its appointed time. If there are centres that do not respond to taijas, then the animal heat of the individual must necessarily decline; then the red corpuscles will decrease in number, the individual will become anaemic, that is one result. The taijas centres are there, but they are atrophied it may be, or paralysed. It may be that suggestion or Some other thing has thrown them

---

1. i.e. The Scottish philosopher, Alexander Bain (1818-1903), author of *The Emotions and the Will* (1859).

out of gear, so that they function no longer. At any rate there is a disease, a diseased condition, which may go on until it actually implicates some of the vital organs. Similarly a deficiency of the apas, and an over-activity of the taijas, centre will produce fever. And so with every disease. And some have said, Can all diseases be absolutely classified? Can an absolute number be set to the diseases to which human beings are liable? And the answer is, Not unless you can classify and number all the colours of the spectrum. For as every colour in the spectrum may be formed of these four tatwas, so every disease has its characteristic colour, and these colours are as many as those of the spectrum, and as imperceptibly glide into one another. Akas, darkness, is the condition of death, and if that be prolonged the death of the individual is certain; and the death of an individual only occurs when the akasa tatwa is in operation in his body. That condition passes certainly every half-hour through the body, and if it be unduly prolonged then death must with absolute certainty be the result. But there are other functions which are familiar to most, at all events by name, and the mention of hypnotism leads naturally to the mention of the psychic functions of clairvoyance and its attendant phenomena. Now, there is one period in the training of occult students when they have acquired a certain amount of sensitiveness, and a certain amount of power of concentration, and so forth, when the teacher directs them at noonday on a clear and cloudless day to look steadfastly into the blue sky. At first they see nothing. At first the eyes will simply grow dazzled, and will be unable to bear the continuous staring into the depths of the blue — a kind of dizziness will pass over, and a sort of grey mist will flow before the eyes. But after a while, if the pupil has attained sufficient progress, he will begin to see pictures in the blue — and, many people will say, 'hallucination'. But it is not hallucination, as has been proved over and over again, when actual scenes and actual occurrences have been seen in this way which were absolutely impossible to be seen by the natural eye, or known of. Now the question arises, Is there any scientific or physical explanation of this? and there certainly is, if we accept the philosophy of the tatwas. Because the atmosphere of the world, its aura in fact, is bounded, and rigorously bounded, at the distance of some few miles from the earth where the air ceases; and there, according to the philosophy of the tatwas, the solar prana passes through the akas to merge into the terrestrial prana. Or, to put it in perhaps a more intelligible form to those who are not familiar with the Eastern language, the blue vault of the sky may be compared to a hollow and transparent glass globe surrounding the atmosphere of the earth. Now, every action of every human being, every motion that is made upon the face of the earth, immediately produces a picture which is carried upon the light rays, on the rays of Taijas. An absolute proof of that lies in the fact that if an electric flash say, or something that you can see a long distance off, is made some six miles away from you, it is an absolutely measurable space of time between the occurrence of that flash, and the time that you see it. During that time the picture of that flash has been travelling along a ray of light, or, as we might say, a taijas vibration, to reach your eye. Well, the picture does not stop as it reaches your eye; it goes on and on, right away into infinity. And now, keep in mind the idea of the hollow crystal ball, for although it is not really a hollow crystal globe, for the purpose of this illustration it produces the same effect. When that picture reaches the interior surface of the hollow globe, part of it goes on and part of it is kept back. I add another illustration. If you are going along in a railway carriage by day, and you look out of the window, you see the surrounding country; but as night comes on and the lamp is lighted in the carriage, you look out of the window, and you do not see the surrounding country, but you see the reflection of the railway carriage. Betwixt and between in the twilight you see both, you see the reflection of the interior of the carriage like a spectral form upon the landscape outside; and even in the broad daylight, you can if you choose see that reflection of the interior of the carriage — and that is a curious experiment, which is worth making because it is very illustrative of the philosophy of the science of the tatwas, that absolutely in certain conditions of light, at the will of your mind, you can either look through your carriage window and see the country outside, or you can look at the glass and see the glass and see the reflection of the carriage within. That is precisely a small analogy of what happens at the confines of the air at the blue sky. The greater part of the picture which is formed upon the earth goes out into the infinite, but a certain portion is reflected back to earth. Thus the sky on a clear day, contains as it were, an enormous reflected picture of every incident that is transpiring upon the face of the earth. Can you see it? Yes, you can, if you can once attain to the proper pose of mind, which is only attained by training. Now that picture is a small picture upon the sky, is a small image of the picture of the globe of this earth, which rays out into the infinite, and is continually passing into the infinite, so that a perpetual string of pictures of everything which has ever taken place upon this globe is passing out at this moment, and has been doing so at every moment since the world first came into existence, and those pictures may under certain circumstances be seen. This is what is called the cosmic picture gallery. And this small experiment, which is one of the first which is recommended by trainers in occultism, is one of the simplest and easiest methods of seeing actually some of these wonderful pictures in the cosmic picture gallery.

Other pictures can be seen. And observe this further, that the man who creates one of such pictures, establishes thereby a tatwic connection between himself and the reflection of that picture, first from the physical sky, and secondly from the larger globe of what is called the sphere of the Zodiac — a tatwic condition which makes that picture, that act of his, a factor, dominant in some cases but not always, but always a factor in all his future life. Thus it is that every act that any person does haunts them, not only for the whole of this life, but for the whole of their incarnations, until its effect is worn out or obliterated by its contrary action; and thus it is that all evil actions have a strong tendency to repeat themselves when certain times recur. When the time recurs at which this picture is again thrown back upon the spot of earth where that person lived, recurs the tendency in himself to repeat the action. When the picture of that action has so far passed from its original positive force as to become negative, it haunts with a constant remorse. That is a similar phenomenon to the seeing of a complementary colour when you have looked long upon a bright colour. Look for a long time at a red disc, and after a bit you will see a green one floating before you. So with a prominent action, an evil action, first will come the tendency to repeat it; as that wears out, and a negative state of that picture supervenes, will come the constant haunting remembrance of that evil action, not now striving to repeat it, but exacting remorselessly the penalty for such action. Thus it is that we human beings are constantly forming the prana, the ocean of the tatwas of this earth; and every action that we do not only tends to reproduce the same action in ourselves, but in lesser degree to reproduce the same action in others. Therefore to that extent is every one of us responsible for the moral conduct of every other, because the ocean of prana, through which these tatwas are constantly playing, is formed by ourselves, and is itself the vehicle of the forming of the character of every other human being, forming in fact a network which links us all together. Now, such is just the very broadest outline of the way in which the tatwas operate upon human beings. It is of course impossible in the time at our disposal to go into any details anywhere, and I have not the slightest doubt that numberless questions must have arisen to most of you, questions of details which do not seem to work out. Well, all I can say is with regard to these, take them patiently, take them slowly. My own experience has been that the system of the tatwic philosophy works in the minutest detail when carefully studied, but a superficial glance reveals only inconsistencies. We must study our electrical engine very carefully, and then, having a very broad idea, a mere schoolboy notion in fact, of the direction and force of the currents which are driving it, we may get a little idea of how best to handle the great machine with which we have been entrusted.

[Paper read on 2 February 1895. Reprinted from *Transactions of the Scottish Lodge of the Theosophical Society*, Vol III, No. 1 (1895), pp. 9-15.]

Polarity of Tatwic Currents

I was asked some time ago to say something about polarity and polarisation. I did not do so at the time, for the simple reason that we had not got then a distinct idea of anything to polarise. And I think it is from that circumstance that a great deal of the confusion of mind which many people suffer from with regard to these words 'polar', 'polarity', 'polarisation', and so forth, arises. But now that we have some kind of notion of the Tatwic currents, I think we can make a sort of shift to get a general idea of what is meant by the polarity of those currents, and what is meant therefore by polarity in general. And I want to give you, if I can, a sort of general conception which will answer for all the different uses of the word. Because it constantly appears, for instance, to a scientific man reading the *Perfect Way*, that the word polarisation is used in a wholly unscientific sense; also when a person who has read a good deal of Hermetic literature, and got accustomed to the use of the words as there employed, happens to take up a scientific book, and to read something about polarised light, for instance, it appears absolutely incomprehensible, as if the word were used in a ridiculous sense. And yet the prime conception is a tolerably simple one, and of course may refer to many kinds of currents; but I propose to take it only on the lines of the Tatwic currents which we have been considering for the last few meetings, and for that purpose I will ask you just for a moment to conceive of the whole solar system being out of existence. Carry your mind back to the time before the solar system, as we know it now, was created, and just imagine this little bit of space where we are, void, an empty space in the centre of the star sphere. Probably there are a great many such spaces. Probably this space is no wider than other spaces. If you went up from here to the nearest fixed star, you would probably find a distance quite as great between you and the next nearest fixed star. But however that may be — which we have nothing particular to do with just at present — we find a hollow sphere to all intents and purposes, studded with stars in all directions. And in this star sphere there is at present no direction because there is nothing to mark it: there is neither up nor down, east nor west, neither north nor south. It is equal as far as the human eye can see, if we can imagine a human eye located in this globe or at the sun, before the globe or the sun were there, and nothing but an eye, nothing but the perceptive faculty. Now through that hollow sphere are running the Tatwic currents which have called those stars into existence. And I will just remind you for a moment of these currents. There is the Akasa, which produces the capacity, the potentiality of motion, which causes the ether — that is to say, the absolutely undifferentiated matter which fills that space — to become so differentiated as to become capable of motion, causes it to become granular. And following that, operates the Vayu Tatwa which sweeps these granules into a circular motion. Upon that again operates the Taijas Tatwa, which sweeps the moving particles into a glowing incandescent mass of fire mist, in fact. And so is born the first nebula, the nebula which hereafter shall take the form of our solar system. Then following upon the fiery Tatwa, the fiery current which has created the fire mist, comes the Apas, its natural reaction, the cold and contracting force which draws this fire mist into whirling balls whirling round an empty space in the centre. And from that again the Prithivi, which gives us cohesion, and which separates the dry land from the water. Again, the run of these Tatwic currents passes through the nebulous mass, now gradually forming into a system, and the remaining star dust, or cosmic matter, or world stuff, or whatever it may be called, is swept by the centripetal forces into the centre, and the sun is born.

Well, such roughly and very broadly and very rapidly is the process of the creation of the nebula and the development of the nebula into the solar system. For fuller accounts of that I may refer you to the admirable paper which Sirius has contributed to the *Transactions*. But I just mention it now in order to recall it to your minds, and to have something to start upon.

But now there is one remarkable thing to notice here, and that is, that the formation of this system has now given us direction; it has given us an up and down. For these whirling balls into which the fiery mass of the nebula first consolidated itself, go round on the same plane. That is to say, we do not have one globe going round in one direction and others at considerable angles to it. We might have imagined something of that kind to have resulted from a whirling sphere gradually coalescing at its outside into whirling balls; but as a point of fact it is not so. The circles are concentric within each other, and all on the same plane, so that you might lay the whole solar system practically on a table, if you had a table big enough. Now that gives us, if we take the orbit of the outermost planet, a great circle, and if we take the centre of that great circle, and drive a line up and down through it at right angles to the plane of the circle, that line constitutes the pole upwards and downwards of that circle. There we have then the solar system as a polar body. Now through that hollow sphere, as we said at the beginning, the Tatwic currents are running and continuing to run always. That is to say, to interpret it into plain English, there are certain currents of force of some kind or sort passing through that hollow sphere perpetually. Now we need not go into details at this stage about that at all, because every one can see that thereare rays of light passing through that sphere perpetually. Thatis one thing also, that there are magnetic currents passing through that sphere perpetually; also heat rays. We need not go any further, because at present these are enough for our purpose. All that we want to assume just now is that there are lines of force perpetually passing, and I think we must assume passing in a fixed and determinate direction, through that hollow sphere. And also it matters not for the present purpose that it is not a sphere — that the stars are at all manner of distances from what we have taken to be our centre. We have imagined this sphere which is void at the beginning and round which are the stars, and within that void sphere we have imagined the nebula coming into existence and gradually evolving into the solar system. We have currents of forces running in definite direction through that hollow sphere; for if they do not run in definite direction, we should have simply lines of force, lines of vibration, lines of effect running about vaguely, hither and thither, and productive of chaos and not of cosmos.

Well, now, if these premises are correct, it is pretty obvious that the precise direction of the plane of the solar system with regard to the stars must somehow or other have been determined by the action of the forces that created it, and by the forces whose operation first whirled the star mist, the fire mist, into a nebulous form, and then consolidated it into planets. If that premise again be accurate, it follows that the precise direction and position of that plane with regard to the star sphere surrounding it must be in some way or other the key to the constitution and nature of the solar system, because it is the key to the operation of the forces which produced it.

Now that plane is the plane of the ecliptic, the plane on which, looking from this earth, we see the sun. And round that plane of the ecliptic, round the circle of stars, that is, which is concentric with the plane of the solar system, and which the plane of the solar system would touch if it were extended far enough, there are certain stars and groups of stars. And it is for that reason that those groups of stars have been always considered to be the ones which most clearly show the constitution and the nature of the solar system; and those groups constitute the belt of the zodiac. Some of the old writers used to say that it was called 'zodiac' in consequence of the imaginary forms of living animals which the ancient Chaldeans fancied that they saw in these constellations, being shepherds of an imaginative turn of mind, and having nothing better to do than to imagine the forms of wild animals among the stars. Certainly I should prefer to think that the word is derived from the Greek word for life, Zoe, and also that it refers rather to the source of life flowing in with the Tatwic currents upon the solar system, from that part of the star sphere which is marked by the belt parallel to and concentric with this plane of the solar system; that is to say, that it indicates the nature of life upon the whole solar system.

Well, now, there you have the polarity of the solar system as a whole. It is polarised towards the pole of its great circle, the pole of its plane. But when we come to look at the individual globes composing that solar system, we find that they are not, as we might expect to find them, polarised in the same way as the great circle. We find, for instance, that our earth has an inclination, that the pole of our earth is not the pole of the ecliptic, but is the pole of its own equator which comes a little bit off the pole of the ecliptic. Very well, now we see that the Tatwic currents affecting the solar system do not directly affect the earth in the same way. If the pole of the earth were the same as the pole of the solar system, then the character of the earth would be the character of the whole system. But it is not. Now certain things we know physically. We know that it is exactly this inclination of the earth's equator to the ecliptic that gives us the phenomena of summer and winter, gives us the phenomena of the seasons. That merely shows us what an effect the fact of the earth not being polarised accurately to its system produces on the mere operation of the terrestrial Taijas, the heat and cold, and with every Tatwic current which flows the result is precisely the same, that is to say, every Tatwa that flows is a little bit out of the characteristic of the solar system. The earth is to that extent in disharmony with its surroundings. The characteristic of the earth depends upon those currents which run, not from the belt of the zodiac, but from the belt parallel to its own equator. Therefore there is in the earth a perpetual disharmony, a perpetual war between this strong characteristic of the whole solar system and the individual quality of the earth. The earth therefore appears in this view like an individual who is out of harmony with his surroundings, as we might say the square man in a round hole; and therefore is the earth always a place of trial and of suffering; therefore also it is that every individual on the earth, every human being, every man or woman who polarises his own or her own individuality in accordance with that of the earth, is in disharmony with the wider and stronger currents, viz., those of the solar system which surround it. Therefore it is that the materialist must invariably and inevitably be in disharmony with all but the terrestrial and material surroundings. Therefore it is that we are told to polarise ourselves to the higher spiritual planes. And therefore again it is that in all occult science we are directed especially to the zodiac in the study of astrology, because that fixes the plane from whence the life of the solar system is derived, not the mere terrestrial life, but the life of the whole solar system. And when we can by mental effort place ourselves in harmony with that life, we draw in vitality from the whole Tatwic currents which are running into the solar system — not merely the material life of the body which we obtain by polarising ourselves with the earth — we draw in the inner and more essential and more vital conditions which, properly assimilated, render us independent of the mere terrestrial currents.

It is of course somewhat difficult to pursue this analogy. It is a metaphor, comparing the material with the spirit, passing from the material plane on to the spiritual plane, from the actual world of flesh and blood on to the thought world; but yet for all students of occultism it is a very real metaphor, a very real transition.

Now in every place and in every connection in which you meet this word 'polar', the meaning of it is exceedingly simple. Anything on earth from the cosmos itself to any planet or star composing it, and down to the minutest atom composing that planet, anything which has two ends is a polar body. When anything is absolutely a homogeneous or heterogeneous or chaotic mass which has no end and no beginning and no middle, well then it is not a polar body; but directly it has two ends it is a polar body; and whether it is accurately or inaccurately polarised depends entirely upon its sphere of action, in other words, upon the plane in which it revolves. If that body points its two ends in the same direction as the poles of the circle in which it revolves — I care not now whether we are speaking physically or metaphysically — it is accurately polarised; otherwise it is inaccurately polarised, it is in a condition of disharmony and of unrest. And that refers to the whole planet, and to every individual on its surface. But with this difference. The earth at present is a place of trial for the individual living upon its surface; therefore the earth is what we may call wrongly polarised. And I use the word 'wrongly' there merely as intending to convey the sense of unrest. It is not ultimately and finally wrong, because it is designed; but it is an unrestful position, an unstable position. And human beings are put in these material bodies which we now inhabit on this planet so unrestfully poised, in order that by the exercise of thought and by the cultivation of their spiritual faculties, they may raise themselves above the material state of unrest, and may polarise their own individualities into harmony with the higher conditions, the conditions of the system into which they are born.

Now you might suppose from that that the ultimate state of this earth would be to get itself straight — in other words, to bring its own north pole into coincidence with the pole of its ecliptic. And that may be so, and it may very possibly be the ultimate destiny of this world that it should go straight. But observe, it would then no longer be a place of trial. Whether it would be a place of bliss I cannot say. My own thought, as drawn from the teaching of the higher divine science of all ages, is that when this occurs — supposing that in the mechanical evolution of the universe it should occur — the functions of the world as a place of human residence will have passed by, that it will then be rapidly approaching the state of a dead planet. I called it my own idea, but I believe it is shared by many occultists. The place of abode of a humanity which has developed itself beyond the necessity for the state of trial in which it now is, will, I think, probably be elsewhere.

To know then the characteristic of the earth or of any planet, we have to know simply the obliquity of its axis, and then to know the exact nature of the Tatwic currents which belong to that plane to which it is polarised. The rules of the old astrologers and the characteristics which they affixed to the star groups give us a great clue. I have not anything like time to go into it now; but any one who has the patience to follow it out can easily do so, and if you look at the direction of the earth's axis, look at the characteristics of the constellations round the pole star and the characteristics of the constellations round the celestial equator, you will see sorrow, suffering, tribulation, and trial, the characteristics of this material plane, and you will see many other things, all of which interpreted will give you a very exact account of the materialist man or woman, the dangers, the troubles, the sufferings that are in store for them. On the other hand, look in precisely the same way at the pole of the ecliptic and at the signs of the zodiac, the constellations round that great belt, and you will see the influx of life, rest, peace, and happiness. So you get a key to the character of systems of worlds and of individuals according to the way in which they are respectively polarised.

It is a very difficult conception to follow, and I fear I have not done very much towards elucidating it; but I shall be very pleased to answer any question, and try to clear up any elementary points that may be left dark; because the conception is such an important one, that I should like you to get a good firm grip, not of the details, but of the conception of polarity, as a key to the future work which I hope we may attempt to do.

[Paper read on 8 June 1895. Reprinted from *Transactions of the Scottish Lodge of the Theosophical Society,* Vol. Ill, No. 2 (1895), pp. 26-31.]

Some Aspects of the Tatwas in Relation to Daily Life

The reason that I put this paper on tonight is that a good many people, members of this Lodge especially, and many others too who have studied the theory of the Tatwas, especially from Rama Prasad's book,[2] have got on comfortably enough as long as they were dealing with wide generalities concerning the coming into existence of the universe in which we are, the formation of the solar system, and the formation of the solar system from a nebular into a system such as we now know it. All that seems tolerably simple, and the theory of Tatwas seems to explain beyond all doubt what was at all events a reasonable and rational theory about the coming into existence of things. Moreover, the analogies which we get, such as of the incubation of an egg, and others of that kind, seem to give us such wonderful correspondences, and the whole line of the story of creation, as developed in the theory of the Tatwas, so exactly corresponds with and illustrates the story as told in the Book of Genesis, and the story as told in the Cosmogony in other races and other religions. There is no getting away from the fact that here is some great system, which, if not absolutely proved to be true, has so much of working probability about it, that we must look upon it as a theory which needs to be critically examined and dealt with. But those who have gone on reading Rama Prasad's book have found grave difficulties when they

---

2. Rama Prasad, *The Science of Breath and the Philosophy of the Tatwas, translated from the Sanskrit, with explanatory essays on Nature's Finer Forces,* (TPS, 1890).

come to try and find out how the Tatwas operate in ordinary daily life; and two of the questions which were asked at the last meeting illustrate that to some extent — those I mean concerning the sun-breath and moon-breath, and concerning Apas and Prithivi. It is quite natural that such difficulties should occur to any one who is merely reading Rama Prasad's book, and has not been thoroughly instructed in the actual operation of Tatwas in our daily life. Moreover, in M. D.'s most admirable paper you find the very same thing — his criticisms are absolutely unanswerable if you take the book itself with no comment — but, as I stated in a note at the end of that paper, none of those things which M. D. criticised were ever stated in this Lodge, and that is an important fact too. I have, in papers and addresses which I have given here, taken considerable pains to state only those things which could be stated without any veil or blind, and which were absolutely and provably true.

But when you come to the question about the currency of the Tatwas throughout the human body, and we come to the question of the breath in the right or left nostril, or the middle, you come to questions which are designedly veiled. They are veiled in Rama Prasad's book more than they need be, and therefore here and there it is possible to raise the veil a little, and this I shall endeavour to do; but at the same time I must remark that there is a good deal in that book which is veiled for exceedingly good reasons, and which no one is allowed to state publicly, for the very sufficient reason that it would give a great deal too much power to people untrained and unfit to exercise such power. That book of Rama Prasad's was primarily addressed to Initiates, and to them every sentence is full of meaning, but a great deal is also perfectly intelligible, with careful study, to the outer world.

Now, the first thing to remember, when you are trying to consider the operation of the Tatwas as we see them round us constantly, when you are trying to identify any particular Tatwa, to know what particular Tatwa is current at the time, and so forth, you must bear in mind what very few people ever do bear in mind, and that is, that as you approach towards manifestation in actual physical and material phenomena so does the perplexity increase. It is very simple when you start with the undifferentiated Mulaprakriti, and you are trying to conceive the breath of God creating the universe therein. You have only one centre, you have the five Tatwas, and five operations of one breath in its dual form of positive and negative. That is the way in which universes are called into operation, but with each stage the perplexity becomes more involved. Thus you have at first a centre developed by means of this operation of the five Tatwas; and that centre forthwith begins to radiate other Tatwic currents of its own; and the radiation of those Tatwic currents from what we may call the great central sun produces other centres, and each in its turn begins to radiate its own series of Tatwas. Thus we have these different series with different times running simultaneously. Now, after a number of such operations, we find our own sun coming into operation as the centre of the solar system. radiating its five Tatwas, the life-source of the solar system. Then that operates upon the earth, but the earth itself is radiating its own five Tatwas each in their particular time, and the solar time and the terrestrial time is very different, and in this I am jumping over a great many intermediate stages, but you have upon those earth centres other centres, each of which is an individual human being, and every human being is radiating its own Tatwas constantly, and those are the Tatwic currents which that human being is conscious of.

So there are an enormous number of Tatwic currents constantly running, every different series from each individual centre running at different rates, and with different times of progression. Thus when you are told that there are a certain number of recurrences of the Tatwic currents between sunrise and sunset, if you are dealing with the solar Tatwas the currents that come from the centre of life of the solar system, which is the sun, that is to say, the vibration of heat, of light, of colour, of electricity, of magnetism, and so on, these come at a particular pace, at certain measured intervals, and succeed each other at measured intervals to the earth.

These produce other currents which radiate from their own centres on the earth; much as the earth magnetism produces the thunderstorm. All these are terrestrial Tatwic currents, and their rate of progress, and the times at which they succeed each other, are not by any means those of the sun, but are quite different. Then, again, each human being is producing his or her own Tatwic currents; every human being is reflecting light, is radiating warmth, shows motion — the circulation of the blood and so forth.

And those lines of vibration proceed at a totally different rate, and at totally different intervals from those of the planet. Now Rama Prasad speaks about sunrise and sunset, mid-day and mid-night, and he asserts certain physical phenomena which take place at these times. Now, many doctors have said that it is not so, and it is not so if you take the time in the heavens for your system of measurement.

Now, what is a day according to the philosophy of the Tatwas? It is not only the day which is measured by the sun; there are many days, some of these Rama Prasad mentions. But there is one definition of a day which answers to the Sanscrit words accurately, namely, the period which elapses between the going forth and the return of the positive effluent and influent current.

That is the 'Hansa' or 'Hamscha', which is the Tibetan Sanscrit word meaning the outbreathing and indrawing of the Great Breath, and this is the period of day and night. Now in the human being we have two such periods exceedingly well marked, namely, the respiration and the circulation. Now the time in the human body may be measured by the conveyance of a blood corpuscle from the heart through the arteries, and the return to the heart again through the veins; that is a day measured by the moon-breath. The moon governs the arterial and vein system, as the sun is said to govern the nerve system, and of the two centres first formed in the animal body, when it first assumes a form at all, the brain and the heart (or what subsequently developed into these), the brain is said to correspond with the sun of the Tatwic currents, and the heart with the moon. Now, as the sun throws its light upon the moon, and as the moon derives all its light and power from the sun, so, thus, according to this philosophy, the nerve force of the human body governs the circulation. And when we are speaking of the human body, we look upon the brain and nerves as the sun, and the arteries and veins (with their centre the heart) as the moon; and the positive and negative states of nerve force are day and night of the sun of the body.

This gives us the modes of measurement of these two functions of the human body, and this is the way we arrive at the primary human day. We are told by Rama Prasad that the terrestrial day and night are merely one small division, that there are a larger day and night, which again are part of the still larger day and night of Brahm. Yet, even so, the day and night of the human organism are a part, even as the pulsations are a part of the terrestrial day and night; and even so we find the pulsation, the circulation, the phenomena of nerve force different by day and night, different in waking and sleeping, and the intermediate stage of dreaming. But inspiration and expiration, and outflow and inflow of blood, the current of life, goes on without cessation day and night, summer and winter, but is modified. Now, that is not explained in Rama Prasad's book. I believe that the word day and night, and the word sun and moon, are used largely as blinds. Yet there is no reason, and I say this absolutely with knowledge, why this amount of knowledge should be blinded at all; because it is, I believe, of very great use in the medical profession if it is carefully studied.

Now then, as we know, the universe is born from the Akasa, which is, according to some writers, of a circular shape, according to others an elliptical shape, according to others an egg shape, but it matters not. Some of the Upanishads have laid down the circular shape, and Babbitt[3] in his theory of atomic philosophy has laid down this egg shape. But whatever shape it may be, there is some definite shape which is cut off and isolated, by the first running of the Akasa Tatwa, the first flutter of the divine breath, etc.

A certain portion of space was isolated which was to become the future universe, and that space was surrounded by an impenetrable shell. Such of those of you who were present at a meeting some months ago, will recollect how the lecturer proved that the physical universe must have a finite boundary. Therefore the universe is not infinite, but is bounded by the Akasa. In that Akasa, then, so cut off, developed gradually two centres. That you can see for yourself, for the infinitely great and the infinitely small are the same. Take a primordial cell, watch it in the microscope, and you will see the tiny cell gradually separating into two centres, a positive and a negative, and thus it polarises. And we know there are two separate centres of force, because they act and react upon one another. That is what I must call the infinitely little in the primordial cell. And so exactly was it in the creation of the universe, and so was it in the creation of man. The two centres were there, the brain and heart. For each human being is the inmost and most material heart and centre of an Akasa of his own — that is to say, every human being is surrounded by a sphere of some sort, which, in theosophical

---

3. Edwin Dwight Babbitt (1828–1905), proponent of Chromotherapy and author of *The Principles of Light and Color: including among other things the Harmonic Laws of the Universe* ... (1878; 2nd ed. 1896).

language, we call his Aura. That Aura is what the human being is conscious of, and he is conscious of nothing else. And in this sphere the Tatwic currents operate.

Now here comes a point — It is a doctrine of the Tatwic Philosophy, that the Aura of each man is the real man. The physical body which we see is merely the Stula Sharira, but everybody knows quite well that the physical human body is not all summed up in the mere material flesh and bones which we share with all animals — there is much of our intellectual and emotional nature which is as physical as the body.

Now how does the Aura make itself felt to others without. As some mystical philosophers have said, the difference lies entirely within, the difference between the man who is a saint and the man who is a depraved and sensual animal is such that it can be felt directly he enters a room. If that be the case, how is it possible to say that the difference between these two men is entirely within; that it is entirely a question of the different mode of arrangement of the grey matter of the brain.

It is impossible that the effect could be produced if that were so; his difference must be in the surrounding sphere, and it must be that surrounding sphere which in the Tatwic Philosophy is called the Akasa of each individual man that we affect one another. Now that is the practical outcome, for it is in this Akasa that the will operates; the will of each individual man permeates the entire sphere of his Akasa, just as the influence of the sun or the moon permeates the Akasa of the whole sphere of the earth's atmosphere. And the sun, you will remember, means, when we speak about a human being, the brain. The moon means the heart and blood-vessels, also the more animal type of emotions. Now then two radiant centres of force permeate the entire Akasa of the man, and when an effect has been produced, there, that effect is perfectly certainly repeated in the human body. When I say this, I do not mean repeated in its full force, for this is never so; even the adept has not the power to mould and alter his body according to his will. But every human being, no matter how little trained, has the power to produce some effect, and the effect entirely depends upon the amount of training, the amount of will put forth, and the amount of faith. That gives you a great clue to the operation of the Tatwas over daily life. For by that very operation of the Akasa acting upon the will of the human being it is possible to call any Tatwa into strong action, or to prohibit the operation of any Tatwa, also to prolong any Tatwa; and there in a large measure lies the key to health and disease. Let the will call into operation and keep in operation the Taijas Tatwa, and a chill is removed, the blood flows more freely, and just in proportion to the amount of training so is the amount of vital warmth attained. So in the case of fever, if the will, acting in the same way, calls into action and keeps in action the Apas Tatwa, the constitution goes back to its normal, and the fever may be surmounted. Now you may say, how is it that a Tatwa may be called into operation? And can the five Tatwas run simultaneously in one continual stream of blended force? Yes, but you must know that great numbers of Tatwas are continually running. A ray of light is white, but it contains all the colours of the spectrum, all those colours are running at a certain rate.

If we want a red light or a red colour, we have to wait until that comes round in the order of vibration. They are all running, together, so to speak, at once, continually passing from the sun, at different rates, it is true, but continually passing. At any time you may, however, from a ray of sun disentangle a certain colour, and so you may disentangle a Taijas Tatwa, and keep it there. Or take your human body, name to me any instant of time which is either day or night of the body, i.e., when the blood is either arterial or venous; both are going on simultaneously; the blood is flowing out from the heart and returning again. Or again, let us imagine ourselves going out from the earth; let us take ourselves to some point in space whence we can look down on the earth, and can any human soul say whether it is day or night? It may be day in Edinburgh but night in Australia. Both are going on continually. So it is everywhere, all the Tatwas are going on simultaneously. The sun-breath and the moon-breath are going on simultaneously. You want one or other for some particular purpose. You want the sun-breath or you want the moon-breath. Well, you can have it. You can bring about that particular phenomenon.

Just as you can go into your dark room and get the light you want, you can have your Taijas Tatwa or any other Tatwa. The human will must be joined with the divine will, and both acting in the Akasa can bring about the operation of any Tatwa which you please. It is true that at certain times you can get your result better than at other times; for understand the Tatwas flow out at regular succession from the sun, and as I told you in a former paper, they begin at sunrise, and they go on in regular rotation from sunrise to sunset, and so it comes about that one or other is more potent in the solar Tatwas at one time or another, just as we may say that each colour is always present, but at sunset the light is red, etc; but at sunrise or sunset we can produce any light we may wish by simply splitting a ray by the prism and isolating the blue or yellow as we require it, but at certain times of the day it is more easy to bring the Taijas Tatwa into operation than at any other time, but the will of man, acting upon his human body, is not susceptible to its external influences; and just as the light of the sun falling upon flowers, etc., brings out their particular colour, so do the Tatwic currents acting upon the earth, bring out their manifestation, and all at the same time. So at the same time we may have the Vayu Tatwa whirling into a spherical form some small whirlwind of the air; and at the very same time and very same place we may have tropical heat bringing into operation the Taijas Tatwa; and at a very little distance off we may have frost and snow — Apas in operation. Or we may watch all the Tatwas coming into operation in the hatching of an egg or the germination of a seed.

So if you wish to watch the Tatwas in daily life you must realise that they are not subject to time. Carry these points in your heads of the meaning of Tatwic time, the meaning of day and night, sunrise and sunset, and the meaning of sun and moon in their different connotation; and also how perplexity arises from so many Tatwic currents, which are continually radiating on to the earth; and also that day and night, summer and winter, are, as it were, mere terms of convenience for measurement according to our limited notation — all are really contemporaneous.

If you think over the work we have done in the Tatwas, you will find that a good many problems will appear much easier than before.

[Reprinted from *Transactions of the Scottish Lodge of the Theosophical Society*, Vol. Ill, No. 3 (1895), pp. 35-41.]

The Tatwas on Four Planes

The subject that I have undertaken to speak upon tonight is an exceedingly wide one, and you must please look upon what I have to say as only the very first glimpse, so to speak, of that subject, because it is not possible to go any further than this in the course of one evening.

We have seen in all the relations in which we have considered the operation of these five tatwas, that the whole philosophy of the Upanishads has been absolutely borne out by modern science, or where not absolutely borne out, then there has been silence. On no point have we found a contradiction by modern science. Therefore we are to a certain extent justified in thinking that what we have found to be a law wherever we have traced it is also probably a law in those further regions where the tracing of it is more difficult.

Now, taking the scheme of the tatwas as we have had it for the last few lectures, and keeping the name, shape, colours, and symbols clearly in your minds, we shall try whether we can trace this further yet. Now, according to the philosophy of the Upanishads, there are four planes. The highest, the spiritual plane, is Ananda. You will remember, those of you who are familiar with the Vedas, the Ananda was the favourite disciple of Gautama Buddha; he occupied the position with regard to him that St John did to Christ. A large school of Orientalists have concluded that when Buddha communed with Ananda he was in fact communing with his own higher self. The next plane is Vijnana, that is what we call the psychic. The next is Manas, or mens, which is the Latin name for what we call the mental; and the lowest is Prana, which is physical life.

Now what we have been considering hitherto has been entirely Prana, that is to say, the operation of the tatwas upon the life of the physical universe. And you will remember that we started with this proposition, that when nothing was, before the beginning of things, the Breath of the All came into being. That breath was the Iswara, the first manifestation of Almighty God in an infinite space of unmanifestation, in an infinite void, the first flutter of the Great Breath. And that flutter, that first breath, was fivefold in the five tatwas. The five tatwas, then, are manifestations of Iswara the Great Breath, and by them He, that is the Breath, created all things. Iswara, according to any Sanscrit dictionary, and according to the Theosophical Glossary, stands for the personal God, also the Breath or the Word; and you will see there the absolute coincidence of the Qabbalistic and Jewish, the Christian and the Buddhistic cosmogonies. The Word which was in the beginning' — therefore it existed before the beginning — 'by whom all things were made'. And this is made still clearer if you study the Hebrew Bible in the light of most modern philology, putting aside the vowel pointing, which has rather blurred and obscured the sense, and also the pronunciation of a great part of the old Hebrew text, and fixing your attention entirely upon the code as it was written on the old scrolls of the law, written in unpointed Hebrew, and making the best you can with the light of comparative philology and of the derivations of the words, you will find that the cosmogony of the Hindu and the tatwas comes out very much more clearly than even in the received Hebrew text, and far more than it does in the English translation, or in any English translation that could be made.

Well now, the Great Breath creates all material substances, the whole material universe. And not only are there the five modifications of the Great Breath — producing first of all Akasa, that is the potentiality of movement; secondly, Vayu, movement itself; thirdly, Taijas, which is a mode of motion, light, electricity, and magnetism; then the reaction of heat and expansion, cold and contraction producing water, Apas, rolling up the fiery incandescent gases of the nebulae into the worlds; and Prithivi, the final form of Apas, the cohesion, which makes the dry land appear from the waters — not only are there these five modifications, but also the positive and negative of each, viz., the Pingala and Ida, and also the Susumna, the point of union between positive and negative. So that during every day — I am speaking of our ordinary solar day — these five tatwas run over and over again their course from sunrise to sunset, producing all their modifications which are known upon the earth's surface according to regular rules. And after sunset the same series runs over and over again on the negative side through the night. And further again, during the bright fortnight of the moon, are the positive tatwas running more distinctly and vividly; on the dark fortnight are the negative running more strongly. And so you get again in summer the positive running more strongly, and in winter the negative accentuated. And thus you get three distinct series of positive and negative of the running of the five tatwas, every one crossing and recrossing, acting and reacting upon each other, and producing an infinite complexity which is only paralleled by the infinite complexity of creation. In precisely the same way was the physical body of man created and built up from the very first germ of organic humanity up to the complete fullgrown adult human being; created, sustained, developed, and built up by the operation of the tatwas bringing him these five characteristics in varying quantities and at varying times.

Here, in order to see how the tatwas operate from plane to plane, I must give a concession which perhaps some may deem to be a concession of their entire position to the materialists. Because, for this purpose at all events, we must grant that everything of which we are conscious is physical. We must consider for this purpose that all thought is but a secretion of the brain, merely a mode of the grey matter of the brain, that everything that we perceive, any object of sense, is merely certain vibrations communicated through a certain sense by the air or what not to the brain, and the modification so produced in the brain perceived and recorded — a group of such sensations, it may be, forming a distinct image — thus the eye giving us a sensation of redness, giving us also a sensation of form, of scalloped and convoluted form it may be; the touch giving us a sensation of velvety softness and the like; the sense of smell giving us the sensation or vibration of a delightful perfume; and the brain combining all these impressions creates a form, to which form we apply the name of 'rose' it may be, in such way that the name afterwards brings before the senses, reproduces, faintly it may be, but still perceptibly, the same run of vibrations and sensations in the brain, and recalls the image of the rest. There is a paper in an early number of the *Transactions* by 'M.D.' which admirably illustrates this. Well, we have to take that to be a thought absolutely secreted by the thinking cells of the brain, and in order to really understand this philosophy we have to get rid, so far as this is concerned, of any notion of higher or lower, or anything of the kind. The thought is a secretion of the brain, just as gastric juice is a secretion or anything else. And, further, all attractions of one person to another are again absolutely physical. They absolutely depend upon the harmony or the discord of the nerve vibrations operating in two individuals, whom for the purpose we must look upon as electric machines or machines of animal magnetism, or something of the kind. If those vibrations are harmonious, there occurs a pleasure in the society of each other, an affection, as we call it; if discord arises, the contrary. Half of the trouble in understanding any of the higher and spiritual philosophies comes from regarding these, which are purely physical phenomena, as being something higher. Those of us whose karma it is to have to try to teach to a certain very small extent a few others who are trying to get along on the path, find that there is nothing which is more fruitful of obstacle and error than this persistent clinging up of every human being to the emotions. There is a kind of natural idea, an error but a natural error, that there are grades in physical life, and that the intellect is higher than the ordinary physical life, and the emotions higher than the intellect, and that one is divine and the other is not, one psychic and the other physical, and so on, and there is an obstinate refusal to realise that they are all physical. But now when we have conceded all that, which is all the point that the most ultra-materialists contend for, let us go on a bit, and the question then arises, Why? And let me say that some of the most valuable discoveries that have ever been made in the world have simply been arrived at by either consciously or unconsciously going on in your train of reasoning until you arrive apparently at an axiom, and then asking, Why? If you are not satisfied until you can answer it, the likelihood is that you are on the brink of arriving at some truth higher than you knew before. If you are content with the axiom you will never get any further, because no knowledge whatsoever is your own until you can demonstrate it. As long as you continue satisfied with the fact that it is self-evident, it is of no use to you.

Well, let us assume all these things to be absolutely conceded to the materialist, and get on to the point of consciousness. A human being is a machine; but he knows it. Why? There is your question, the solution of which must lead you somehow or other to the conviction that there is something above this most elaborate machine. And if the fact of a machine which will work at all, must necessarily bring within its own conception the idea of a designer and a maker thereof, what have we to say of a machine which is so absolutely and truly constructed that it will meet every possible circumstance of human life, and meet it truly? Does not that more conclusively than ever demonstrate some higher power beyond, which could have conceived and executed such a machine? If you take the materialist's argument and push it to the materialist's conclusion, what does it give you? It shows you a magnificent and absolutely ordered kingdom, and it leads you beyond that kingdom face to face with an empty throne. Is that reason? It cannot be. There must be something beyond. Now can we reach, can we know anything whatsoever about that something? The physical universe is absolutely limited and finite, but not so the mind. The mind of man can conceive and has conceived infinity. The mind of the mathematician has not only conceived infinity, but has reasoned about it, and has told us a good many of its qualities. There, then, lies the difference between our two bottom planes, between Prana and Manas. And in Manas must reside somehow or other the cogniser, that which knows the machine, that which recognises it. But how again we are met with a peculiarity, because in Manas also is every human individual separate. It is not one mind looking down upon thousands and millions of human beings constituting the inhabitants of these planets and watching how they all go, conscious with the consciousness of every brain, but it is one individual manifestation of Manas conscious of the going of one particular human body, and conscious also, or with a potential consciousness it may be, of infinity above.

Now why is it that we should apply the names of higher and lower to different functions of the mere physical body? Well, it is on account of what the Easterns call the law of Vasana; and the law of Vasana is this, that when the Tatwic vibrations have operated along any line of vibration, there will be a tendency for that series of vibrations to recur along that particular line. And that is a characteristic of the Prana or physical life; it is also a characteristic of Manas or the mental life. Suppose, for instance, that a man learns to play a particular tune on any instrument, and practises incessantly at that tune. When he is not thinking, his fingers will involuntarily run on to those particular movements, and with difficulty on to others. Another common illustration is the difficulty and the pain which occurs when we try to bring unused muscles into operation in attempting any unusual exercise. So with the brain. A certain series of vibrations have run through the brain over and over again. Start the first note of that series, and there will be a tendency to repeat the whole series, and with difficulty to take up, or be sensitive to any other series. Now that is the law of Vasana. It applies to all living organisms as distinct from inanimate objects; and it is a characteristic, one of the modifications, one of the forms of Avidya or ignorance, because it is one of the greatest obstacles to true perception. Directly the brain or nerves are started on a particular line, they will tend to run along that line, and reject or refuse to perceive the impressions which should be coming into them from external sources. Therefore arises false perception of external thought.

Now to apply that. The Manas plane sends its vibrations primarily into the brain. Gradually there comes, by the law of Vasana, an impression into the individual man or woman that the brain is the intellect. The brain is nothing of the kind. The brain is the instrument which the intellect uses, which the Manas uses in order to function through that material human body. Now it follows from this, that outside of ourselves, and on a higher plan altogether, exists an intellectual, a mental counterpart of ourselves, of each one of us, which perceives, recognises, and directs this physical body. You will, no doubt, ask, how then does the physical body come into manifestation on the physical plane, and what is the connection binding it to the mental plane, the plane of Manas? Well, you may find the key to that, which is very difficult to put into words, by an attentive consideration of the cosmic pictures. A picture is formed upon this earth's plane. It goes off into the air. From the limits of the earth's atmosphere a quick reflection is sent back. That is very slight. The bulk, the strength of the picture, goes out beyond the earth's atmosphere, out into the void, so to speak, and becomes, so to say, latent. But at a measured interval, which interval can be calculated, that picture returns; and returning, and coming within the earth's atmosphere again, and within the influence of the terrestrial Prana or life of this planet, it remanifests itself. I daresay some of you have seen Edison's latest invention, the Kinetograph, by which, taking photographs at intervals of a tiny fraction of a second, of a man doing any particular act, and reproducing these through a magic lantern in rapid succession, you appear to see on the sheet before the lantern a moving figure actually doing the act which the man had been photographed in doing. Well, that series of pictures illustrates what I mean. We are all of us perpetually forming such a series of pictures, and they pass away into the void, into the Akasa. But they do not vanish. They produce there a synthetic whole, a character; and at the appropriate time that character returns to earth once more, and coming into the earth plane, it tends to remanifest, still remaining in connection with the mental being on the plane of Manas which produced it. That tendency, then, having come into the earth plane, at once begins to manifest itself by forming an infant, coming to birth with a certain character impressed upon it by those cosmic pictures, which had flown off from the earth hundreds of years before, it may be — one does not want to be particular as to the precise time, because it varies very much — but so coming into manifestation, that is to say, collecting to itself material particles, so as to make that which was merely a mental picture before a physical picture, by degrees a human being is built up and grows to maturity, but always with the Manas as its real self. And when I say that, I mean the real self in comparison with the Pranic manifestation which we can see and talk to in this earth plane. And therefore, the idea that I want to drive home at this moment, and the only idea that I really want to drive home, is that, behind every one of us, above and beyond, is a real self; that the human being whom we know, whom we call a friend or relation, or what not, is a phenomenal and very transitory body, behind which, on the plane of Manas, there is a real self-governing, modifying, and moulding it with more or less of success. What is the contact between the two, you will ask? Well, I do not think it is possible to put it into words. It is no physical contact. When we talk of the shining thread and other things, we are using the language of metaphor; and perhaps the nearest illustration I can give you would be this. If you have a musical instrument laid upon the table, and a violin tuned so perfectly into accord with it that every note struck upon the violin would produce a corresponding vibration and thrill in your instrument upon the table, you have a sort of rough image of how by some strange sympathy which can scarcely be even expressed in words or in thought, the Manas body governs, and controls, and modifies, and moulds the physical body. That is the task of the Manas body, the mental individuality, the mental reality of every one of us. It is a more or less faulty instrument that is given to that Manas body to operate upon. It has its heredity, its hereditary diseases it may be, its acquired diseased, its limitations of brain and of intellect, its nerves, its nervous affections, all these things, all its limitations and hindrances. The task of the Manas substance, of the real man, is to mould that physical body into more of a likeness with itself. And I say 'more' advisedly, because it is impossible to do more than to get a step or two forward in one incarnation. If the Manas body, so to speak, succeeds upon its physical instrument to such an extent that it leaves the earth just a stage or two better than it enters, a success has been won. Therefore it matters not what this physical body is, because the task of Manas is to bring physical matter into subjection to itself. If, therefore, the Manas body, the real man, undertakes the body of a tramp in the Grassmarket, or a savage in Central Africa, or of the greatest saint or greatest philosopher in the West, or the greatest Mahatma or guru in the East, still it matters not. The task is to improve that body, and by doing so, to educate itself. As an art student may paint hundreds of pictures and spoil acres of canvas, every one of the pictures may be absolutely and utterly worthless in itself, and only fit to light the fire with; but the training which the artist's hand derives from that work is of incalculable value. And that is the work which the Manas body is achieving everlastingly upon every one of us.

Well, now, the last question with regard to this point is, taking ourselves to be self-conscious, and endeavouring to assist in this great process, in this great transmutation, how are we to do it? Well, by uniting ourselves with our higher self. That is the eastern uniting Praha with Manas. Manas is striving always, the Manas body, real and substantial and veritable, mind, is striving always to mould and to raise this physical body. As far as self-consciousness resides in this physical body, the process can be helped by the raising of the physical body to a union with the higher body of Manas on the mental plane. And that is by killing out the self, by getting rid of everything which can be traceably found to proceed from Prana. For why? Prana with the Sthula Sharira, with the physical body that is, lasts us only for this short life. We leave it behind, and it is no more use to us after we have learned our lesson upon it. Therefore everything which is born within that body is not only useless, but a hindrance to us. All its desires, all its affections, all its emotions, are hindrances to us, so far as they demonstrably arise from the physical body.

And here again we find a great deal of the road to health. Because if the physical body get out of gear, if there is disease or sickness of any kind, it arises from some disharmony in the tatwic condition; and the great healer of all, the *medicatrix naturae*, resides in Manas, and it is by the stilling of the physical body that we arrive at that yoga, at that union of the physical and the mental, whereby Nature herself restores the lost harmony. Take the case of the neurotic, take the case where Taijas is over prevalent in the nerves, and you get restlessness and exhausted nerve centres — loss of tone, as they say. The ignorant practitioner, now I am happy to say getting much fewer than he was before, piles on tonics, piles on change of air and so forth, and gradually increases the mischief, because he knows no better. But he who has either studied occult science, or, as is often the case, and is practically quite as valuable, has intuitively grasped it, will do nothing of the kind. He will see the necessity for the yoga in such cases — whether he calls it by that name or not — and he will probably apply depressants.

Well, now, as I said, the Eastern doctrine tells you to raise yourself to your higher self, the Western Hermetic doctrine says unite yourself to your higher and divine genius — that is a higher plane still, Vijnana. Now it is impossible at this time to follow out that process or even to indicate what the plane of Vijnana means, save that as Prana is to Manas, so is Manas to Vijnana. As the mind is to the body, so is the soul to the mind. And the soul governs the mind just as the mind governs the body, and it is real and substantial with regard to the mind. Now as the physical body is made up by the courses of the tatwas in its form, in its functions, in its colouring, in everything connected with it, so on the plane of Manas is the mind, the mental man, made up by precisely the same rules. You get mental activity from Vayu, and mental fire and genius, invention and discovery from Taijas. You get receptivity and the plastic turn of mind from Apas. You get the firm and steadfast mentality, admirably sane and founded upon a rock, from Prithivi. And so you may trace the mental condition of every human being, and you may know precisely what tatwas have operated to produce that particular mind. And the finer thrills which run through the mental plane, the Manas plane, and which are to Prana about in perhaps I might say the proportion of the thrill of the finest nerve in the human body to the thrill of the biggest string in the violoncello — that is somewhere near the proportion — it is all a matter of proportion — brings us to a number which is the spiritual soul where you may know, by the absolute obliteration not only of the self but of the Ego, that everything is yourself, in Ananda. But the reaching of that transcends the plane of the highest adeptship. It is only dimly known as a vista of what may be in the extreme future.

But the thing to carry away is the idea of the substantial human being lying behind and governing the phenomenal, formed precisely in the same way and governed by the same laws; and the realisation of the transient and phenomenal and comparatively unimportant character of the phenomenal physical body with which that being is now concerned, and through which it manifests.

[Reprinted from *Transactions of the Scottish Lodge of the Theosophical Society*, Vol. 3, No. 4, (1895), pp. 51-58.]

18. The Science of Numbers — Kabalistic and Hermetic

The subject of Numbers is a very wide one, branching out into every possible domain of science, history, legend, and mythology, and also of occultism. If one knew the whole symbology of numbers, and the whole meaning and interrelation of numbers, it would not be necessary to know anything more; for then would be known absolutely the top and bottom, the ground-work as well as the consummation, of every science on earth.

In various systems different numbers are given, which at first blush appear to be irreconcilable; and people get puzzled, being told in one place perhaps that there are four principles, in another that there are seven, and somewhere else that there are ten, and so on. And this, in fact, is the principal reason why I was asked to speak on the subject.

There is no doubt that numbers are the key to a great many things. Taking, for instance, the ordinary matter of science, everyone knows that if a crystal is broken, one can tell by the shape of the fracture what type of crystal it is; each particular crystal breaks in its own particular way, and will not break in any other. In botany again, the ordinary type of an ordinary group of flowering plants — the exogens — are always known as being grouped in either 4 or 5; the endogens, on the other hand, are always in threes or multiples of 3 — usually 3 or 6; and so their pistils, stamens, ovaries, etc., all follow these numbers. There we have the key number to a group of plants, and it is not necessary to go any further to know the nature of a plant — whether it was an exogen or an endogen — having found its key number. Then there are the periods of time, which are very well known in disease: these follow their key number with considerable accuracy. Or again, if we look at the animal kingdom, we find the five points of man — two arms, two legs, and the head; or the four legs and the head of the quadruped, or the six legs of the average insect: these are key numbers to the various classes. Again, taking chemistry, we see the almost universality of what is known as Prout's law, that the combining weights of the various elements are multiples by integral numbers of the unit element hydrogen; but not exactly so. If, however, we take the preliminary element to be half hydrogen — i.e. take H to be 2 — Prout's law is found absolutely exact, allowing for a slight inaccuracy in observation. And so there we get key numbers again of the different elements. The paper on the Septenary Law and on Mendelejeff's Table amply showed how that worked out, and how numbers were the key thereto.

Then as to the various modes of dealing with numbers. In physical science we get the square of numbers constantly occurring; for instance, the attraction of gravitation in the inverse ratio of the square of the distance is a commonplace law. There are a great many more cases where a number is found to be the key to some fact. Now the Kabalists observed these facts, and concluded that there must be some general key number to the whole universe, one number which keyed everything; and whether by patient analysis and synthesis of every science they arrived at it, or whether — as the Kabalists themselves said — they got it by divine revelation, and found out afterwards that every science keyed into it, I cannot say, but at all events they arrived at the conclusion that the key number of the entire universe was 10, the decad. And as everything had to be set down so that the profane who might chance to light on any of the records or hieroglyphs would not find out anything, they symbolised the doctrine thus: There was unity, that is the Eternal Silence, because 1 is necessarily alone; it cannot multiply or divide. Directly, however, the unity comes into manifestation, it emanates the ten Sephiroth, and not in any particular order. If one might symbolise it by an earthly image, when the time for manifestation arose the whole ten Sephiroth flashed forth at once. These ten Sephiroth consisted of the one and the trinity in unity, therefore the three transcendental, supernal, and uncognisable by man, and the seven cognisable by man. Here we have the seven principles of man. Seven is the key to the Mosaic condition, and there we get the second key: the 7 days of creation, the 7 principles of man, the 7 great planets, the 7 archangels, and 7 angels, and so on, symbolised in every great religion; the 7 great gods and the 7 demons; and these 7 great gods answer precisely to the 7 archangels of the Gnostics, Hermetists, and, later on, of the Christian scheme. They existed before the time of Christ, and were — if not actually worshipped — looked upon as mediators. But at the Incarnation of Christ, those who believed that here was the prophesied fulfilment of the Pleroma banished the 7 great gods from their position of being worshipped, the 7 being now included in one, as returning to the primitive unity. There is again another aspect of that. These 7 belong to the four planes: the archetypal plane of Atziluth; the physic plane, or plane of Briah; the plane of formation, Yetzirah; and the material plane, Assiah. This may be illustrated as follows: A sculptor desiring to make a great statue first conceives of it in his mind — the first plane, Atziluth. He then conceives of a picture, or something of that kind, which he may sketch on paper, or perhaps only see as a mental picture; that is a further materialising of the idea, bringing it into form, though not yet concrete and visible form, and that is the second plane, Briah. He then proceeds to make a clay model; that is the third plane, Yetzirah. His conception is then incarnated in the permanent marble, where it is to remain, and that is the final plane of Assiah, the most material of all. And thus we get the four. Now the four is also, as will be found in a great many books on occultism, the number of the letters of the great name of God in Hebrew — Yod, He, Vau, He. There is a peculiarity there, for there are only three letters really, the He being repeated; and one naturally asks, seeing that in the Kabala and in Hebrew nothing is done in vain, why is this? That brings us to the meaning of the number 4. This number is the number of creation also, and it typifies the two opposing forces; the letter Yod is the active, the energising, the fire; while the letter He is the passive, the receptive, the water — the Spirit of God moving on the face of the water, the fire moving on the water. Hence we get warmth and moisture, which are the basis of all life, and without which life is impossible; also the male and female principles which pervade all nature; and we get the letter Vau, which is the union of the two, completing the triangle, and making the divine sign. But the second He is the term of transition, the passing from one world to another. The plant grows and flowers, but concealed within the flower lies the seed wherein is the potentiality of an infinite series of plants of the same kind. That seed is the second He. The metaphor may be carried as far as we please, to any manifestation of life, either spiritual, psychic, or material, and the analogy is found to be perfect. There must be the triangle — the two opposing forces, active and passive, energising and receptive — and the third which unites them, and the term of transition. The figure 4 itself symbolises this, for it is composed of the straight stroke with the triangle on top of it, — symbolising the triad of life and the term of transition coming from it, symbolising also the man standing erect, or figure 1, and bearing on his head the triangle of supernal wisdom. There is another peculiarity of this fourth term, which can only be explained by referring to the Kabalistic method of dealing with number, or rather two methods, the addition and reduction.

There are a great many of such processes. One is to add together all the numbers up to the number required; and if the number arrived at is a compound consisting of a certain number of digits, these may be again added, until one digit is arrived at. Treating every fourth term of the ordinary arithmetic series of numbers by this process, the result is unity. 1+2+3+4=10, and 1+0=1; 1+2+3+4+5+6+7=28, and 2+8=10 or 1 as before. And so on up to any number, every fourth term will bring out unity if treated in this way; and that unity, according to the Kabalists, is the germ of the new series — it is the seed out of which a new tetraktys will come. That is just one translation of this great name, the Yod, He, Vau, He. The same thing is found in the cards of the Tarot: the four suits mean the four letters of the great name. The four honours of the Tarot pack are the King, Queen, Knave, and Knight; and these four correspond, the King to the active or energising force, the Queen to the passive or receptive force, and the Knight to the juncture, the union, completing the triangle. The Knave or Squire (German, Knabe) is the term of transition. These again refer not only to the letters of the great name, but to the four worlds or planes of Atziluth, Briah, Yetzirah, and Assiah. Assiah, the lowest of all, is the key corresponding to the 4 knaves of the court cards; and these knaves are the terms of transition, as the material world is the term of transition standing midway between the divine world, which is above and the world of demons which is below. The 3, which is supernal, and the 4, which is human, constitute together the 7 principles, the higher triad, and the lower tetraktys, symbolised by the triangle above the square. And again, these are divided into the four worlds of the Kabala; and not only so, but each of the four worlds (so say the Kabalists) has its 10 Sephiroth, and each of those Sephiroth is again subdivided into 10 sub-Sephiroth, if one might so say, as each of our seven principles has its septenary. Thus we get in each world 10 Sephiroth, each containing 10 sub- Sephiroth, that is 100 in each, or 400 in all; and 400 made up the number of the Hebrew Tau, the Tau cross, and the number of perfection and finality.

That leads us to another treatment of numbers. Each number is related closely to its multiple by 10; 1 is related closely to 10, as we have seen that according to the Kabalistic theory from 1 sprang forth all at once the 10 Sephiroth, without running through intermediate numbers: there is a sudden transition from 1 to 10, and from 10 to 100. Now that is put down in the Kabala in what is called the Kabala of nine chambers. The Hebrew letters and symbols are arranged in a cross formed of two lines drawn vertically and two lines drawn horizontally, making nine compartments # are also used for the symbols contained within them. Masons will recognise that a superficial and rather rough form of this is used as a cryptogram in arch-masonry. The full and complete explanation and working out of this Kabala of nine chambers belongs only to the Hermetic and Rosicrucian temples, and can only be fully explained to initiated Hermetists. But, as a cryptogram, they claim to understand what it means, and perhaps I may say that the outline of each compartment symbolises the letters referring to the numbers which are so related together. Thus the Hebrew letter which signifies 1 is Aleph, the Hebrew letter which signifies 10 is Yod, and the letter which signifies 100 is Qoph. In the same way, the letter which signifies 2 is Beth, that which signifies 20 is Kaph, and that which signifies 200 is Resh. And that is simply the name for the Kabala of nine chambers. Most of us have probably had some experience in the forming of magic squares — which used at any rate to be a popular game among children, — arranging figures so that whether added up or down, diagonally or crosswise, the result will be the same. There is a much deeper meaning in the Kabala than the childish game which is derived from it, as many of our childish games are derived from the deepest mysteries of the ancients. But according to the Kabalistic theory and treatment of numbers, every planet, and therefore every number, and every one of the great gods or archangels, had its own key number; and making a magic square out of this key number, you arrive at other numbers, the sum of the column, and the total sum of the numbers and so forth. By substituting the Hebrew letters for the numbers certain names are obtained — and thus for Mercury we get the name Tirial, as the key number for the great number Taphthartharath, which is the name of the presiding spirit. Now those names were simply given because to the Jewish initiates they at once gave the key number of that

Taphthartharath. They added up the numerical value of the letters, and thus arrived at the key number, just as if doctors were to agree among themselves upon some secret language which would not be understood by their patients. In such a case one doctor might say to another the name of a word which signified 40, and another word which signified the key number of heat or fever, and the interpretation would be at once a fever of 40 days' duration, the patient being none the wiser. That is an indication of one way in which these Kabalistic names and numbers were used by the Hermetic initiates in communicating knowledge to one another, without letting the outside world know in the least what was meant. As another example of that, the name of the spirit which is formed from the key number, the great number of the sun, is Sorath, which indicates the number 666, the number of the beast of Revelation, about which a great deal has been written with very little understanding.

Taking the numbers individually, there is not very much that one can usefully say. The dual was always looked upon as a very particular number, because it was the first number which emerges from the great silence of unity, and therefore called by Pythagoras and his disciples the number of audacity, the number which dares the bridge. And therefore it was specially regarded by the Greeks; so we find singular and dual, but no number signifying 3 or 4, or anything else in Greek except the plural. Then the number 3 is called the mistress of geometry by Pythagoras, because the triangle is the most useful and universal figure in geometry; and the 3 is found prominent in all sciences. We find it in music, the 3 notes which form the chord, and the octave which repeats the base note, which might be taken as the term of transition to a new chord. The 3 again is found in time — past, present, and future. There are also three dimensions of space length, breadth, and thickness; in fact, we cannot get away from the 3. In Royal Arch Masonry it is the triple Tau: whoever can turn that has the key to all the sciences. The turning of the triple Tau may be accomplished by a perfect knowledge of numbers. Then 4 is, as I said, the great name: also the 4 elements and the 4 orders of elemental intelligences, or elemental beings or powers, of fire, water, earth, and air. 5 was pre-eminently the number of marriage among the Jews — 5 gifts, 5 blessings, the guests were admitted by fives, 5 wise virgins and 5 foolish in the parable. And 5 is the human number — the 5 points of the human being, the 5-pointed star, as well as the human hieroglyph the Pentalpha — which is not the seal of Solomon as some people think, but which is the symbol of health. The true seal of Solomon is the interlaced triangle, which signifies the atonement. And there again we get the relation of the number of the 7 principles. 7 is the key of the mystic creation, 7 is the number of man according to his principles. Consider the destiny of man: it is to draw up the material into the divine. The final purpose of all creation is the inbreathing the reunion of everything now separate with the one Eternal Unity; therefore translating that into the microcosm, the union of the material, carnal, and earthly man with the higher self or higher triad. Now what keeps them apart? It is Kama Rupa, the bar of self. When that is removed the self is cast out. Then the material in man is the emblem of matter, viz., water, the lower triangle. Hydrogen, or the root of hydrogen, may be the final primordial element, the half hydrogen of which I spoke before, but this drawn up into, intertwining with, and interlacing with, the higher triad. And that is the final atonement, or at-one-ment, the re-union of the material with the supernal, of the human with the divine, the perfected atonement, when spirit and matter, no longer separate, shall be one. Therefore is the interlaced triangle the seal of the great Solomon. The 6 thus is the key to the 7. The word seven comes from the Hebrew Shebo, the 7, or completeness or abundance. The periods of life are worked into terms of 7 years, as every physiologist knows — 7 principles, 7 planets, 7 days of creation; the number is found, in fact, wherever we go. About the next two numbers, 8 and 9, there is a great deal to say, but it would take a great deal too long; but the principal numbers to remember, and the key numbers, are those I have mentioned. 9 being the square of 3, 3 times 3 comes in with very great distinctness in all those calculations which involve the square of numbers. After the 9 we come again upon the 10, the number of completeness, the tetraktys, the triangle of Pythagoras, which was an equilateral triangle enclosing 10 yods. The arrangement of the 10 in the Tree of Life is another branch of the subject altogether; that belongs to the Kabala, and an elementary view of it will be found in a paper in the third number of our Transactions, where the Tree of Life, and also the names of the ten Sephiroth, are fully set out. The full illustration of it belongs entirely to the Hermetic mysteries. (*Transactions of the Scottish Lodge of the Theosophical Society*, Vol. 1, p 37, 1892.)

I trust enough has been said to show where the key comes in to different numbers being used in different systems, and that no one will henceforth be puzzled to find 4 principles of man laid down in the *Perfect Way*, and 7 laid down in the *Secret Doctrine*, or *Key to Theosophy*, and other Oriental works. You will be able to see now pretty clearly that both the 7 and the 4 are absolutely views of the same thing, and so also is the 10, the 10 Sephiroth of the Kabala.

[Paper read on 3 December 1892. Reprinted from *Transactions of the Scottish Lodge of the Theosophical Society*, Vol. 1, Part VI, (1892), pp. 92-7.]

19. The Tarot Cards

The strange, weird-looking cards known as the Tarot, with their bizarre designs, have interested and puzzled archaeologists, mystics and occultists for over a century; and many books have been written, from ponderous and learned tomes to popular manuals, from M. Court de Gebelin's *Monde Primitif* in 1781 to Mr A.E. Waite's *Key to the Tarot* in 1910. Yet the mystery remains unsolved. What was their origin? What do they mean? Are they primarily an occult treatise told in hieroglyphics, or merely the implements of a game of chance or skill, used as an afterthought for purposes of divination? Was their origin Egyptian, or Indian, or Chinese, or some as yet unguessed source? There is no reliable evidence, though there is plenty of bold assertion. The fact remains that we know they existed in the fourteenth century, and prior to that they are wrapt in impenetrable obscurity. Having read all the books, I could get access to on the subject, and studied many theories and speculations, I finally arrived at the Scottish verdict of 'Not proven'. Under these circumstances I should hesitate to intrude into the distinguished, circle of writers on the Tarot, even to the extent of an article, but that it so chances that I have one or two slight contributions to the study, which may be of interest to inquirers.

Many years ago it was my privilege to examine at leisure the magnificent collection of playing cards made by my friend, Mr George Clulow,[1] one of the greatest living experts on the subject. That collection is now in America, where I am told it is the model for all such collections. The item that chiefly interested me was a splendid series of Tarot packs of all ages and all countries. And the point that struck me most was the continuance of the designs throughout, often it is true corrupted, where an ignorant engraver, copying from a copyist, and obviously unable to understand a symbol, had expressed it by an unmeaning flourish, or substituted a flower, or some object he was acquainted with, for an uncomprehended symbol. Thus the Bateleur who in the oldest examples had

---

1. George Clulow (1836-1919) was the manager of Charles Goodall & Son, one of the principal makers of playing cards in the United Kingdom at the time. He was the author of a book on *Peculiar Playing Cards* (1893) but wrote nothing about the Tarot.

magical implements before him, came to have a shoemaker's tools. But by comparison of one pack with another these could easily be rectified. Occasionally some local or political cause had produced variations, but these also were detected without trouble. One such occurs in a modern French pack in my possession, where a strong antipapal bias has occasioned the substitution of the figures of Juno and Jupiter for the original La Papesse and Le Pape. Now and then some enterprising innovator has redrawn the entire pack to suit his own ideas of the symbology, as did the fantastic peruquier Alliette, who under the pseudonym Etteilla (being his own name spelt backwards) posed as an illuminated adept. But these have attained no vogue, and are now merely of interest to collectors, for they embody, not the ideals, whatever they may be, of the old Tarot, but only Etteilla's notion of what they ought to be. Discounting however these variants, the persistence of the designs through some five centuries, and many countries, is, to say the least of it, remarkable. And whether or no those designs are comprehensible, one feels thankful that the redrawers have not succeeded in displacing the old traditional patterns.

That the cards have long been used in Italy, and perhaps elsewhere, for a game is certain, and that before ever they were written about as occult emblems or implements of divination. Lord Mahon, in his *History of the Forty-Five*, quotes an English lady who met Prince Charles Edward in Rome in 1770 at the Princess Palestrini's, when he asked her if she knew the game of Tarrochi, and she spoke of his handling the Tarot cards and explaining them. But one may conclude from the designs that they were originally intended for more than this. As played in Italy today the 22 Atus or Trumps are often omitted, and many packs are sold without these. But taking the ordinary pip cards, if they were simply used for a game, the ancient designs, which have persisted through so many years and in divers countries, would seem meaningless. The numbers of pips as in the common English packs would be sufficient. Why, for example, should the two of pentacles have a serpent coiled round the two pips in the form of the algebraic symbol of infinity. And here we may say that those well-meaning writers who have redrawn the cards have gone on the wrong tack. Admitting that we have no evidence of the original meaning (there may or may not be a secret tradition, I wish to make no assertion as to this) it is surely the part of wisdom to preserve the ancient symbol as clearly as we can, and await enlightenment, rather than to assume a meaning, and form a new symbol consonant thereto, which may be miles away from the primitive intention. This at all events was the thought that came to me on examining Mr Clulow's wonderful collection, and noting the persistence of the designs, and the variants of which I have spoken.

With regard to the 22 Atus or Trumps the case is different. It would be impossible in the compass of a single article to go into all the various interpretations that have been put upon them, nor am I sure that it would serve any good purpose to do so. In the absence of evidence as to the intention of the original designer they must remain as merely the speculations of individual writers. But there is much to be said for the idea of Eliphaz Levi that they were to be referred to the Hebrew alphabet. Students of the Qabala, who are familiar with the symbology of the Hebrew letters, have often been struck with the correspondence of some of the Atus with some of the letters. There can be no doubt that these cards are hieroglyphics of some kind, though the meaning seems to be in dispute; but whether they represent a series, such as the history of the soul, or cosmical evolution, or the grades of training of an initiate, or a synthesis of all of these and possibly others, there seems no positive evidence, but a great wealth of speculation. The connection with the Hebrew alphabet would largely depend on the attribution, and as twenty-one out of the twenty-two cards are numbered, the position assigned to the card marked zero called le Mat, or the Fool, must be the crucial point; and as to this there is wide divergence among the commentators. The wise student will maintain an open mind, and wait for further evidence; Eliphaz Levi appears to take one a certain distance, and then slams the door in one's face, but whether because he did not know, or whether, knowing the secret tradition, he was unable to tell more, who shall say? In any case all are agreed as to the fascinating quality of his work, and undoubtedly no one can read it without having his interest profoundly stirred in these ancient cards.

It is generally supposed that they were unknown in France, or at all events in Paris, prior to M. Court de Gebelin, who it is said, found and introduced them to the French occultists.

This, however, may be doubted. I have in my possession a French Tarot of the early eighteenth century, a very interesting feature of which is that some of the cards have MS inscriptions of their meaning, and apparently the records of an experiment in divination, which from internal evidence would seem to be Pre-Revolution. This, so far as it goes, would support the theory that they were known in France before M. de Gebelin wrote about them. I would not, however, press this further than as a warning against too confident dogmatism concerning the date of the Tarot, and the history of its introduction into Europe.

The cards have been called the 'Tarot of the Bohemians', and have often been popularly spoken of as the gipsy fortune-telling cards. As a fact, however, when gipsies lay the cards for the fortune of an inquirer it is the ordinary pack that is used, and it seems certain, as Mr Waite points out, that the Tarot cards were known in Europe before the arrival of the gipsies. Moreover gipsy folklorists, with the exception of Vaillant, have very little to say about the Tarot.

The only evidence on this head that has come under my own observation was from a woman of pure Romani blood, whom I knew many years ago, a Mrs Lee, but of what tribe I cannot say; she was reputed to be an Epping Forest gipsy, but she said herself that her people belonged to Norwood, and only left there when Norwood became a wilderness of villadom, and their old haunts were desecrated by the incursion of Cockney residents. She once showed me an old tattered and much thumbed Tarot pack, of the ordinary Italian design, and told me that these were the cards she used among her own people, but never for Georgios. She also gave me the principles of interpretation, not under any seal of secrecy, but with a general request that it should not be published, and this, needless to say, I have honourably observed. I may, however, state that it was a thoroughly logical and complete system, the four suits representing the four elements, and the four temperaments, and being judged according to their position. Thus wands representing fire and the sanguine temperament, a wand card occurring in a bad position would indicate danger from rash and hasty action, anger, or quarrelling; the same card in a good position would show noble and generous action, courage, energy, and the like. Curiously enough the numbers of the pips were interpreted on a system very much akin to the Pythagorean system of numbers, especially in regard to the occult meaning of odd and even numbers. Mrs Lee laid particular stress on the arrangement of the pips on the cards, pointing out its similarity to the arrangement of spots on dice and dominoes. (The connection of this with the Pythagorean system is obvious.) In the light of this explanation the appropriateness of the serpent in the design of the two of pentacles is manifest.

Whether Mrs Lee's explanations were common to the gipsy tribes, or merely a system of her own, I cannot say. She seemed to regard it as very private, and only shown to me as a special mark of favour.

The last time I saw Mrs Lee was some twenty years ago at Yetholm, when the son of the late Queen Esther was crowned Gipsy King. Mrs Lee was very contemptuous of the Yetholm gipsies — 'Tinker trash,' she said, 'not a hundred words of Romani among the lot.' This, however, may well have been the prejudice of a different tribe.

I was interested to find that what she told me of the Tarot was well known to another friend of mine, the late Mrs Florence Farr Emery, who herself claimed Romani descent, and had a great store of strange learning. She it was who first pointed out to me the correspondence of the interpretations of the pip cards with the Pythagorean system, greatly to my delight, for the meanings usually ascribed to the cards had seemed merely empiric, and founded on no system, as indeed are the meanings ascribed to cards by the ordinary type of fortune-teller today. More doubtful were Mrs Emery's suggestions of Egyptian correspondences. She was a diligent student of Egyptology, though perhaps not quite as much of an authority as her friends claimed, and with natural enthusiasm was apt to see ancient Egypt everywhere.

Another unexpected gleam of light came to me from a friend of the late Charles Godfrey Leland, who told me that Leland had some special knowledge of a peculiar system of Gipsy Cartomancy, which for reasons known to himself he was not at liberty to divulge, and of a special pack of cards used by them. The friend who told me this had never seen the cards, but from the evidence of the Tarot pack shown me by Mrs Lee it seems more than likely that these were in fact the Tarot cards, and that the interpretation thereof had been communicated as a secret to Leland. So then there appears to be a probability, in spite of the scepticism of the folklorists, that the connection of the Tarot with the gipsies may have a solid foundation in fact, and on this also we must await further evidence.

Meanwhile a guess may be hazarded that, although the cards arrived in Europe before the gipsies, they may yet have a common origin. Both the tribe and the cards arrived roughly about the same time, from an utterly unknown and mysterious source; and though the cards arrived first, there is no evidence to show that they did not come from the same origin. This will be a problem for future investigators, and a problem that I would humbly suggest is to be solved, not by negations, but rather by careful and open-minded examination of all the minutest traces of evidence available. It may be perfectly true to say there is no evidence of the Egyptian origin either of the cards or the people. But like other negations it takes us no farther. It may be right to deprecate the hasty dogmatism and superstition of those who proclaim loudly, on the very slenderest authority, that the secrets of the Universe have been laid bare, and the key to universal knowledge is in the hands of some certain mystic writer or teacher, who poses as a divinely inspired final authority and revealer of mysteries. There be many such nowadays, specially of the discredited German brand. But in this deprecation we should beware of falling into the opposite error, and because there is no proof, rashly assume that there is no evidence. It is by the patient examination of minute, almost invisible, and nearly obliterated traces, that true scientific investigation triumphs at length. There are traces, faint and infinitesimal it is true, of an Egyptian origin both of the gipsies and of the Tarot cards; and until some clearer indications of another origin are discovered it is wisdom to preserve these, and make the most of them, examine them with minutest care and search for others, meantime not neglecting any other clues pointing in any other direction. Above all, the careful examination of the designs of the cards, from the very earliest that can be discovered, with all their variants, must be an essential part of the inquiry. No good end can be served by redrawing the cards, however skilfully or artistically it is done. They will remain nothing but an evidence of the taste, and skill, and opinions of the artist, or his inspirer. But anyone who can in any way contribute to a reproduction of the original designs as they were, not as he thinks they ought to be, will do a real service to the study of the Tarot. Even the well-known and accepted symbols on the best of the current packs, well-drawn and coloured, and well printed to replace the crude and poor examples which are the best we can get now, would be a boon to Tarot students, and would demand neither archaeological nor mystic learning.

In common with many Tarot students I welcomed Mr Waite's little manual, and found therein as I expected, and as one always expects from his work, the result of careful research, set forth in graceful and elegant diction, an invaluable summary for those who have not the time or the patience, perhaps not the opportunity, to study the original works, of which he gives an excellent bibliography. But after all it carries one very little farther. *En passant* I was rather surprised that he should have taken the swords of the Tarot as the prototypes of clubs. So learned and accurate a writer must have had some authority for this statement, but none is given, and the obvious idea that in Italian swords is *spadi,* and the form of the pips in modern cards suggest a conventionalized drawing of the Roman broad sword, is not so much as alluded to. The original symbology as I have said remains unknown, and is open to any conjecture, but it must be said that the form of the club pip is singularly unlike a bludgeon or quarter staff. But if we take the suit of denarii, or pentacles, to represent earth forces, and suggest that money or coins might symbolize material powers, and that the clover or trefoil leaf, as a product of the earth, might also symbolize the earth forces, it might be as good symbology as the derivation of bludgeons from swords. In any case it seems to be generally assumed the cups are the prototypes of hearts, and sceptres of diamonds, and if swords or *spadi* became spades, there is only left the correspondence of Pentacles with modern clubs.

There are then three ways in which we may regard the Tarot cards. Firstly the most obvious, as implements of a game of chance or skill, and this is only historically interesting. Secondly as a book of hieroglyphics, revealing, if properly interpreted, some great mystic truths. It may be some cosmogony, or history of evolution, either of the universe, or the human soul. And thirdly as a means of divination. Clearly the second of these depends entirely on our having the correct order of the cards; and as to this at present no light comes from antiquity, and modern authorities differ, as we have seen. The third, or divinatory use, depends on the chance laying down of the cards, the order in which they turn up after certain prescribed shufflings and cuttings by the querent. Mr Waite inclines to the belief that the series of 22 Atus, or Trumps, were solely referred to the second of the above ways of regarding the cards; and the 56 pip cards, which he calls the lesser Arcana, were for no other use than for divination or fortune telling. This may be correct. Certainly there are examples of the Atus alone without the pip cards, and there are packs of pip cards sold now in Italy for the playing of Tarrochi with no Atus. Yet there are early examples in Mr Clulow's collection of packs containing both, and clearly related. One form at least of the game is played with both, the Atus have a very special power justifying their name of trumps; and certainly also the system of divination shown to me by Mrs Lee made use of both. I can only say that after examining all the evidence — that cited by Mr Waite as well as some others — I have myself come to a different conclusion, but I consider the point still open to investigation.

As to divination or fortune-telling, there are many ways of laying out the cards; I have myself been shown over a dozen, and I am persuaded there are many more, some of them peculiar to individual diviners. The first method described by Mr Waite has long been familiar to me. It was sometimes used among others by Mrs Florence Farr Emery, but the divinatory meanings were entirely different. Rightly or wrongly they were logically formed by the combination of the general meaning of the suit with the mystic properties of numbers, which Mr Waite apparently disregards. This divinatory meaning is broadly borne out by the old symbolic designs. The theory, therefore, is that the Tarot was in its origin a symbolic book, whose meaning can now only be remotely guessed at; that the original designers worked upon the fourfold division of all created things, whereof well-known examples are the four beasts of Ezekiel's vision, and of the Apocalypse, the four cherubim, the four archangels, the four letters of tetragrammaton, and many others; to which they added the mystic virtues of numbers, and upon each page of the book they placed a symbolic design still further to elucidate it. Each page on this theory would in fact form a chapter in the book, describing the good and evil influences operating from the spiritual on the material world. By the theory of divination the process of shuffling and cutting the cards according to the prescribed method would indicate the influences operating on the querent. We may perhaps compare the symbolic designs to the vignettes illustrating chapters in the Egyptian Book of the Dead.

If this theory is in any way correct it is obvious that it is of supreme importance to preserve by all means the ancient symbolic designs, and if possible to restore them to the state in which the original designers intended to set them forth. Archaeological research is continually bringing to light new and unexpected discoveries, and it may well be that any day some fresh evidence may be forthcoming on the forms of the Tarot, before the earliest that are now known, evidence that perhaps will without doubt connect these mysterious cards with one or other of the great races of antiquity and the great systems of philosophy or prove the fallacy of this idea. I trust that Mr Waite may some day find time to tell us from whence he derived his interpretations, and the designs illustrating them.

Taking as an example the two of pentacles, of which I have spoken before. Pentacles represent the earth forces — the material influences ruling our mortal life — and two according to the Pythagoreans is the number of divided councils, of Good and Evil, the first number to separate itself from the divine unity, hence associated with the dual nature of the serpent, or the two serpents, the serpent of the temptation, and the brazen serpent of healing lifted up by Moses in the wilderness, which was a type of Christ. Appropriately then in the old designs is the two of pentacles illustrated by the serpent coiled in the symbol of infinity. The interpretation may be true or false, I claim no special inspiration for it. It is merely a suggestion. But from whence comes Mr Waite's dancing man? If he belongs to any of the old forms of the Tarot, or is in any way connected with the original designers, he is worthy of serious consideration. But one would like to know his origin and credentials. And the same remark applies to the other designs.

I am aware that my contribution is exceedingly small, but in tracing a path so obscure the faintest gleam of light may be of great value. I wholly agree with Mr Waite in deprecating the attitude of those who assume a mighty air of mystery, and hint that an they would they could tell much. This is not the attitude of the real occult student. Those who know the secret tradition (supposing there is one) should either set forth their knowledge, if they may, and are not restrained by any pledges or honourable understanding, or should be silent; and those who have any interpretation to give should give their authority, or if the source be their own intuition or clairvoyance, should frankly say so. If all commentators would follow these simple rules of scientific investigation, we might be nearer to solving the two mysteries of the origin of the Tarot cards, and the origin of the gipsies, and either proving or disproving their alleged connection.

[Reprinted from *The Occult Review*, Vol, XXIX, No. 2 (February 1919), pp. 90-8. Brodie Innes's article stimulated a response from A.E. Waite and a subsequent series of articles and letters, by various authors, printed in issues of *The Occult Review* throughout the following year.]

Magic and the Golden Dawn

20. MacGregor Mathers: Some Personal Reminiscences

In November of last year, almost unnoticed by the general public, there passed away in Paris a very remarkable man. What was he — a great adept — a great scholar — a great impostor — a great rascal? I have heard all opinions, confidently, even dogmatically, asserted. As many and as contradictory opinions as were pronounced of Cagliostro. I knew him intimately; and perhaps a close friendship of some thirty years may warrant my giving a few personal reminiscences that may help to a better understanding of a most interesting personality. When I first met with him he was in charge of the Horniman Museum at Norwood, and even then the contradictory accounts I heard of him roused keen curiosity. Some eminent archaeologists told me that, from his wonderful learning in strange by-paths of knowledge, there was no man in Great Britain better fitted to arrange and catalogue such a Museum as the Horniman. Others denounced him as a superficial charlatan, whose learning could only deceive the ignorant. His very name was in doubt — was he MacGregor — was he Mathers? Yet even the slightest knowledge of Highland history would solve this. The name Macgregor was proscribed after the 'Forty-five. His ancestors took what was in effect a by-name — Mo-Athair's — "The Posthumous" — from the infant son of Alastair Macgregor of Glenstrae, who, born after the murder of his father in 1603, was installed as Chief of Glenstrae. This name was anglicized into Mathers, which was borne by his ancestors. But the true name was, of course, MacGregor. His grandfather had fought with great gallantry at the siege of Pondicherry, with Lally Tollendal, and received from Louis XIV the title of Count MacGregor de Glenstrae, afterwards confirmed by James II, a French title which naturally was not used in England.

As soon as I came to know him well the mystery of the varying opinions with regard to him was apparent. MacGregor was a Celt of the Celts, a type which no Englishman of the Teutonic strain has ever yet been able to understand or to appreciate. To very many indeed this type is as a red rag to a bull. There are those to-day who will outdo Dr. Johnson in abuse of everything Celtic or Highland. MacGregor had all the Celtic fiery temper and pride of race. He would pick a quarrel on a point of punctilio, a real, or even a fancied, slight to his clan or nation, and fight it out with the keen zest of a mediaeval knight, but always at a disadvantage, for he was above all a chivalrous Highland gentleman, and in all his nature was not one grain of malice, but among his opponents were some who disdained not the use of very underhand weapons — any stick good enough to beat a dog. Such a nature, familiar to me as a Celt, was incomprehensible to the average Saxon. Vanity doubtless he had, but it was the harmless vanity of a child. Credulous too, and liable sometimes to be taken in by an impudent impostor, for he who hated deceit was slow to suspect it in another; but unsparing in his denunciation when he found it.

Of his scholarship it is not for me to speak, so far was it beyond my own, yet I know it was as frankly acknowledged by some competent authorities, as it was bitterly denied and depreciated by his opponents. I once showed some of his letters to me on the Kabalah to my own first teacher in Hebrew, a Rabbi and an advanced Kabalist, and he said "that man is a true Kabalist. Very few Gentiles know as much, you may follow him safely." When he arranged a Temple of Isis for the Paris Exhibition, an Egyptologist whose name is world-famous said "MacGregor is a Pharaoh come back. All my life I have studied the dry bones; he has made them live." These are but two examples out of many. Yet there have been those who have said that his Kabalah and Egyptology were shallow and superficial, a rehash of other men's work. Who shall decide? Yet I do know that many questions I asked him were answered at once, and satisfactorily, with abundant citation of authorities, showing intimate acquaintance with the subject, and never have I detected a mistake.

This is not the place to retell how he was taken in by the famous (or infamous) Horus pair. The story is well known, and the trial may be read by the curious; — that he should have been thus deceived is an instance of the faults of his qualities.

Of his occult knowledge and power I can speak more confidently. He had the rare gift of making clear-cut and luminous those deep inner teachings, so often veiled in nebulous vapourings and prolix verbiage, wherein one plods through leagues of slush to pick out a few gems. His astrological knowledge was exceptional, as is abundantly proved by many horoscopes that have passed through my hands, in which the accuracy of his judgment as evidenced by events was convincing. He had also the second-sight of his race developed to a remarkable degree. Of this I have had many proofs. Ceremonial magic of many ages and countries was familiar to him, and I have been told by eminent scientists that his explanations of the power and effect of ceremonial were extremely clear and logical. That he was the head of a Hermetic Rosicrucian Order is well known. But of this nothing can be said. The pledge was given in full in the Horus trial. All members were bound by a solemn oath to divulge nothing concerning the Order, or its members, or what took place at its meetings. Anything therefore that has been published as to this Order can only have been obtained by the wilful perjury of some member, or evolved from the imagination of the narrator. I may, however, say of my own knowledge that, in spite of dissensions and secessions in the past the Order has gone on and flourished. It has spread over many lands, and the loyalty and affection of its members for their chief was probably greater at the time of his death than ever before.

For many years he lived in Paris, and while in France he naturally and properly used his French title, which he had dropped while resident in this country.

Seldom, I suppose, has a man inspired such love and devotion, and such deadly animosity. For myself I can but speak of him as I knew him, the true and loyal friend of well-nigh half a lifetime. Often I have written to him some question relating to my own literary work, and with unselfish readiness he has laid aside other work to search the Paris libraries and museums, and copy or translate page after page from MSS. inaccessible to me, or frankly to place at my disposal the stores of his strange learning and his patient researches. I was not blind to his faults, which lay on the surface, and were patent to all. Yet seldom, I think, has a man had a more faithful and cordial friend through many changes of sunshine and shadow than I had in MacGregor Mathers.

Dear, impulsive, hot-headed, warm-hearted Highlander, he had all the defects and the qualities of his race; misunderstood, reviled, and revered, brave and loyal to the last, bearing no malice to any, scarcely even resenting the many baseless falsehoods freely circulated about him, I am glad of this opportunity to add this one little leaf to the wreath laid on the tomb of my dead friend.

[Reprinted from *The Occult Review*, Vol. 29, No. 5, May 1919, pp. 284-286.]

> Formal
> Statement of the Tenure
> by which
> the members of the G.D.
> in
> Edinburgh
> do agree to accept, and to hold
> the
> Warrant for
> Temple N.° 6.
> named
> Amen Ra
> By the assent of the G.H. Fra Lux in Tenebris;
> Signed and issued by S R M D.
> Chief Adept G.D. of Anglia;
> and - Na. O. M. Registrar

Mathers' and Westcott's formal statement about the warrant for 'Temple No. 6, named Amen Ra' (June 1893), with the assent of the mythical Dr. Thiessen (Lux in Tenebris)

> June 1893
>
> We the undersigned members of the Isis-Urania Temple of the Hermetic Order of the G.D. in the outer viz.
>
> John William Brodie Innes (Sub spe) (5°)
> Charles William Pearce (Sapientia Felicitas) (4°)
> Isabella Duncan Pearce (Animo et Fide) (4°)
> Frances Annersley Brodie Innes (Sub hoc signo)
> George Dickson M.D. (Fortis fortuna juvat) (0°)
>
> who have petitioned the G.H. chiefs of the second order for a Warrant to form and hold a Temple of the Order in Edinburgh to be under the immediate control of "the College of the adepts" in London do hereby agree and do bind ourselves to accept the Warrant and to retain it upon the conditions here specified. It is further agreed by us the same signatories jointly and severally that we will return the Warrant and close the Temple, if we be required so to do by the G.H. chiefs of the second order, or by their representati[ves]

Formal acceptance of the Warrant by the founders of Amen Ra Temple (The Warrant, or Charter, has not survived)

21. Concerning the Revisal of the Constitution and Rules of the Order R.R. et A.C.

Very Honoured Fratres and Sorores,

As the original proposer of a revisal of our Constitution and Laws, may I address to you a few words on the present logical position of our Order, and the questions which must ultimately rest with you for decision.

You are aware that, originally, the Second Order in this Country was governed absolutely by three Chiefs. Ultimately their authority all devolved on one; our late Chief, the G.H. Frater, D.D.C.F. [*i.e.* Mathers], who was practically recognized as Autocrat. When, for reasons I need not enter into, the Order deposed and expelled him, the authority devolved on the whole body of Adepti who chose to remain connected with this branch of the Order; *i.e.* all who signed the form of adherence, and whom I now address.

By this form you declared that the authority heretofore possessed by G.H. Frater, D.D.C.F., should be vested in an "Elective Council," thereby delegating the authority that vested in yourselves to a Council to be chosen by you, but only delegating it *when such a Council had been chosen.* At the time when this form was signed a Council was in existence, which assumed provisional authority and responsibility, it was, however, not an *elective* or *elected* Council; you, as a body, had no voice in its constitution. It is for you now to consider whether or no you will confirm the acts of that provisional Council; these acts are at present not binding on you.

You have decided, by signing that form, that you will be governed by an elective Council, but you have not decided how the election shall be conducted, by what majority members shall be elected, or even the number of the Council. These points must be settled before any Council can bind the Order.

Up to this time, therefore, no elective Council exists. The present so-called Council is not elective in any sense, for (1) it consists of six members in whose election you have no voice – viz., the Officers of I.U.T. [Isis Urania Temple] – and of ten members who are said to be elected. (2) Moreover, by the process adopted of nominating a candidate for a particular post as teacher of Divination, Chess, or the like, if only one candidate is nominated, or only one accepts nomination for a particular office, that one must be elected, there being no contest. Thus, if only three offices have a single nomination each, it is obvious that out of the sixteen members of Council, there are nine (a clear majority) in whose election you have no voice. Plainly the authority devolving on you is not delegated to this Council, and their whole acts are invalid until confirmed by you by unanimous vote. This Council being, therefore, *provisional* until confirmed by you, it follows that no legal act can be done by any of its officers, not even a legal receipt or discharge for money, or any other property, can be given by any officer, which is binding on any but the individual members of the Council who appointed him.

It rests with you, therefore, now to decide whether you wish to retain any voice in the affairs and government of the Order; or, assuming that, having deposed and expelled one autocrat, you desire to come under the sway of another, it rests with you to decide whether you wish to exercise any choice as to who that autocrat shall be, or to leave it to chance for the first strong hand to seize the reins.

Secondly, if you wish to retain any control over the Order, it rests with you to decide whether you will be governed by three Chiefs, as was the original form; by one Chief, which was the form you repudiated; or by an elective Council, which was the form you consented to; or by any other as yet untried form; and, whatever is your decision, to take measures to carry it out.

I need hardly point out the method of nominating candidates to special teaching posts, and electing them by general vote, has little to recommend it. How, for example, can those Adepti who as yet know nothing of Chess decide whether A or B is the better teacher thereof? Yet these Adepti, whether they know Chess or not, have an equal right to elect to the Council. Again, an Adept may as a good man of business be extremely valuable on the Council, yet be unable or unwilling to teach any specific subject. Such a one would be ineligible at present.

It rests with you, then, to decide whether you wish your elective Council to consist merely of teachers of the Second Order and Officebearers of I.U.T. (in the choice of the latter of whom, at all events, you have no voice), or of persons chosen by yourselves as capable of ruling the Order wisely and well. A possible and not unusual arrangement would be that you should elect ten members of the Council, leaving it to them to appoint their own Warden, Moderator and Scribe (if such are the office-bearers you decide on), also leaving it to them to name teachers of different subjects (these to be either members of their own body or not as they choose, but if not members thereof, of course to have no voice on the Council), and similarly to appoint office bearers of I.U.T. (who also would have no voice on the Council unless duly elected thereon). Your duly elected representatives would then absolutely control the Order, being responsible to you only, and the system would have the merit of simplicity and practicability.

If you decide that the Order should be ruled by an elective Council, headed by three Chiefs, one might be responsible for the general administration of the Order, one for teaching and the conduct of ceremonies, and the third for the correspondence and finances. This is merely a suggestion of a logical division of duties.

When the Constitution has been thus settled according to the general wish of the Adepti, it will be necessary to pass rules and bye laws. For example, the rooms at headquarters and all the furniture and property therein are *yours,* and every one of you has equal rights to the use of them; they vested in you when you signed the form under which you now exist as a body, and are maintained by your subscriptions. Careful regulations are necessary to ensure the use of the rooms to all of you for all lawful purposes of the Order, and to prevent your property being monopolised by a few.

Again, the rights, privileges, and obligations both of the officebearers of I.U.T. and their sub-officers, how and by whom they are appointed, and their tenure of office, and also of the officers of your Council, need to be definitely settled, and some form of suspension or degradation provided in case any members persistently break the rules and defy the authority of the Order.

Many other subjects readily occur which need to be provided for by rules and bye-laws, but such might well be left to the elective Council when formed, only observing that every rule, to have any binding force, must have the assent of the whole body of Adepti.

It is obvious to any one who has watched the progress of the Order in the last few years, that with us, as with every other institution that has any vitality, there are two parties – one desiring to preserve all our old customs and rules, even where notoriously faulty, the other desiring to make a clean sweep of all that we have, and make an entirely fresh start. It is well, and a sign of the health of the Order, that these should both exist. I say not which I think is right. Probably neither are absolutely right; but I do strenuously assert that the party in power should be the one which commands the general assent and confidence of the whole body on a free and unfettered expression of opinion.

This expression of opinion you have never had an opportunity of pronouncing, and until such opinion is pronounced, there is no Council, no government, no rule or order that is of any more than provisional validity, waiting for your confirmation.

In saying this I have taken simply the legal and material view of the question, as of a purely human institution; I seek not to bias your judgement in any way, but merely to point out the questions on which, if you were dealing with a purely human institution, you would have to pronounce a decided opinion. I do not forget that ours is an occult and magical Order, and I for one firmly believe in the guidance and supervision of higher powers (whether you call them the Third Order or by any other title), and I believe that such higher powers will take care that all that is worth preserving in the Order as we know it will be preserved. But I also believe that whether our particular branch is worth preserving depends entirely on whether we do our duty – whether, having accepted the responsibility that devolves upon us, and taken upon our shoulders all the authority formerly exercised by Frater D.D.C.F., we each and all of us do our best to maintain the Order by forming the best judgment we can on the questions coming up for decision, taking a vital interest and actual share in the concerns of the Order, and, if defeated, agreeing willingly to the desire of the majority and loyally insisting upon that desire being carried into effect..

If we do this faithfully, I believe the Order will flourish and go on from strength to strength and from knowledge to knowledge, and that the Masters of Wisdom will guide our counsels. But if we fail herein, and supinely allow the affairs of the Order to drift, and say to ourselves that "others will manage them," I believe that our branch will perish as no longer worth preserving.

Personally, I can only say that my best services are, as they have always been, at the command of the Order, and therewith I remain.

> Yours always fraternally,
> Sub Spe, Th.A.M.
> *Former Imperator of Amen Ra.*

[Printed privately and circulated within the Order in June 1902. The text was first published in George Mills Harper, *Yeats's Golden Dawn*, 1974, pp. 271-275.]

22. Some Notes on the First Knowledge Lecture

The newly initiated brother of our Order, receiving this First Knowledge Lecture, experiences an involuntary feeling of disappointment — 'Is this all?' he will say to himself, 'After all the promises, the elaborate ritual, the pledges of inviolable secrecy. A few symbols to be found in scores of books.' But let him take heart. It is not to jest with him that this lecture is put forth in this way. Our curriculum is an elaborate system of occult education and training, designed many centuries ago, to lead men step by step to the highest advance they are capable in this life of attaining, and to the diligent student we can promise the unfoldment of the Spiritual Life, the development of all the faculties, and the power to fulfil the purpose of this present earth life and to enter with confidence on the future.

I who write these few words have myself been a student of the Order for near on thirty years, and I can say with absolute truth and conviction I would not be without one atom of the teaching I have had. Nor do I regret one hour spent in the study of its learning. Let him therefore not be discouraged at the outset. This First Knowledge Lecture indicates the plan and scope of his first studies, and gives him as it were the alphabet of the sciences he is to learn. And this alphabet must not merely be known, it must be as familiar to him as the letters of the English alphabet.

If you set about to read a work on any science you are desirous to master, where would you be if you had to go back to your primer to learn the form of a letter? You would make but small progress.

Now at the root of all occult learning lies the knowledge of the elements. Not only our own bodies, but the whole created universe is composed of the four elements, and from them is drawn even the great secret Name of God Himself. By the knowledge of the elements we may attain control of our physical bodies (called self control in common speech), and having attained this and being fit to exercise wider powers may attain to the mastery over the elements. But the symbols of the elements — the ordinary alphabet used in instruction — must be perfectly familiar, otherwise much valuable time is wasted.

So again the influence of the universe of stars on this earth and on the nature and destiny of man, has been known and recognised in all ages. I am not speaking here of the popular manuals, and the half taught pretenders who have brought an ancient science into somewhat undeserved disrepute, but to the profound knowledge possessed by the Chaldeans of old, and still accessible to the diligent student.

The importance of this knowledge can hardly be overestimated for our own progress and development, and to this again the familiar knowledge of the alphabet is essential. The symbols of the Zodiacal Signs and of the Planets must be so perfectly known as to become instinctive, and the elementary terms of the science of Astrology.

The third important subject of the first beginning is the Hebrew Alphabet. The great Jewish system of occultism known as the Cabalah has survived and been proved for thousands of years. It is not necessary for the student in the early grades of our Order to acquire any knowledge of Hebrew as a language, but a knowledge of the letters and their meanings and their numerical attributions is essential. And here I may interpose a hint to the beginner. Learn from the very first to be very careful in the formation of the Hebrew letters. Never by any chance allow yourself to try and write them cursively as you do English.

A few hints here may be useful to the beginner, and save him much time and trouble hereafter.

The general idea of the Hebrew letters is the square formation, the horizontal lines being thick, and the perpendicular lines thin. The easiest way to acquire this is from the first to write with the pen held in the direction of the lines and to press heavily on the horizontal, lightly on the vertical. Also copy every letter as though it were a mechanical drawing. In the examinations that follow each Knowledge Lecture much credit is given for good Hebrew writing. When the alphabet has been learned, I advise the student to take a text at random from a Hebrew Bible and name aloud each letter, disregarding the dots, marks, accidents, etc. noticing only the letters. He should not be satisfied till he can do so easily and without hesitation. When he is perfectly familiar with the forms of the letters, he may read with advantage my paper on the 'Symbology of the Hebrew letters in the First Pentad'. There will be much in this that he will not yet understand, but it will serve to impress his mind with the importance of attending to the exact form of the letters and the comprehension of what is taught therein will be gradually unfolded to him as he proceeds.

These three subjects then should be impressed on his mind:

1. The four elements and their natures.

2. The starry universe, or what is outside of himself and influences him from without.

3. The Hebrew letters, which are to give him a key to a more perfect understanding of both.

Having got thus far he recurs to the Ritual of Initiation, and here he may with advantage study my address on the Ritual, wherein the meaning of that ceremony is set forth as fully as at present he is able to understand it.

There are also some eight lectures on various subjects connected with our teachings which he may have on loan at this stage.

It is however only necessary for his advance to the next grade that he should be thoroughly acquainted with the First Knowledge Lecture, and should pass an examination thereon. The lectures I have mentioned he may study at any time. But it is better that he should take them as soon as he conveniently can. It is important that he should from the very first remember his pledge of secrecy, and he should therefore provide some box or receptacle that can be kept locked in which the MSS can be kept. It is also convenient for his future work that each MS should be separate. It is not good to copy a number into one book.

A number of small MS books of the same size will be found hereafter the most useful. I am personally always willing to reply to any questions or difficulties which any student may find in the course of his studies. Any of the above mentioned lectures may be and should be copied, but the originals should be returned as soon as possible. And note that the student must also recognize and undertake that the copies he makes are not his own property, but in the event of his ever leaving the Order, they must be considered as a loan which he is honourably bound to return to the proper officer.

There is no obligation to attend any meeting. But on receiving an invitation he should reply at once whether able to attend or not.

The two Equinox ceremonials are considered of special importance, and every member should make a special effort to attend.

To the protection of the Lord of the Universe I commit our newly initiated brethren, in the firm hope and trust that they will prove true and excellent fratres among us.

SUB SPE.
Imperator of AMEN RA.

[Issued for members of the Amen-Ra Temple of the G∴D∴ c. 1895.]

23. Essay on Clairvoyance and Travelling in the Spirit Vision

The best theory of the phenomena of Clairvoyance seems to be founded on the relation between Man as the Microcosm and the Universe as the Macrocosm; regarding the former as a reflection in miniature of the latter, as in a grass field full of dewdrops each drop might present a perfect tiny image of trees and mountains, the sky, clouds, the sun and the stars.

If, then, everything in the Cosmos is somehow reflected or pictured on each man's own sphere of sensation, or Akashic envelope, it follows that if he could but be conscious of the pictures so reflected or imprinted he would at once be possessed of all actual or potential knowledge of everything in the Cosmos, and further assuming that time itself is merely an illusion, and that the reality of things is, as it were, one vast picture along which we travel seeing point after point in succession and producing the idea of lapse of time, then it further follows that the full and complete knowledge of all that is reflected in our sphere of sensation includes all knowledge past, present and future.

The reason, then, why we have not such knowledge consciously to ourselves must be from the obtuseness of the Sensorium, the actual physical brain, which cannot perceive the images on the sphere of sensation. If, then, all knowledge lies within each man's own sphere, it is by looking within, or intuition, that such knowledge is made available.

Know thyself and thou wilt know everything. But seeing that the brain and sensorium are physical, it is necessary at first to use physical means to produce the sensitiveness necessary to consciously perceive the images on the Sphere of Sensation. And the readiest and safest means is the use of a symbol. This is familiar in everyday life, but so much as to escape notice.

For example – to a depraved and debauched person an obscene word or figure – carelessly drawn and seen by chance, is a symbol calling up a host of unclean images and ideas. To a lover the name of his mistress spoken by chance in his hearing – the sight of a colour she usually wears, or the scent of a familiar perfume will suffice to raise the image of the beloved form almost visibly before him and to produce quickened pulse, heightened colour, etc.

To the soldier the sight of the flag of his country or his regiment, produces visions of martial glory, ideas of devotion, loyalty, patriotism and unflinching courage.

In all these cases ideas and visions are produced in the brain by the symbol, and if the above theory be accepted it follows that the effect of the symbol is to render one portion of the physical brain more sensitive, or it may be more translucent, so that the image lying within the corresponding region of the Sphere of Sensation may be dimly perceived (such sensitiveness of brain may be produced in other ways, such as by Hypnotism or self-induced Trance, by Obsession, Disease, etc. – but the method by symbol seems to remain the surest and the best).

This theory is made use of in the practice of inducing Clairvoyance.

A large number of well known and recognised symbols have a definite relation to certain portions of the Sphere of Sensation and the corresponding regions of the Cosmos, and also to the regions related thereto of the physical brain.

The experimenter should know thoroughly the attributions and meanings of the symbol employed, as this knowledge produces an immediate concentration of thought, of vital energy, of nerve force, and of actual physical blood on the tract of the brain related thereto, and thus materially aids the establishment of a special sensitiveness there.

Thus if the Tejas Tattva card be taken, the knowledge that it belongs to fire will at once charge with nerve force and with blood all the centres of the brain relating to fire, and will involuntarily recall the various Divine and Spirit names which the experimenter has learnt connected therewith. The actual speaking of these with the solemnity and impressiveness of the Vibration will increase the effect – gazing fixedly at the symbol and touching the appropriate implement which is also a symbol of the same brain tract, momentarily increases the force – vires acquirit eundo[1] – until every other brain cell is shut down, muted and inhibited; the whole consciousness is concentrated on the perception of fire.

The physical brains thus become sensitive and translucent in this respect and able to perceive dimly in the Sphere of Sensation the reflection of the Macrocosmic idea of fire, with all its connotations.

---

1. 'It acquires strength in going'.

The sensation is as though one stepped out through a window into a new world.

The reality probably is that the new sensitiveness enables the actual physical brain to become conscious of ideas and pictures hitherto unknown.

At first it seems as though everything thus perceived were just the product of one's own imagination – i.e. that one simply took scraps of memory, scraps of other men's ideas gleaned from books, pictures, etc. and built them up at will into a composite picture. But a little further experience generally convinces one that the new country one has become conscious of has its inviolable natural laws just as the physical world has: that one cannot make or unmake at will, that the same causes produce the same results, that one is in fact merely a spectator and in no sense a creator. The conviction then dawns on one that one is actually perceiving a new and much extended range of phenomena; that, in fact, which is known as the Astral World or Astral Plane.

Here, then, comes an experimental confirmation of the theory above set forth, which will probably be deepened and intensified with every experiment which is carefully made.

Personal experience confirms the foregoing: On taking any symbol whereof I know the meaning, such as a Tattva – or Tarot card, the abstract idea of the symbol comes first – as fire, or water in the abstract – and a pose of mind cognate and sympathetic thereto, a desire for that particular element – not keen but perceptible – gradually the feeling of the physical effects of the element – as of warmth – moisture – etc. – and especially the sound as of the roaring or crackling of fire, the rush – or patter, or ripple of water. Gradually the attention is withdrawn from all surrounding sights and sounds, a grey mist seems to swathe everything, on which, as though thrown from a magic lantern on steam, the form of the symbol is projected.

(This I conceive is due to the withdrawal of blood and nerve force from other centres of the brain and their consequent inhibition.)

The Consciousness then seems to pass through the symbol to realms beyond but, as above-said, I think it more probable that visions and pictures from beyond come on the hypersensitive brain centres and, as these have been sensitised by the symbol itself on the grey mist, so they seem to take the form of the symbol and to pass through it. At all events the sensation is as if one looked at a series of moving pictures, although there are beings in this new world with whom one can converse, animals that one can dominate, or that attract one, yet to me personally it is all no more solid than the pictures of a Kinetoscope or the sound of a phonograph.

Yet when this sensitiveness of brain and power of perception is once established there seems to grow out of it a power of actually going to the scenes so visionary and seeing them as solid, indeed of actually doing things and producing effects there.

This what I imagine is termed Travelling in the Spirit Vision.

Whether it is more than an extension of the power of perceiving the pictures on the Sphere of Sensation or Akashic envelope is very difficult to determine. The sensation, however, to me personally is first to become, as it were, dimly conscious of a figure walking among the scenes of the new country – or the Astral Plane – gradually to become conscious that it is my own figure I am looking at – gradually, as it were, to be able to look through the eyes – and feel with the sensations of this *doppelganger*. Further to be able consciously to direct its motions, to control it, to inhabit it, and in this body to be able to visit the scenes and persons I had previously only looked at, as it were, through a telescope.

It is as though my Consciousness had extruded from my own body to take possession of a body which I had either created for the purpose, or invoked out of the Astral Sphere as a vehicle for myself.

It seems, however, almost more probable that as the Sphere of Sensation reflects everything that is in the material Universe so it must needs contain a reflection also of the material body of the percipient and if this be so it is not hard to suppose that such reflection can be made to travel about within the Sphere of Sensation and visit all things therein reflected with as much ease (or more) as the will of the man can make his physical body travel to material places on the earth.

The Perception of the Astral plane seems to be peculiarly liable to delusions, arising probably from defects in the sensorium or physical brain – as an object seen through faulty glass is distorted, that is to say the personal element, or what scientists call the 'personal equation', becomes so strong as to produce actual error.

As the brain can be rendered sensitive in a particular direction by symbol – so can these errors also be corrected by symbol. The various qualities in each man's nature are symbolised by the planets – hence when this symbology is well known the planetary symbols may be used to correct errors arising from the particular quality attached to each. Thus the error could be that visions are merely compounded from memory.

In this case build up in brilliant white light in front of any image you suspect to be merely a product of memory the letter Tau, the symbol of the Path of Saturn, 'The Great One of the Night of Time' – whose sober and steadying influence will cause a memory picture to disappear. Similarly Beth for Mercury formulated in the same way will cause to vanish any product of lying intellectual delusion – or Daleth for Venus is used for the result of intellectual vanity – Gimel for Luna for a wavering mind – Resh for the Sun for delusions of haughtiness, vanity, etc., and Kaph for the path of Jupiter against imagination, and Peh for the path of Mars against revenge, hatred etc.

[Flying Roll XXV was originally a 'Notice re Stamping Letters', dated by Westcott '27/1/94'. Brodie Innes's *Essay*, which replaced it, was probably circulated in 1895 – the year in which Edison introduced his 'Kinetophone', a device that united the Kinetoscope, for presenting apparently moving images, with the phonograph that provided a sound accompaniment (both of which are referred to in the Essay). The text was printed in Francis King's *Astral Projection, Ritual Magic, and Alchemy. Golden Dawn material by S.L. MacGregor Mathers and others.* (1987, 2nd ed., pp. 85-89).]

24. Notes of an Experiment in Exorcism

For some time my wife had been troubled with an obscure illness, some form, as I think, of influenza — nerve weakness and prostration, with cold and sore throat and general feeling of exhaustion. This baffled and was curiously persistent. Finally it began to attack me also.

In concentrated contemplation true knowledge came to me with increasing certainty "This is the obsession of some vampirising elemental", and I seemed from time to time to hear a voice saying "Cast it out". Not yet being very familiar with the details of the G.D. ceremonies, and especially not having any implements consecrated, I was minded to ask the help of some higher adepts.

Thinking over this alone one night, in intensely concentrated contemplation, I seemed to hear a voice almost, but not quite audibly saying "You must do it yourself, and now, under my instruction". Thereupon I became conscious of a presence in the room, as of a man of stately presence in a black robe with some shining insignia, but what I cannot say.

I neither actually saw on the retina the figure, nor actually on the tympanum heard the voice, yet both came so closely into my consciousness — I cannot explain how — that I could have drawn the figure and transcribed the words with ease. I gave the figure the sign of the Portal and of the 5=6, at which he saluted gravely. I cannot say if he gave the answering signs, but he made some gestures I could not easily follow.

From this time my guide, as I will call him, seemed to take possession of me, and as soon as I had resolved to act under his guidance, I had no desire to question anything. The instructions were partly by signs and partly by words — I cannot quite distinguish which was which, for they seemed intermixed, as it were, but every order was clear and unmistakeable.

The first was to lower the gas — this I did — and the figure of my guide seemed now clearer and more visible. The next was to "burn incense". I had no incense holder handy, but I took a hot coal from the fire, with the tongs and sprinkled some incense and while it was smoking I was directed to trace [banishing pentagram] with it towards the East.

There was a pause before the sign of Leo was traced in the middle — then to use the name Adonai-ha-Aretz. Then after returning the coal to the fire, to face East again and make the Kabalistic Cross. Then in default of magical implements, to trace with a sharp knife the invoking pentagram of [Earth] and at the same time to call on the foul thing that troubled us to appear manifestly before me. I forget the words — they were simply an impression, not dictated to me, but, as I think, spoken through me — for I had composed no form of words and none was suggested, yet I seemed to say them without hesitation.

As I did so, there seemed to be a vague dark blot before me, more like a floating scrap of London fog than anything I can think of — and my guide seemed to come close and stand at my right hand with his arm raised in the attitude of giving the sign of 1=10.

I was then ordered to command its appearance again, using the names Yod, He, Vau, He; Adonai; Eheieh and Agla. The mist seemed to thicken itself to a certain nucleus, but did not grow more definite. Then my guide said "use the Name of the Lord Jesus", *i.e.* Yeheshua, Yehovashah. I did so, commanding in that name a fuller manifestation. A shiver seemed to run through the mist and a dim outline formed, gradually becoming visible as a ghostly and dim but most foul shape — something as near as I can describe, between a bloated and big bellied toad and a malicious ape. It was very dim but quite distinct.

Then a loud clear voice, this time absolutely audible said, "Now smite with all your force" and again "use the Name of the Lord Jesus". I remembered then the Flying Roll on "Imagination" as used by V.H. Fra. Resurgam [E.W. Berridge], and also the instructions of V.H. Soror S.S.D.D. [Sapientia Sapienti Dono Data, *i.e.* Florence Farr] and I gathered all the force I possessed as it were, into a glowing white hot ball of electric fire, and calling on the Name of the Lord Jesus, I projected it like a lightning flash upon the foul image before me.

There seemed a slight shock and puff, as it were a momentary foul smell, a dimness for a second, and the thing was gone utterly and completely disintegrated, as I think. My guide was also gone. The effect however had produced a great tension of nerve in me and a disposition to start at the least thing, which lasted for about half an hour. (*You ought to have brought back to yourself the ray you projected. N.O.M.* [Non Omnis Moriar. *i.e.* W. Wynn Westcott])

This was past midnight, and the house, except for the light in my room, was quite dark. I went upstairs in complete darkness and seemed to see floating balls of fire in various directions — but they may well have been hallucination. My wife was sleeping quietly and with no fever — apparently quite well.

Next morning she told me the illness was gone. She did not know and does not know yet of the above described experiment, which I have communicated to no one, until this account was written for the adepti of the G.D. I thought the cure should have been sudden and perfect (*No, the effect was first upon the Ruach and then later upon the Nephesch. N.O.M.*) but in meditation the message seemed to be given to me "The unclean spirit is gone out, but it remains to purge away his traces from the house of life".

The above is as nearly as I can describe, an account of the experiment. I ask for any suggestion, advice or remark of any Fratres or Sorores of the Second Order, which they may think helpful or appropriate thereon.

Sub Spe, 5=6

Remarks

It is not always permissible to destroy completely an Elemental. You should not do it on your own responsibility. But what you did was to disintegrate a collective built up form. It was not one Elemental but many, built up into one. Always invoke the Highest forces first, angelic as well as Divine.

D.D.C.F. 7=4 [Deo Duce Comite Ferro = S.L. M. Mathers]

[This undated text, with the title as above, was one of the 'Flying Rolls' – teaching documents circulated within the Second Order of the Golden Dawn, the *R.R. et A.C.* It was numbered as Flying Roll XXXIV, (originally 32) and probably issued during 1895, the last dated Flying Roll, No. 29, having been issued on 8 November 1894. Brodie-Innes entered the Second Order on 6 April 1893, and from his admission that he had not yet consecrated any magical implements, it can be assumed that the 'experiment' was conducted shortly afterwards, probably during the following May or June. The text survives in a copy made in 1898 by Colonel Sir Henry Edward Colvile (Frater Tenax Propositi); it is now held in the Library and Museum of Freemasonry in London. An abbreviated variant of the text was printed in Francis King's *Astral Projection, Ritual Magic, and Alchemy*. (1987, 2nd ed., pp. 40-42).]

25. Letters and Notes Relating to the Solar Order (The Cromlech Temple)

1) *J.W. Brodie Innes to an un-named frater (William Wynn Westcott), 21st July, [1896]*

Care V.H. Fra

If you have time read enclosed m.s. before Friday night.

It was compiled by me from some brief notes & a study of the rituals of ☉ in order to explain the line of colour symbology used, so that the candidate may understand the symbology. The Church allusions are my own entirely & no part of the teaching of the Order.

The message that came this morning was that "We (*i.e.* the authorities) gladly welcome the Candidate proposed". The ceremony is fixed for 9.15. [The 'enclosed m.s.' is missing]

      Yrs.
       S.S.

2) [The following 'Notes' appear to be a revised version of those referred to; Westcott has annotated them 'J.W.B.I. on ☉ order. Recd. Sept 8, 96'.]

Notes by Fra Δ on the Ritual of Initiation of ☉°

The foundation of the Ritual appears to be that the physical phenomena of the influence of the Sun on the Earth bear exact correspondence to the influence of the Divine Source of Good on the Human Soul & that by an intelligent & inspired study of the former the true method of Spiritual Development may be learned.

Thus the ☉ is the only perfect symbol of God.

The modes of action of the ☉ are Sevenfold, whereof two are too high to be perceived in our present state.

Hence there are 5 Officers or Priests with two Masters who are said to be invisibly present to make up the Seven.

Of the 5 manifest the highest is Δ who represents the synthesis of all the forces of the ☉ as manifest to man.

The next [pentagram symbol] represents the glittering radiance of ☉ These two are manifest yet scarcely definite. Hence they have gold & silver rather than colour for their states & their symbols are mathematical rather than ideographs.

Initiation is called the Vehicle of El Shaddai, hence the more manifest of the Supernals – Neschamah – the Highest part of the Soul in the most exalted of the Human planes. Therefore these two symbolize the link between the human & Divine. The purely manifest powers of the sun are Magnetism, Light & Heat & the symbolic colours of the States of these Officers denote their functions.

Their symbols are scientific instruments for measuring or analyzing these powers – viz. the Magnet, the Prism & the Thermometer.

It is a tradition in the Order that the ancient symbol of the last was an alchemic furnace & that the Thermometer was substituted by Robert Fludd who was said to have been a Companion of the Order.

Fra Raphael (symbol), Blue stole, seems to = Zeus – Lord of the Thunderbolt – also the Angel of ☉

Frater Anael (prism symbol) = Prism, the connecting or carrying Ether – Vehicle for the transmission of Light. An Angel of the Powers of Venus. Urania – the pure Heavenly Love or Hermetic Love.

Frater Agni (thermometer symbol) = Thermometer = the more earthly love, warmth which should be pure but may be the reverse, hence showing the danger lying at the threshold of all occult work.

I am told that the resemblance of his symbol to a Phallic Emblem is not accidental but enshrines a deep truth & that certain schools which have developed Phallicism & Black magic of the sexual type have precisely failed to pass Agni & taken the downward path indicated in their invocation of the Red Ray. It was said to me "If you know aright all the mysteries of Agni you have won the first grand initiation and your feet are safely set on the path. Then & then only do you truly pass the first golden bar of the Veil"

"Therefore is red the first light you see."

I believe there is a special meaning in his name alone being Indian. But that has not yet been given to us.

The prohibition of the use of wool in any material used in the Ritual is I believe Egyptian.

The name on the front of the Altar is (Aleph & Nun) which Hurwitz gives as a form of Adonai. I have found it nowhere else.

3) *Psychic communication through, and in the hand of, Frances Brodie-Innes, July '96*

Let each one every morning before beginning the work of the day as before directed bring his body to perfect stillness – regulate his breathing to the fourfold rhythm (all of which should by this time have become very easy of attainment). Then let him recall in thought the other companions as he and they knelt together at the Shrine of Mithra, holding the red cords of the veil. Let his mind – with body still, eyes fixed & slow regular breathing – recall every item & the faces of his companions. Then let him say slowly silently – but emphatically "To this Holy Companionship & to the cause of humanity is all my being pledged. Witness the radiant Sun that I here renew the pledge – Accept it Thou Infinite Supreme – This day & all days to come I will obey the commands of the Master in all things."

It may well be that if this is done regularly & faithfully after a while the savour of incense will float across the senses. This if it occur will be a sure sign that the Veil dividing thee from the Masters is getting thin & that thy labour is near fruition & thy services accepted.

The rhythmic movement & regulation of breathing are potent aids to harmonizing the body to the spirit & should be practised whenever occasion serves.

4) *J.W. Brodie Innes to William Wynn Westcott, August 16, 1896*

By the way the symbol is thus ⊙⁼

The 2 strokes under the small ° symbolize the 2 steps which lead to the grade – viz. conquest of the body & conquest of the thought-world.

This however is only to members of the Order, if we ever use the symbol to others it is simply written O [with dot in centre] in the ordinary way.

The symbol of our own Temple is [drawing of a cromlech] a Cromlech in allusion to some Druidical Temple where the same or cognate mysteries were celebrated at or near Edinburgh ages ago.

Yrs. ever
S.S.

5) *Communication in the hand of J. W. Brodie-Innes: Recd. 23rd Sep: 1896.*
☉♀ [and Cromlech symbol]

Say unto Frater [Hebrew letter Samech]
   Not in vain Brother – nor unknown to the Supreme Masters of Wisdom hast thou been left to strive through thy life-work alone. Strong was thy Spirit in the luminous realms, strong & confident & when it demanded this test of standing alone with no sympathiser near it in its strivings for the higher life & the Divine Light the demand was granted because the Spirit was strong enough to bear the strain, the effect whereof would be to enoble & glorify it.

   For weaker spirits the sympathy of those near and dear to them in their occult working & spiritual aspirations is given as a support, to others who have already striven & overcome it is given as a rest after their labours. Blessed are those strong souls who stand in the midst of trials & buffetings in their own strength and fail not – Great shall be their reward. Fret not then therefore when prop after prop shall be removed from thee – It is but as an athlete casting from him one by one his artificial supports. Thou art strong & shall prevail.

   We warn thee however in one direction. Near to thee in thy working – junior to thee yet trusted by thee is one who deserves not confidence. We may say no more – be thou ware – trust not overmuch to any & so fare thee well.

Under the Sign of Three Chiefs
[Symbol of three Calvary Crosses on an arc]

[This was probably directed at Westcott at a time when he faced dissension within the Golden Dawn. The identity of the untrustworthy member, 'junior to thee', is impossible to determine with any certainty.]

6) *Communicated by direct transmission to Frater Δ & thus imperfectly recorded by him. 20th Nov.* [1897 ?] ☉♀ [and Cromlech symbol]
[Attached slip, also in Brodie-Innes's hand, reads 'Please return to Fra Δ direct']

Letters and Notes Relating to the Solar Order

Grieve not for our Fratrix.

The task undertaken by the higher soul by reason of the strong materiality of the physical body, wherein was bound a lower type of ♀ Spirit was too heavy; and the physical was exalting itself over the spiritual and dominating it.

For years although the struggle was hard the Equilibrium was maintained, but just before her admission to our Order the scales were reversed. Planetary & other influences gave great power to the lower Intelligences & Elementals of ♀ and the Spiritual nature was weakened by the determined assault of Evil Potencies in the higher planes inclining our Fratrix in her human personality to listen to the lower rather than the higher counsel both on the human & the astral plane & to be deluded thereby.

Therefore was it by deliberate counsel of the Chiefs of our Order that at that moment she should be admitted a Companion, in order that great strength might be infused into the higher soul so that it should not become entangled in the lower body.

The struggle was then severe for all the potencies of the lower body arose in wrath and dire & strong were the temptations & alluring the hopes held out.

At this time in the higher planes did the higher will deliberately consent to the loss of the physical body so soon as it should be certain that the power of controlling it could not be regained.

During the bright fortnight of the present moon the higher soul has been absent from the physical body which has been in effect dead all the time – kept functioning only by the elementals dwelling therein. The higher soul has been guarded & protected by the Chiefs of the Order till, after a period of rest, the higher will might decide whether again to renew the struggle or consent at once to the loss of the physical body.

With that determination none may interfere – yet know that unless success crowned the effort of the higher soul the life would be one of incessant & increasing misery. Victory would give a bright future – yet hope not & wish not for life without it.

We will give all our powers to fortify the higher soul, whether it remains united to the body or not. And the fervent prayers of the Companions in the name of the Most Holy Master of Masters will also avail much.

[This communication appears to relate to the breach between Brodie Innes and Isabelle de Steiger. He failed to understand just why she had supported Peck in Amen-Ra Temple.]

[These Solar Order letters are currently in a private collection]

Novella

The Old House in the Canongate

THE AUTHOR'S FOREWORD
THE following narrative is rather an experience than a composition. The author, who is very familiar with the old parts of Edinburgh, noticed some time ago, with curious distinctness, the sensation of Spain which he has endeavoured to describe, hanging around a peculiarly squalid close, and finding that other persons quite independently had experienced the same and that no written or well-known oral tradition would account for it, he sought to pursue the subject and get clearer mental pictures. Thus bit by bit the old house, as described, grew up in shadowy form, and here and there sufficiently clear indications came to bear verification from local history and tradition, such as coats of arms of old Scotch houses standing out distinct over the shadowy gateways with dates and initials superadded. In this way a few historic facts were pieced together on which again shadowy pictures built themselves up. These pictures referred obviously to various dates, yet with little to show what was their historic sequence. Wherever verification was possible the story was borne out by recorded facts. Obviously, however, it was utterly impossible to observe any of the ordinary rules of construction in telling such a story; the only thing the author could attempt has been to set down the various pictures in as clear sequence as circumstances admit of. Those who have had similar experiences will recognise the difficulty. It only remains to say that as the portions of the story which were actually verified, involved more than one well-known Scottish family, the names, etc. have been altered, but the reader may rely on it that only absolutely necessary alterations have been made.

THE WRITER'S PROLOGUE
It was a great many years ago, while still the old town of Edinburgh retained its quaintness and picturesque historic flavour, which the march of civilisation has so largely destroyed of late, that there stood, just off the Canongate and fronting on one of the curious characteristic closes that branch off on either hand, an old house; so old that the very legends of its first foundation were blurred and dim. Bits of carved tracery round

a window niched into one angle of the basement indicated ecclesiastical art of a date considerably older than Holyrood, and above this, in strange contrast, was sculptured the coat of arms of a noble Spanish family, whose very name had perished more than two hundred years ago in the land of their birth. The first storey projected on carved beams as in many of the old Edinburgh houses, and above were fantastic gables, pepper-box turrets, and dormer windows, looking like a strange architectural nightmare, wherein the old Scotch baronial style was blended with much of the Moresque. At the time I write of, however, the old house had fallen on evil days, dirt and neglect were over it all, for some years it had been shut up altogether, the lower windows boarded over, many of the upper ones broken; previously to this it had been long in the sole custody of an old half-caste servant, who sternly refused admission to any person whatsoever.

At this time I was deeply interested in the history and antiquities of Edinburgh, and priding myself, as I did, on knowing something of every building in the city of any pretension, my curiosity was greatly piqued by this queer old rambling mansion, the inside of which no one seemed to have seen, and whose story no one seemed to know, save that it was commonly rumoured to be "uncanny," if no worse.

On one special morning in the late autumn, as I was passing down the Canongate, I noticed an unusual stir, and quite a little crowd created about the head of the close I have mentioned, and drawing near enough to gather their remarks I soon learned that the authorities had condemned the old house as unsafe and that it was to be forthwith pulled down. "Now or never! " I said to myself, "if I am to see the inside of that house while it yet exists there's no time to be lost." As if in answer to my thought there bustled through the group of idlers Mr. Evan Fraser, the worthy bailie, and probable Lord Provost of no distant date, the man who could procure the realization of my wish if anyone in Edinburgh could; portly and important, rather red in the face, his hat tilted a trifle back, his heavy gold chain and bunch of seals jingling in front across his broad expanse of waistcoat, and panting slightly as he elbowed his path away from the old house ; to him I addressed myself.

"See over yon hoose," he said; "aye! aye! to be sure, weel ye ken, laddie! its no just in my own hands, and the proprietor, he's no vara fond of letting folk gang through — something no quite the thing aboot the hoose maybe. Oh ! I'm no saying anything, mind ye, that should na be said, perhaps it'll be the drains that's wrang, or something like that. Still, as the hoose is to be pulled down, and seeing that ye're interested in a' that rubbish o' coats o' arms and sic like trash, and a' the world'll be seeing the inside o' it in a few days now, I dinna think there can be muckle harm, an' I'll write a note to Mr. Dalrymple, that's the proprietor ye ken, and tell him I'd taken the liberty. Aye ! aye! just come ye this way."

So saying the worthy man turned back with me, and leading the way to the door, he knocked; it was cautiously opened on the chain.

"Open the door, ye donnered auld fule!" said Mr. Fraser. "Have ye no the sense to ken my knock yet? "This," he continued, turning to me, "is Mr. Dalrymple's servant, who has known this ramshackle auld place ever since he was a boy, haven't ye, Peter? and knows all the ghosts about it, just as well as he knows the whisky shops in the Canongate."

"Oh, Mr. Fraser!" said Peter as he closed the door behind us, "for the love of the Lord! dinna ye mak' fun o' they? Man and boy I've been here these sixty years, and they never harmed me yet; but eh, mon, they're ower near to us to flyte at."

"Weel, Peter, I canna stay to hear your auld world stories now, but look ye! this young gentleman wants to see all over the auld place before it's pulled down, and you must just tak' him round and let him see a' there is, right away, ye ken, frae the cellars to the attics, and the secret chambers if there are any, and tell him all your auld stories, if he has patience to listen; I will answer to Mr. Dalrymple."

The door closed on the energetic Bailie, and I was in the entrance-hall of the old house I had so often longed to see. I looked with some curiosity at my companion; notwithstanding his broad Scotch tongue, he had unquestionably more than a dash of foreign blood in his veins; he was tall and slight, with great grace of movement, a sallow olive complexion, hair and moustache grizzled with time, long, restless, taper fingers, and piercingly, black eyes. I had not time, however, for a prolonged scrutiny.

"Come awa'," he said, "if ye want to see th' auld hoose, no that there's muckle to see, its a' falling to bits noo, but I mind the day when it was a real, bright, bonny hoose, about the time Mr. Dalrymple was married Aye, and before that, when the auld laird was here."

"I've heard Mrs. Dalrymple was very pretty," I said.

"Aye, was she, puir body; a bonny lass! Folk'll tell ye," he said suddenly turning round on me, "that it's her that walks, don't ye believe it I've seen them that walks in this hoose, many and many a time, aye, before ever Mr. Dalrymple married, before Mrs. Dalrymple, puir thing, was born, and those that were here before me kenned them, lang ere ever I came to Edinburgh. Na, na, Mrs. Dalrymple lies quiet enough, God rest her soul," and the old man crossed himself devoutly. "Come awa'! " he said quickly leading the way up the broad uncarpeted stairs, whose rotting and worm-eaten boards looked singularly insecure.

I am bound to say I was disappointed with my tour round the old house; clearly the outside was the most interesting part of it. Suites of rooms that had been handsome once, but decorated in the worst taste of the later Georgian period, and now with all the tawdry plaster wreaths and Cupids crumbling away, the paper hanging in festoons from the walls, and dragging the mouldering plaster with it, some rooms partly furnished, but with carpets and hangings riddled by the moth and falling into rags from very rottenness. Everywhere it was the same, the vulgar commonplace crumbling into sordid decay.

"Mr. Fraser spoke of secret chambers," I said at last, "do you know of any such?"

"Na, na," said the old man, " it's just his duffing; there may perhaps be a passage or so, for the wa's are gey thick, ye ken, and maybe a hiding-hole or the like, they did queer things in th' auld times, but nane o' them's known at present, and troth those that walk dinna need any hiding-places or secret chambers; many a time I've seen that puir lady coming doon these vera stairs towards me wi' the black lace over her bonny face, and the cross-hilted dagger in her breast, and many a time when I never saw her, I've felt the swish of her satin gown go past me on the stairs, but never past the seventh step from the bottom, she just seemed as though she passed into the wa' there. Come awa', sir, ye've just seen the whole of it noo."

"No Peter," I said, "I haven't been in there," and I pointed to a door on the left of the first landing.

"Oh, ye've seen that," he said; "besides, there's naething there, just a room, the auld laird's room it was."

I fancied I detected something in the old man's tone as though he wished to deter me from entering, and this of course redoubled my anxiety to see the room. I sprang up the stairs again, turned the handle and entered. A commonplace room, sure enough; a huge four-post bed occupied a great part of it, deeply recessed windows gave but scanty light, a huge mirror confronted me, rusty and dim, its silvering largely worn away and its frame broken, some sombre kind of brown patterned paper covered the walls, a dreary room altogether; as I walked into it, the door closed behind me, not with a slam, but slowly, gently, noiselessly, as though some unseen hand were shutting it quietly. Then curiously, notwithstanding the dismal gloominess of the room, I began to be conscious of a strange exhilaration and excitement; my heart beat thick and fast with an emotion distinctly pleasurable, and I became conscious of a faint and almost indescribable odour, recalling at one moment the scent of burning wood, then a subtle aroma as of incense, blended with a suggestion of orange flowers, and through it all an unmistakable whiff of garlic. Where had I smelt that smell before? for it came to me as perfectly familiar, and then in my brain rose clear the memory of an artistic ramble in Spain some years before. Yes, it was Seville, that that strange subtle scent belonged to, and as it permeated my senses, the room I stood in seemed dream-like and unreal, the black-robed priests, the peasants, the dark-eyed donnas of Spain were all around me. In the embrasure of the deep window, or was it in the tall mirror? — I could not say — was reclining a graceful form — amber satin, and a black lace mantilla. My brain seemed growing dim, a clammy perspiration was in the palms of my hands, yet my pulses throbbed with the excitement of a coming adventure. I know not why I murmured the name of "Juanita," an old sweetheart of the old wandering days in Spain. That instant the door was thrown open and old Peter appeared. "Best come oot o' there, sir," he said, "that room's no' wholesome."

"What do you mean? " I asked.

"Oh, nothing! just it's th' auld laird's room. I mean they say it's over the drains, ye ken, and they say there's some effluvium."

"Perhaps what I smell," I thought, but why these memories of Seville? However, I was glad enough to get out on the landing and draw two or three deep breaths to revive myself. Peter looked at me curiously. "Was I long in the room before you came in?" I said, for to me it had seemed like ages.

"'Deed no, sir! I just followed you as fast as an auld man can follow a young ane!" he said.

At this moment my eye fell on a small picture which I had not previously noticed in the entrance hall; an old, old portrait, as would seem from its frame, the paint almost obliterated by time and dirt, yet it was impossible to disguise the strange, powerful lineaments, the piercing eyes, which, even in its present state of neglect and decay seemed to glow from the canvas and to exert almost a mesmeric influence.

"Who is that? " I asked.

"Sorrow o' me kens, sir," he answered, with a queer tremble in his voice. "There was a man came here once — it was soon after Mr. Dalrymple was married, as like that picture as two peas in a pod; Signor Hernandez, I think they called him, and he looked at that picture. 'Aye, aye,' he says, 'that's my grandfather, or my great-grandfather, or something. Fergusson, his name was, and ought to be mine by rights. Then he gave a little laugh, but I give ye my word, sir, that night that he was here I saw them as walks here, them as I've told ye of, sir, just as plain as I see you now, plainer than I ever saw them before or since, and sic' cruel, wicked looks among them. Puir Mistress Dalrymple, she was ill that night, too, and Mr. Dalrymple was nursing her; I just laid down here in the hall, sir, on a sofa in case I should be wanted, and whenever he came out he just shuddered and gasped like a man going to die. 'Deed, sir, but I was glad when that Signor Hernandez took his leave. If he wasna just Auld Clootie, he was no vara distant kin, o' that I'm sure."

I pressed a half-sovereign into Peter's hand with an intimation that I might, perhaps, be glad to have another look over the old house before it was finally demolished.

"Thank ye, sir," said Peter, "I'll be glad totak' ye round any time ye like to come; ye're the first stranger that's set foot in here for thirty years, forby some o' the town council, and they don't count, puir feckless bodies; there's no ane amang them a' has wit eneugh to keep himself warm, unless it's Mr. Fraser."

So I went back, as the evening was now fast drawing on, to my lodgings in Northumberland Street, where my good landlady had a brisk fire burning, and very soon a comfortable little dinner. Yet for all I could do that vision of Seville haunted my brain; not a thought of the old house, scarce a memory of Peter and his quaint stories, but a constant memory of the sunny streets and the lovely girls of Spain.

"After all," I said to myself, "it's the only place for real life, I must go back. Ah! how I should like to see my little Juanita once more. I'll go, as sure as fate, as soon as I can get away from this old country. I'm off for sunny Spain, marry Juanita, turn orange grower, or something."

I put on my hat, lighted a cigar, and strolled out, humming a Spanish love-song, with my brain full of old memories and fancies, finally turned into bed, and, as might have been expected, dreamt of Spain and Spanish demoiselles, and of kneeling with Juanita before a gorgeous altar, while, the clouds of incense floating upwards veiled the candles and the golden shrine, and then wandering with Juanita under blooming orange trees; then a nightmare, I cannot clearly remember what, but a cross-hilted dagger stood out plain against wreaths of dark, lurid cloud, and I awoke, gasping for breath, and bathed in perspiration.

Next morning came a feeling of strong curiosity about the old house, and I determined to seek out Mr. Dalrymple. Evan Fraser's chance words had informed me he was in Edinburgh, and to Evan Fraser therefore I betook myself as soon as possible after breakfast.

"Aye, aye, laddie," he said, "ye'll find him here in Queen Street." He gave me the number; "he has a suite o' apairtments there; just for the time, ye ken. Stay, tak my card, wi' ye? He's no vara keen for seeing strangers."

In ten minutes more, by the passport of good Evan Fraser's card, I was ushered into the presence of Mr. Dalrymple. A very tall, very thin man, with a face as white as marble and perfectly white hair, kindly hazel eyes of strange brilliance, a very prominent, hooked nose, seeming much too large for his pinched face and sunken cheeks. He stooped terribly, and his clothes seemed to hang loosely on his shrunken frame, and as I entered he raised a handkerchief to his lips, as though to check a fit of asthmatic coughing.

There was a look of kindly interest in his eyes as I told him of my architectural and heraldic studies and my fondness for old Edinburgh, but when I spoke of the old house in the Canongate it grew troubled, as though painful memories were stirred within him. I told him how the outside of the old house had attracted me and how I had at last procured access to it, and what a loss I thought its intended demolition would be to Edinburgh.

"Better so! better so! " he said, "the town council have done well to condemn it, the old house has been a curse to all who have lived there — tell me, did you go into the room on the left of the first landing?"

It was my turn to start now, he looked at me so curiously and intently. "I did," I answered, "a melancholy room, it would give me the blues to live there."

"It was not always so," he said, "I loved that room better than any room in the house forty years ago. My bridal chamber it was."

"An unhealthy room, I fancy," I replied, "it gave me a most curious sensation. I suppose it was the closeness or damp, or a drain smell or something, I felt like fainting."

"What! there's more than this! tell me what you felt? did you think of any country, of any place ? did you dream of anyone?" cried Mr. Dalrymple, strangely moved. "Pardon me. I have a motive for asking."

"Well, yes," I said, "I smelt something, a drain perhaps, but it somehow recalled Seville, the drains are not over good out there you know, and then, I suppose from the association, I began to think of Spain till I half fancied I saw a lady in an amber satin dress and a black lace mantilla in one of the deep window recesses. 'Pon my word, I'm ashamed to tell you the story, it looks so ridiculous in broad daylight."

"Not to me! not to me!" he said with a heavy sigh. "You must be intensely sensitive. Tell me," looking straight into my eyes, "What are you thinking of doing for the next few years."

"Well," I said, rather taken aback by the suddenness of the question. "I have an idea of trying orange-growing in Spain."

"Ah! just so," he murmured, "and of marrying a Spanish lady and settling down for life in the sunny South. 'Tis a lovely dream."

I stared, his words so exactly followed the current of my own thoughts.

"Tell me," he continued. "When did you form this project — last night, was it not?"

I could only nod again. I was too astonished to speak.

"Ah!" he said, "the old curse of the house — it's terrible! it's terrible! Stay a moment, sit down where you are."

We had been standing by the fire all this time. As he spoke he pointed to a large arm-chair. I could not resist, almost without my will as it seemed I sank into it. Mr. Dalrymple laid a cool hand on my forehead, and his thin white fingers seemed to touch my hair caressingly, a grateful sense of coolness flowed through my brain, my thoughts grew clear and luminous, the feverish haze which haunted me melted away.

"Well!" he said, "what do you think of orange-growing?"

"Oh!" I answered, "a lovely dream, as you said just now, but I don't fancy the reality would be so charming. I've been in Spain and it's a fine country for a holiday, when you're young and have nothing to do, but I don't care to go back."

"Nor to marry a Spanish lady?" he queried with a slight smile.

"Oh dear no!" I said, "that is a lovely dream too, but Heaven forfend it should be more."

"Yet," said Mr. Dalrymple, slowly and impressively, "that very thing you would have done if Providence had not sent you in the nick of time to me. Look here, my young friend, I never saw you before, I may never see you again, but for the sake of my dear old friend Evan Fraser I take a great interest in you, and therefore I warn you, there are influences all round us, of which the bulk of mankind, happily for themselves, are wholly ignorant, and which they only feel very vaguely, and when they do probably ascribe them to indigestion or drains or some such thing. You are abnormally sensitive, and it may embitter your whole life as it has done mine. Now will you light a cigar and sit down and listen patiently to an old man's garrulity, and I will tell you as well as I can the story of my own life, and of the old house in the Canongate, which, please God! I will never enter again. Mind you! I can't explain it; I can only tell you literally my own experiences, which I would never have told anyone but that I see in you a person even more sensitive than I was myself, and I believe you might develop into a spirit medium of the kind they call under-control, from which may God in His mercy preserve you, and all other sane men."

Heartily I thanked him, and lighting an excellent cigar disposed myself to listen to Mr. Dalrymple's story, which ran thus:

MR. DALRYMPLE'S STORY OF THE OLD HOUSE
"The house has belonged to my family for many generations, in fact it used to be called Dalrymple House some hundred years ago, though this name seems to have been dropped since. I don't quite know why. No one knows its earliest history; there are legends in the family about some monastic foundation; you know the corner window looking up towards the Canongate, well, that is said to be the remains of some very old ecclesiastical building, older than anything else in Edinburgh,

founded on the site of some Druid altar or temple. I never had much turn for archaeology myself, so I can't tell you much about it; my own personal experiences I can tell you, and perhaps you may be able to interpret them. My father never lived in the old house. I question whether he ever set foot within it; he was a merchant much engaged in the Indian trade, but as he died soon after I was born, all my knowledge of him is but hearsay. I was sent to school in France, then brought home and sent to school in England, then to Oxford where I took a fair degree, but until I was two and twenty I never was in Edinburgh, and, beyond the fact that my family possessed a town house there, I knew nothing whatever of the old house in the Canongate.

"During my minority it was inhabited, that is when it was inhabited at all, by my uncle, a bachelor and a man who was generally looked upon as a *mauvais sujet* in the family; though my father had confidence enough in him to nominate him as my guardian. Except however for paying for my education and keeping me liberally supplied with pocket money, my uncle did little for me, and thus it chanced that until I was twenty-two I knew but little either of the house or my uncle. After I had taken my degree, however, I determined to go North, and take possession of my property, and make myself familiar with the old traditions of my race, and the places with which for so many generations we had been associated.

"My uncle was always called, and I believe is called still, the Auld Laird, but he never had more than ample income left him by my father in recognition of his trust on my behalf.

"I was just twenty-two at the time I begin my story, as happy a stripling as you often see, with magnificent health, ample fortune, and not a care in the world. I had just taken a good degree, I had troops of friends, I was engaged to a sweet girl, the daughter of my old College coach. My first wish on leaving Oxford was to know more about this old Edinburgh house, the most curious bit of my possessions, as I gathered from some notes left my father, relating to my grandfather who had lived there. It was a cold night in January when I first arrived in Edinburgh, but my uncle's welcome was warm and boisterous. 'Welcome to your own home, my boy,' he cried, his jolly old red face beaming with pleasure, 'you're master here now. By gad, Sir! I'm glad to hand over the reins to you, but if you'll let me have a corner in the old place,

I'll be obliged to you, for I've got fond of it, and an old man's like an old tree, suffers if it's transplanted you know.' 'Indeed, Uncle,' I said, 'I hope you'll stay here all your life.' 'Well, until you're married, my boy!' he answered, 'and look here, I've told them to put you in your proper place, in the Laird's room; I've been sleeping there myself lately, but only to keep it warm for you.' Talking like this he led me upstairs to that room we were speaking of just now at the left hand side of the first landing; a cheerful fire burnt in the grate, but that huge bed with its dark hangings made me think of a hearse somehow. "There was tapestry on the wall then, and that old mirror was new. By the way, did you notice the little door leading out of the room, up one step, a queer looking door?" I had not noticed it. " Well, it's there," continued Mr. Dalrymple, "if you go again, go through it, it opens on a little landing; there was some lumber piled there the night I'm speaking of and a pile of old books; there's a narrow stair leads up and down from that landing; so much I saw, but I hadn't time to explore further; the place might have been damp, at any rate it gave me the shivers, so I picked up a book thinking if I were wakeful I could read myself to sleep as I often did, and returned to the fire; at that moment I heard the clock chiming a quarter to six, and six was the dinner hour; no time to be lost; I pitched the book on to the table by the bed and rid myself of my travel-stained garments and put on an evening suit with all the haste I could muster. My uncle and I dined alone that night, and I am bound to say I found him capital company. I wanted to hear about the old house, but not a word would he tell me; time enough to explore in daylight, he said, and I should probably live there a great deal in the future, and come to know it all by heart. So he discoursed generally and genially about his travels, and about books and famous men whom he had known, and the time slipped by till bed time. I retired to the stately old room, very handsome I thought it then, for the hangings and decorations, though not new, were fresh and in excellent preservation. I sat down by the fire intending to write to Edith Challoner, my fiancée, and I commenced a letter; but never, since we were engaged, had my words flowed so sluggishly; measured and commonplace sentences such as one might write to the merest acquaintance were all I could frame and even these with difficulty; what a contrast to the free outpouring o f thought and feeling of my letters to her of only a week ago.

"'Pshaw!' I thought, 'I am overtired, or the champagne was too good or something. I must just turn in, I shall be all right after a night's rest." I jumped into bed and blew out the candle, but no sooner had I done so than a most unreasoning fear of that door on to the little stair came over me; an apprehension growing to certainty that something would come out from there made me sit up and strain my eyes at the door, and as I did so the feeling lessened and almost vanished. I must say here that I was not previously imaginative. I had never known any sensations of this kind before, though I had slept in so-called haunted houses, and had laughed to scorn what seemed to me superstitious fears. No sooner did I close my eyes again than the same idea came before me; something gruesome and horrible was behind that door and would open it Physically, I was no coward. I was afraid of nothing I had ever seen — of nothing I could imagine. I was afraid that some new shape of a horror I had never dreamt of, would appear to me — the tension was growing unbearable. I jumped up — plunged my head in cold water and the feeling vanished as soon as I was broad awake; I put on my silk-lined dressing-gown and sat down by the fire, taking up mechanically the volume I had brought out of the landing with me — by a strange chance it was Don Quixote. I read and read, and the scenes grew more and more vivid. Spain seemed to lie all round me. So clear was it that I actually thought I saw the waving boughs of an olive tree, till I realized that it was only the dark green arras stirred by a passing breath of wind.

"I looked up from my book and my eye fell upon that long mirror with a start and a tremble as I saw what seemed to be a dim figure faintly outlined in its depths — amber drapery and black lace — clearer and, clearer it grew, till I saw, or thought I saw, a pale lovely face, with great limpid black eyes raised half piteously, half coquettishly to mine. That face burnt itself into my brain as no living face had ever done, yet when I looked again there was nothing there but the reflexion of one of the figures on the tapestry.

'This won't do,' I said to myself 'my brain is getting out of gear. I've been working too hard I suspect.' But while I thought this, an irresistible drowsiness passed over me — my eyes would not keep open — my brain refused to act.

"When I awoke I was lying in the great funereal bed; how I got there I never knew, the sun was streaming in at the window, it was near eleven o'clock.

"My uncle did not fail to chaff me on my late appearance, and asked me in a bantering tone if any of the old Lairds' ghosts had disturbed me; but not wishing to be ridiculed as a superstitious dreamer, I kept my own counsel, though half resolving to leave Edinburgh that day on any excuse rather than face another night in that room. As evening drew on however my thoughts changed. I began to feel an intense interest in the lady of the mirror, a feeling like that of a lover who has a tryst with his mistress. My better nature reproached me with disloyalty to Edith, but I put the thought aside, saying to myself: 'What nonsense, why it is but a shadow!' Nevertheless I knew that the memories of Edith were growing very thin and pale and that the shadow was to me a far more substantial reality.

"That night I sat again by the fire reading Don Quixote, and ever and anon glancing in the mirror I saw the reflexion of the figure on the tapestry, but nothing else. However towards the early hours of the morning a faint rustle seemed to come behind me like the very light trail of silk over the carpet, a faint odour as of sandal wood and a cold air as the rustling sound seemed to pass me. My heart beat fast. 'She is there,' I thought. 'Come to me, darling!' I said half aloud, stretching my arms. And I thought I felt a warm breath on my cheek, and then the same drowsiness as on the previous night.

"I must have been in a parlous state of mind and brain at this time, for my whole waking thoughts seemed to turn on these experiences, and whatever questions I had to decide on the most trivial matters of business connected with my property were mentally referred to this. Since that first night, I saw the form in the mirror sometimes, but never so clear again — often I was conscious of the frou-frou of the sweeping dress, passing over the carpet, the cold air and the scent of sandal wood — sometimes it passed me on the stair, once it seemed to linger beside me in the hall, when I stood looking at that picture of Hernandez. I had projected a trip abroad, now I thought with dread of any separation from the dream lady. I was obliged to visit my estates in Ross-shire, the night before I left I was wretched. I sat by the fire as usual and heard the silken rustle. 'My darling,' I whispered, 'shall I hear from you while I'm away?' I fancied a soft 'yes' breathed on my cheek, and I went away half consoled. When I reached the market town, I stopped to order some toilet necessaries I had forgotten to be sent out to me. I was to stay at the factor's house. The parcel did not arrive till next morning. When it came it was brought up to my room with my shaving water. I opened [it carelessly enough, but as I did so the well-known scent of sandal wood came on my senses, and a tiny scrap of pink paper fluttered down. I seized it eagerly. It bore simply written or lithographed the word 'Mercedes' — nothing else in the parcel had the scent of sandal wood — but as I inhaled the sweet fragrance from the scrap of paper I seemed to know that my lady of the mirror had kept her promise — and more — for she had revealed her name. 'Mercedes! my darling! 'I murmured, 'true love! when shall I meet and know you?'

"I must stop for one moment here to say that no single thing had happened to me which plain and common-sense people would not have accounted for by the most commonplace of reasoning; whatever of the supernatural there was, if there was any, came from within and was quite personal to myself; this may perhaps throw a good deal of light on the state of my mind at the time.

"We were living then much as the bulk of well-to-do Edinburgh folk lived; my uncle and I went out to dinners, heavy, stiff and formal, and heavy, stiff, formal people came to dine with us, and often drank a great deal more than was good for them. My uncle, however, was very abstemious, much to my surprise, for I had heard he was terribly dissipated in early life. We knew many people whose names are household words now, but with these I do not trouble you, nor did I trouble myself at the time. I was deeply in love with a shadow. I still wrote fitfully to Edith Challoner, and now and then had pricks of conscience, but ordinarily my dream love monopolized all my thoughts and fancies. I should say here that never since that first night had I any return of the feeling of shrinking horror from the little door on to the stair that I have mentioned, save once, when I felt the presence of Mercedes, as I had now learned to call her, at that side of the room; but it was not the stately sweep of the dress like a queen moving through her throne-room, rather the fluttered and excited rush of a terrified woman fleeing from danger. My own heart was strongly stirred and agitated, alarm for her rather than myself moved me, but all that night I had that vague terror of that door. I could not take my eyes off it, once or twice it actually seemed bulging as though pushed from the other side with enormous force. I felt sure something wicked was behind it. I longed to go and look and reassure myself, yet — coward as I must appear to you — I dared not. Next morning the bright sunlight drove away these visions and the little landing looked commonplace as usual, but a strange thing happened, for I dropped a sleeve-link and feeling about for it on the floor I came upon a loose board in the wainscot, and pulling it away I saw something glitter behind it; I pulled it out and found a cross-hilted dagger, or rather stiletto. See here it is, I never part from it."

Mr. Dalrymple as he spoke drew from the breast of his waistcoat a tiny dagger, hilt and all about eight or nine inches long; the hilt was of old fashioned silver work of Moresque pattern, shaped like a cross, the point of the blade broken off, some strange characters were engraved on the blade which I could not see. He kissed it devoutly, as a Catholic might the relic of a Saint, and softly murmured the name "Mercedes."

"Yes," he continued, "it was that morning I found this and put it in my pocket as a curiosity; as I pushed the board back it creaked and I suppose there must be some hollow spaces behind, for the creak echoed down below, like the wild laugh of a mocking fiend, or so it seemed to my excited imagination. I started in horror, broad daylight as it was, all my veins running cold, for that moment, the floor, the walls, the whole landing seemed to be oozing forth some ghastly exhalation hostile to human life; a stain on the wall with which I was perfectly familiar, appeared like a great splash of blood. I turned and fled hastily slamming the door behind me, and rushed into my uncle's room. 'Look here, uncle,' I said. 'what I've found!' He turned the dagger over curiously, poising it in a strange way point upwards between his fingers, then he pressed it on his forehead. 'Very wonderful!' he said at last. 'Tell me, nephew, have you studied the occult sciences at all?' 'What do you mean?' I asked. 'Clearly from that question you haven't,' he said. 'Well, look here! I'm a bit o f a conjurer and this dagger can do strange things, I fancy; just give me your hands a moment.' I gave him my hands, the dagger was lying on a little round ebony table between us. In an instant I felt an intense vibration run through both hands and up my arms, a thrill like that of an electric shock; my uncle raised his hands and mine, holding them above the dagger, which to my intense surprise began to move, and at last stood up as It were balanced on its point, swaying its cross hilt to every movement of our hands.

"Such phenomena are now the stock-in-trade of every spirit medium, and are scarcely deemed even startling; but at this time no such things as mediums were known as public performers, and I was deeply impressed and slightly alarmed. I felt, however, that, in some strange way, a magnetic attraction raying forth from our linked hands was the cause of the motion of the dagger, but I was more astonished to see its point moving, apparently by its own volition, and tracing geometric figures of a kind new to me, on the polished surface of the table. I have the table still with the cuttings on it, the import of which I understand now. As the designs grew complete, it seemed to me as though the black surface of the table was like a well of clear water of infinite depth, through which, deep down, I could see strange, fantastic forms; gradually one image detached itself as though floating upwards, white and still, and as it grew clearer and clearer I saw the face of Mercedes — but pale as ashes — clearer still and I saw it was the face of death ; and would to God it were death only — for that white face floated up almost to the surface with a more awful expression of extreme agony than I ever conceived or dreamt could have been on any human face. I gave one shriek and wrenched my hands away from my uncle's and that instant the dread white face vanished — the dagger fell with a clatter on the floor, and my uncle, angry for a moment, exclaimed, 'You pitiful young fool! do you know you might have killed us both by such an absurd caper?' 'Rather that,' I said, 'than see again what I saw just now.' 'See !' he said, 'you don't mean to tell me you saw anything, you poor ignoramus — the place was full of lovely forms — lovelier than any women of earth, but no untrained eye like yours could see them. Come! come!' he added in a gentler tone, 'you're overwrought — you want a little distraction. Lady Scott's ball is to-night you know; we'll go!' I was on the point of laying I would do no such thing, but some undefined impulse of the moment prompted me to assent. I stooped to pick up my dagger — it was burning hot — too hot to hold. 'Ah,' said my uncle, 'the magnetism is in it yet,' and he passed his hands over it once and handed it back to me, now cold as well-conducted metal should be."

"I was not sorry to go to the ball that night, if only to escape the horrible associations which the former night and that morning had left about the little landing.

"Lady Scott's house was sumptuous; every appointment beyond praise, she herself an ideal hostess. The ball-room, with its exquisite decorations and masses of tropic flowers and ferns (then far less common even among the wealthy than they are now), was. a dream of beauty. You may perhaps have heard of Sir Robert Scott; he claimed some kinship with Michael Scott, the wizard; he had been knighted for some service or other in the East, where he acquired fabulous wealth. And so they blazed the comets of a season in Edinburgh. The chief attraction of their house, to me, was a noble library, arranged on the best of all systems, the cellular, with a low vaulted roof and rows of small compartments, wherein one could bury oneself in one's favourite authors, without fear of disturbance. But I am wandering away from the ball. I danced a good deal and for the time forgot altogether the strange experiences of the last few weeks (it was then, I think, only six or seven weeks since I first came to Edinburgh).

"The evening was wearing on; heated and somewhat tired, I walked out into the entrance-hall for a breath of fresh air. Suddenly my pulses stood still a second, then every vein in my body throbbed at express speed; through the foliage of a great magnolia that grew in a large wooden box at the foot of the marble staircase, I caught a gleam of amber satin and black lace, and the well-remembered and now to me almost sacred odour of sandal wood, floated on my senses. In an instant it was gone, but something whispered me to follow. The library lay in that direction. I hurried into its cool, dimly lighted recesses, the seventh on the right hand had been on previous visits my favourite haunt, containing Spanish books, mainly of a mystic character. To this recess instinctively I bent my steps, and so highly strung was my mind, that I was scarcely surprised to see there, half reclining in the semi-darkness, the same form I had seen in the mirror at the old house; the same amber satin and black lace, only now with the addition of a ruby-coloured fan, and now no shadow, no phantasm, but a warm, living, breathing reality. I sprang forward. 'Mercedes!' at last, I cried; she drew back slightly, the fan pressed close to her lips, while she extended the other hand towards me; for my life I could not have ventured nearer to her, I sank on one knee and covered her hand with kisses. 'I expected you,' she said softly, 'but not here, not thus do we meet or part. Come to me in the Cathedral, at Seville, two months from to-day; you can do me a great service, which no one else can do; now adios, remember!' She withdrew her hand and stately as a queen she glided out of the recess. I turned to follow, but she was gone. Not among the guests that night, nor anywhere in Edinburgh at that time, did I again see my beautiful Mercedes.

"Needless to say I resolved at once that, come what might, I would not fail of the tryst. Two months seemed an interminable time to wait, yet as I sat half dreaming before the fire in the stately old room, I thought, or rather I felt, that the spirit of Mercedes was close beside me there, but that if I went away I should be separated from her. My uncle too grew more confidential and I was surprised to find in him an amount of knowledge and scientific research I had not suspected in that avowed viveur and man of the world. Spain was evidently very familiar to him, especially Salamanca. 'T was there,' he said, 'I met my dear friend Hernandez, a connection of ours I think.' My eyes turned instinctively on the portrait, you remember it, hanging in the hall. 'Aye,' said my uncle, interpreting my glance, 'it's very like him, that's his great grandfather though, Fergus Fergusson. He was one of our family and lived here, I believe, somewhere in the seventeenth century or sixteenth or something. Then he or his son went to Spain and changed the name to Hernandez — why, I can't tell you, I never knew much of these old family stories — however, I met Hernandez at Salamanca, he was a professor when I was a student; he's coming here to Edinburgh and I want you to ask him to come here.'

"'Why, of course. Any friend of ours is welcome. But he must be old.'

"'Old, bless the boy, he's about 40!'

"'O come, uncle, if he was a professor when you were a student, he must be older than you at any rate, and you're a good 65, I know!'

"'God bless me, you're right,' said my uncle, 'I never thought of that. I suppose he is; I can't think of him as past 40 though. Why hang it! he must be 75 if he's a day, wonderful man, wonderful!

"I didn't see that a man of 75 was necessarily wonderful, but I held my peace.

"One day my uncle asked to see my little dagger again. I brought it from where I kept it, for I didn't carry it about with me.

"'It's a pretty toy,' he said, looking closely at the handle, and as he spoke he touched the extreme end of the handle which seemed to tremble under his finger; he pressed it and the strange carved work of the hilt parted into an egg-shaped garland, then into a perfect circle. My uncle held it up in triumph, then pointing to the characters on the blade he read them off. I will not weary you now with all he told me of the use of this dagger and the symbolism wrought into its handle and written on its blade, and the faiths of old archaic nations which were, as it were, crystallized in this curious old weapon, legends of Isis, of Ashtoreth and Aphrodite, and of the great temple of Cyprus, for my uncle was a man of wide culture and extensive travel. I was glad to some extent to hear him talk, for his words partly dispelled the feeling of superstitious dread with which I had regarded the dagger since the vision in the ebony table. At some points, however, I must have smiled incredulously, for my uncle said, 'Come now, let us put it to the proof.' I dreaded any further visions in my uncle's company after the last, but somehow I was unable to make any resistance, and I followed my uncle into his little sanctum, by the way, that queer ecclesiastical-looking window belongs to it. I had never been in here before — my uncle seemed greatly averse to intrusion — and I had always desired to humour all his whims. It is a queer stone-vaulted little room, but it looked like a bric-a-brac shop, so thickly was it hung and strewn with curios of all kinds, but what most attracted my notice was a series of seven silken curtains of the seven prismatic colours, which as the full sun shone in seemed to dazzle my eyes, till I almost seemed to fancy a strange mist between me and them, like the appearance of the white of an egg dropped into a tumbler of water.

"My uncle lighted a small lamp, notwithstanding that it was broad noonday, and set it on a little geometrically-shaped table, and soon a rich heavy sensuous perfume filled the room. My uncle laid the dagger in the palm of his right hand, and directed me to place the palm of my right hand over it, while his left hand and mine rested on a little table which stood between; very shortly I felt my hand and arm begin to burn and tingle, the heavy scent stole up to my brain, sensuous images began to rise in my thoughts. My uncle grasped my hand closer and murmured some kind of Hebrew or Arabic chant, the prismatic curtains seemed swayed by some breeze which we could not feel, and the opalescent mist moved and stirred and coagulated, forming itself gradually into lovely forms of women, floating, gliding here and there. My senses were entranced with a wild rapture, though I felt at the same moment as though all my vitality were being drained away. Momently I was growing weaker; with a violent effort of will at last I said to myself 'this won't do: What can be happening to me? I shall faint in another moment.' I drew in a long deep breath, shut my teeth and my lips hard and held my breath a moment, as I looked steadily and firmly at the fleeting shapes, and wherever I looked, there then were none of them, a void hole as it were, with circling forms all round; through one of these voids I saw the amber of one of the curtains, and as it were a simulacrum of black lace over it. Instantly I became conscious of a new power in the force of my will. I put forth all its strength, commanding the obscene herd to disappear. As I did so I felt my uncle's hand grow cold and clammy; he loosened his grasp and the dagger fell to the floor; he was panting and utterly exhausted. I filled a glass of liqueur from a small silver tray that stood on a side table, and in a few moments after swallowing it he was himself again. But for me, never again did I pass the door of that little room without a shudder.

"A few days later Señor Hernandez arrived. I have seen this remarkable man often since, but never can I forget the first impression made upon me: my uncle's account had prepared me for an elderly gentleman, instead I saw a man apparently in the prime of life; not a grey thread in his jet black hair, not a wrinkle in his clear olive-hued face, the finely-cut features of which might have been wrought in metal so impassive were they. I tried hard to greet him as an ordinary guest, but the curious mixture of terrified repulsion and yet a curiosity amounting almost to attraction was such as I had never felt before, and made it impossible to treat him as a simple casual acquaintance. He looked hard at me with piercing eyes which seemed to dazzle all my senses, and made me feel as in a trance. 'So you are the owner of this old place now,' he said. 'Well, many have come and gone since my — my ancestor's — portrait yonder was painted here. You ought to have some powers — eh? Clairvoyant I should think, perhaps you might tell me some things I want to know.' But the experiences of the past with my uncle had warned me, and I replied that I would never play with such subjects. Señor Hernandez, still looking fixedly at me, said it was a wise resolve. We were standing all this time together in the hall. 'Your grandfather wished he had made such a resolution,' he said, 'before he brought that Spanish bride of his home.' I started, I could not help it — so there was Spanish blood in my own veins then — I had not known of this before. 'Oh, yes,' said Señor Hernandez, 'a lovely girl she was — by the way, you are going to Spain, I may see you there. You wonder how I know. Thought travels quicker than light, and there are those who can read thoughts, even as far off as Spain.' I thought to myself that this man was a very transparent humbug pretending to extraordinary powers, and that he had somehow heard of my intended journey, and made the most of the information. But as I stood talking to him a most strange faintness came over me, a great swell of magnificent organ harmonies seemed surging through my brain, I gasped for breath, my eyes grew blinded; all at once I became conscious that Hernandez was holding his right hand opposite my forehead, and that innumerable threads as it were of pale blue luminous gossamer were streaming from it into my brain. Faint and dim and far away I heard his voice — I was just conscious of sinking into an arm-chair — I heard the distant voice enquiring what I saw, and then, clear as a picture, came the vision of a desolate ridge of a hill with a precipice on either hand, and, mistily outlined in the background, the familiar form of Arthur's Seat: on the midmost point of the ridge stood a species of cromlech, and at its base, a large flat stone, a troop of wild men and women with gipsy faces and wild matted hair pressed around, a form bound with seemingly interminable networks of linen bands interlaced with swaiths of willow was laid on the stone, an old man with flowing white hair and beard, and a crown of green leaves on his head, raised a large knife; then to my horror I saw the victim was a young girl — a mist came over the altar stone — I could see that it was raised — but I could see no more, save that cruel ghastly rills of blood rippled round it; then, as it faded, the face of Hernandez showed through the mists with a diabolical expression of triumph.

"Again the mists seemed building themselves into pictures, and now I heard the swell of a Christian hymn, and I saw a little chapel with kneeling worshippers, all draped in dark-coloured, coarse woollen clothes of no particular shape, all rough and fierce-looking, both men and women, yet bending in humble adoration. To my intense surprise, I recognised the mouldings of that little room which formed, as I have told you, my uncle's sanctum. I know not how, but in some strange way I was conscious that under the altar there was a hollow, and that into this hollow I ought to see.

"It seemed, also, as though Hernandez stood beside me, saying, 'Look below the altar'; but ever that strange, blinding mist floated there and baffled my best endeavours; but as I strained my eyes, a form seemed to float between me and the altar — a kneeling figure, amber silk and black lace — and the faint perfume of sandal-wood floated towards me instead of incense, and in a second all my senses rallied. Some hellish art had overcome my will, and forced me into a trance condition, but I would break from it, even though the effort should tear every nerve. I strove with might and main to free myself, to cast off the heavy cloud that seemed resting on my brain. It felt as though ten thousand tiny filaments all embedded and entangled in the sensitive mass of the brain were being slowly dragged out, each with a separate pang, but the unreal vision vanished; I felt as though awaking from a heavy sleep, and at that moment I heard the voice of Hernandez saying, 'A thousand devils! the boy's too strong for me!' Far away the voice sounded. With a great gasp I came to myself; I was sitting in a big arm-chair in the hall, my uncle and Señor Hernandez standing over me, the former, with a glass of water in his hand. 'Why, nephew,' he said, 'what on earth has come to you? What do you mean by going off in a dead faint like that and scaring us out of our wits?'

"Hernandez said nothing, but a faint smile, more sinister than ever, came round his mouth, but moved no other feature of his face.

"There were but a few days left before my departure for Spain; in those days of slow travelling and probable delays I resolved to allow at least a month, lest by any chance I might miss the tryst at the Cathedral of Seville. Of those few days I remember little, save that the old house seemed more eerie than ever, and the forms, whose presence I dimly felt sometimes on stairs or landing, appeared more palpable, and charged with a magnetism whose evil influence sometimes almost dominated my will, strive as I would. The image of Mercedes, too, seemed now to press close beside me, as though seeking protection, but two days before my departure it disappeared altogether. Left alone in the old haunted house (for my uncle and Hernandez almost lived in the little sanctum, save at meal times), you may guess I was glad enough when I embarked at the Port of Leith for the sunny South."

THE WRITER REVISITS THE OLD HOUSE
Mr. Dalrymple paused, and rising from his chair, said, "I fear I must have wearied you, and you must think it strange that I should thus disclose the deepest and most sacred history of my life to a complete stranger — a history which has never passed my lips before. The cause is simple; you are, whether you know it or not, a natural sensitive, gifted

with abnormal powers, and you are the first individual for many years who has penetrated into that old house. Hence you are exposed to dangers you have not the least idea of, and to me, the duty of warning you is as clear as it would be to lead a blind man whom I might find ignorantly straying into a nest of robbers and cut-throats, or wandering on the brink of hideous precipices. The duty is made still plainer by the fact that the house is mine, and therefore I am morally as responsible for the evil caused by it as though I kept a man-eating tiger. True, it was by no will of mine you were admitted, still you have been there, the influence has seized you to some extent, and I must protect you if I can, and I can do so only by telling you my own story, painful and gruesome as it is. I see, however, that my time is up for the present. Will you pardon me now, and come again to-morrow, if you are not over-wearied with an old man's tale, which no doubt sounds to you much like the wanderings of a superstitious dreamer lapsing into dotage."

I hastened to assure him that, on the contrary, I had listened with the utmost interest, and longed to hear the end of a tale more wonderful than anything I had ever read. Meantime I begged that I might be allowed to visit the old house once more.

"Yes!" he said, "there can be no objection now you have been once, only beware; keep your will active and your senses about you; there are many influences and they are evil. Allow them no foothold, yield not for an instant; the house is accursed, and the dwellers therein will be restless so long as one stone remains on another."

He bowed and was gone, and I slowly walked out into the bright sunshine, with a strange eerie feeling of having been in some other existence and of some great change having come over one. It was past midday, and I made my way as quickly as possible to the old house, determined to lose no chance of exploring it while it yet stood, and before the workmen had begun to despoil and ruin the old-world flavour of it. The temporary excitement of the previous day seemed to have departed, only the ordinary High Street loafers were prowling about, the old house stood grim and secretive as ever, looking as though a whole world of secret wickedness were hidden behind its dull heavy walls. Strange, I thought, as I looked at it, that Mr. Dalrymple's experience should so curiously tally with my own, or rather that the influence, which evidently had dominated all his life, should have been felt by me, a total stranger, and felt at once on entering the house for the first time. Strange, too, that as he half indicated, his experience should be in a way the repetition of that of his grandfather; the whole thing seemed weird whatever way you turned it, and though at that time I always wanted, if possible, a material explanation, and strove hard to find one in this case, the complicated chain of coincidences appeared almost greater than the mind could grasp; yet I could not lay my finger on any one point in the story and say it was supernatural; everything might be explained by coincidence, nightmare or hallucination, allowing of course some latitude for imposture. It was the extraordinary hanging together of it all that made it seem the most improbable of all possible theories to attempt a materialistic interpretation.

With these thoughts in my head I knocked at the door; once more it was cautiously opened by old Peter, who looked cautiously out, and seeing who it was took down the heavy door-chain which he had kept up meanwhile and admitted me.

"Eh, sirs," he said, "but ye're sune back. Hae ye seen Mr. Dalrymple?"

I replied that I had and he had given me permission to come to the house as often as I pleased.

"Weel, weel," said the old man, "it's the first time I ever heard o' the master doing the like o' that; however I suppose it's all right, but tak' ye heed, young sir! ye cam' unco near seeing some o' them that walks here the last time ye were through the hoose, and min' ye though yon puir leddy, that folk say is Mrs. Dalrymple, is harmless eneugh, there's other's that's aboot as wicked as old Clootie himsel'; no' that I've ever seen them, they never interfered wi' me, and I dinna heed them, but I ken far awa' doon among the foundations somewhere, there's that that a man shouldna name."

"Nonsense, Peter," I said, "down among the foundations I expect there are some beastly rotten drains, that ought to be dug out and disinfected as soon as possible."

The old man shook his head and muttered low: "Aye! aye! Youth thinks it knows everything."

"Now Peter," I said, "I want to explore a bit, by Mr. Dalrymple's leave, and I won't trouble you; it's just this little room beside the hall, and what you call the Auld Laird's room that I particularly want to look at."

"Gude save us!" said Peter, "the verra twa places that ye'd better let alone. Weel! weel! Wilful youth maun hae its way; but see ye, if anything flegs ye, just ye cry on to me. I'll no be very far awa'."

So saying he gravely and solemnly withdrew to the back premises, and I walked eagerly towards the little room with the strange ecclesiastical mouldings; as I did so a strange scent came floating towards me, at first the musty smell common to all old houses, a smell of dust and decaying wood, yet withal faintly aromatic; the aromatic quality increased as I laid my hand on the carven door; it was a subtle, sleepy, sensuous perfume, suggesting luxurious vice, immorality in trappings of purple and fine linen. I opened the door; the light was dim, a fragment of what once had been a rose-coloured silk curtain hung over part of the window, the lower part had been boarded, a tiny bit of stained glass filled one space of the curious tracery. I suppose the dust and dirt and decay were as conspicuous here as in other parts of the house, but in the dim light they were not so visible; in fact the miscellaneous litter and rubbish of the room assumed strange, quaint and beautiful shapes. Still that curious perfume, which reminded me somewhat of patchouli and of musk, but was not gross as these are, but rather the inner soul of the scent as it were. Something moved on the wall — I started — it was only an enormous spider; the room felt hot, probably from the fact that the afternoon sun now just caught one angle, shining full on two of its outside walls, and one ray penetrating through a broken pane shot clear across the room, making a strange track of light on the floating dust and motes, and gleaming full on a strange-shaped brass implement, the like whereof I had never seen before, engraved with curious figures, and something like Hebrew letters within a double circle. I sank into a tattered arm-chair to try and take in the curious scene. Old Peter had carefully kept me out of this room on my previous visit. As I did so a fresh cloud of dust rose from the ancient cushions and circled round my head, gleaming in the sun and vanishing in the shade like living things, and all charged strongly with that strange clinging perfume. My eye fell on a torn scrap of writing close to my hand. I picked it up and tried to gather its contents; it was in a woman's hand and seemed to contain passionate pleadings by the writer, to some person of whom she stood in great awe, not to drive her to the commission of a crime.

"Is it not enough," so ran one passage, "that you have forced me again and again to go through the same horrible scenes — must I in yet another body expiate the old sin? Let me expiate it and go. I cannot and will not do that horrible thing again. The centuries that sap your forces have given me a new birth and increased strength."

Here the writer broke off into some incoherent phrases of Spanish, and as I was trying to master these I felt my hands tingle as though from an electric battery. The shock seemed to run right up both arms, nearly paralysing them, and at the same moment a sensation like a cool delicate hand grasping my right wrist, and a distinct attempt to pull the paper from its grasp. I had almost lapsed into a state of dream, but this experience roused all my energies. I remembered Mr. Dalrymple's injunction, to allow no foothold to the influences, and with a great effort I shook off the sleepy feeling and got to my feet. I suppose I must have been half dreaming, and perhaps my arms resting on the elbows of the chair had got cramped, but when I got up I felt just as though I were waking from a troubled dream, with a half remembrance of having seen troops of beautiful ladies dancing in gaily decorated halls. Still there was the paper in my hand, and I carried it off with me. Sooth to say, I was afraid to stay in that queer little room any longer. As I passed out through the hall, my eyes fell on the picture said to be like Signor Hernandez; a ray of brilliant light from the now low westering sun fell upon it, and it gleamed with a strange distinctness, every line seeming to be thrown into strong relief, and at the same moment came across me the memory that in my dream in the little room that face had bent over me, while the beautiful ladies were dancing behind, those cruel sneering eyes had dominated my will, but how? or why? for I had never seen the original and until this moment his features had never appeared plainly to me. A dreamy feeling was coming over me which I did not like at all. I drew several deep breaths to try and banish it, but, instead of the renewed vigour I expected and looked for, I experienced a very curious sensation, as though with such breath the old house became more and more part of me —or I of it — I could not clearly tell which it was; my consciousness seemed, as it were, to pervade every hole and corner of it, till I thought I could see every room, every passage, at once, and feel and touch them all; those who have ever experienced the feeling will know what I mean; those who have not will never realize it from any amount of description; this, however would not do; it was plainly morbid and unhealthy, moreover I felt like falling asleep or into a trance; instinctively I doubled my fists and struck out several times as though boxing; anyone who had seen me would have thought me a lunatic, but it had the desired effect, I became calm and reasonable and wide awake again, and went upstairs to pursue my investigations. It was the room off the first landing that I naturally went to first, the Auld Laird's room as they called it, all just the same as when I was there before, and the same subtle aroma which even more instantly than yesterday suggested Spain to me; but in the rusty old mirror all was dim, no Spanish demoiselle now reclined there, or in the room.

I recalled Mr. Dalrymple's story, and resolved to open the little door which was in the corner beyond the bed, on the other side from the one by which I had entered, the looking-glass being in the opposite corner diagonally. Never in my life had I felt such repugnance to anything as I now did even to go near that door. I would have given almost anything to turn and flee out of the house altogether, only pride kept me from doing so. Something horrible was there I felt; an exhalation as it were exuded from it and while it made my flesh quiver, and stirred the roots of my hair, yet it drew me with a certain ghastly fascination; I obeyed, and bracing myself as though for a supreme effort in a race, I went to the door and opened it. I was surprised, and if you will a little disappointed, to see nothing — a little landing, an old wooden stairway going down to the kitchens or offices probably, a few shelves with some worthless tattered books — novels of fifty years ago and the like — a little window looking on a sort of back green, such as was not quite unknown in Edinburgh at the time I write of, the whole papered in a dull sombre brown; but as I stood looking down a strange feeling of sinking or floating away came over me, a feeling that my body was too light, such as I once felt when under the influence of opium, and then I became vaguely aware of a figure descending the steps. I did not see it with mortal eyes but just became aware of it, as sometimes one becomes aware that a person has entered the room, though one's back is to the door. Immediately all my senses became vividly alive, and my attention was fixed with a concentration, which had in it something of horror and apprehension, on the descending figure, and the impression of it became more and more clear, till I seemed quite certain that it was myself who was going down into the unknown depths. This strange duality I had felt before in dreams, when I sometimes seemed to stand apart and look at my body with curious pitying eyes, but never when broad awake before; at the same time I felt icy cold, and as though all my vitality were being drained from me, the palms of my hands grew clammy, and I felt my hair growing moist. Still that figure, that was myself, descended the stairs, and still my consciousness followed it, though to the eye the lower part of the stair was invisible. At the foot of the stair was a large flat stone, part of the stone paving of the offices, and this seemed to the eye of my waking dream to grow transparent, as though its scarred and stained surface were but slightly tinted glass. It was a curious effect, which dreamers may perhaps recognize, but few others — at the top of the stair just inside the door from the Auld Laird's room stood I, myself, that is to the ordinary eye of the world, and I suppose any friend who had been there would have said that beyond all question I was there in as full material presence as I had walked down the High Street an hour ago; but far down below, and at that moment passing through the flagstone, as though it had been but a magic-lantern image thrown on smoke, was this phantasm of myself, my Doppelganger as I suppose the Germans would call it, and to my own consciousness what seemed I myself was conscious of both, of the material body leaning helpless in semi-trance condition against the door, with wide-open staring eyes, a body which, though I saw and knew every portion of it, I was utterly powerless for the moment to affect or control, and that strange phantasm which was my body too, descending those dreary depths, drawn by I know not what horrible fascination, and with a growing terror, which seemed to react on the material body, whose cheek blanched, and a terrified cry seemed strangled in its throat. It was a horrible nightmare, intensified by the broad waking consciousness, but such as I am persuaded we sometimes go through in sleep, when we wake exhausted and terrified, yet mercifully oblivious of what we have been through. Vainly I strove to regain control of my body, to move, to cry out. Vainly I tried to recall that strange projected phantasm which seemed to have sucked out my vital force — my will was paralysed, only perception was enormously more acute and the horrid dream, if dream it were, went on.

Down! down! by a corkscrew stair below the flag stone, clean and dry at first, but soon becoming dank and slimy, full of odours of death and loathsome creeping things. Down! down! now the stair became a species of cleft in the solid rock, through the sides of which black waters oozed and glistened on the surface; eyeless, almost formless reptiles tangled in hideous knots; on and on; my consciousness more and more seeming to unite with the phantasm which was drawn by some grisly magnetism into these fearsome places, and the more I became as it were conscious through the phantasm, the more did the living rocks that seemed to prison us grow transparent, and this increased the horror; for though they formed an impermeable prison, which not even the Doppelganger could now pass through, they allowed us to see all the hideous deformities and shapes of corruption and decay, looking like incarnate pestilence and sin and death. The Doppelganger too seemed to be growing more material and tangible, and I thought with horror that my actual corporeal body was giving off its atoms and particles in some strange way to materialize the phantasm; and the strange thought came to me that perhaps my whole mortal frame might thus be sucked down and reunited into a waking life, or say rather a ghastly and horrible death, in this awful place. I was powerless to avert it, and the nightmare dream went on. Through the solid rock and the streaks of sodden clay that filled its interstices, now grown transparent, then seemed floating as it were strange black objects, long and narrow, over each of which a green phosphorescent light gleamed fitfully; my attention, in spite of myself, was riveted on these, and instantly I knew them for coffins, of great antiquity probably. Among others some bore Spanish names. At this moment I became conscious again, as in a flash, of my material body, away up in that little landing, bloodless and pale, as though dying or dead: it seemed in the very act of falling to the ground. My horror then was realised, and here in this living grave, among these ancient coffins, and unclean and hateful things, I must drag a material existence till death relieved me. And death! what death of the body could touch that Doppelganger, and the strange ghastly consciousness, that, made all that came within its perception as terrible as though the body itself were there, but without any power of will to avert it or to turn the attention to any other matter. My consciousness, which hitherto I have spoken of as hovering, now became so sensibly united to the phantasm that I regarded it as being myself, and though its motion was still independent of my will I was conscious of the weird force which drew it, and which I can only describe as a resolution against the will, a determination to do an act from which consciousness shrank, which all the faculties knew to be evil, to do which there was no temptation or desire, even as though the resolution on which the limbs acted were formed by some exterior will, whose tendencies were all evil. Close by me (I speak now in the person of the Doppelganger) lay a mouldering coffin, once of solid oak and bound and clamped with iron; but age had rusted the iron to mere red dust and the oaken boards looked as though they might crumble at a touch. A will within me which was not mine put forth a hand to rub the angle of the lid: it crumbled, and a renewed horror took me that my dream was growing real; unless I had been here in flesh and blood could the decayed wood have crumbled to my touch? And if here now, why here for countless ages, among the rotting bodies and the evil magnetic phantasms of the long ago dead, to take my place there conscious, alive, material, yet dead and prisoned: it was an awful thought.

The coffin I had touched seemed to quiver or shake; a jagged hole where my fingers had rubbed away the rotten wood seemed to let through a bluish phosphoric light, and it seemed as though something inside were struggling to emerge; then suddenly, as a large rotten piece fell out, a leg bone protruded, green with age, and far within appeared gleaming eyes, blazing with all the concentrated malice and spite of a hundred demons in torment, and above sprang into sudden and vivid prominence the face of the picture in the hall. Then, as it were a voice, the first sensation of sound I had perceived in the awful gloom. "Run! run! or it will catch you." An awful terror seized me that the demon of the terrible eyes would enter in and possess my phantasm which was now myself, and would drive it through torture and madness while sensation was abnormally acute and all will or power to resist was dead or paralysed. I turned and fled — the first act of will that had been possible for me since the sundering of my consciousness. Then succeeded a terrific time, ages upon ages, as it seemed to me, fleeing through endless caverns, through the sea and through the fire, away into the boundless regions of space, pursued by troops of demons eager, as I felt, to possess even that poor fleeting fragment of a body which was left to me, being themselves bodiless and unable therefore to gratify the lusts and passions which tormented them. Suddenly and with a start I felt my consciousness no longer attached to the phantasm. I was again looking on my material body, which fell with a crash at the top of the stair in the little landing. So all the long and complex series of visions I had been through must have taken place within the time of my body fainting and falling to the ground. But where was the Doppelganger? I felt, though I did not know, that it had re-united with the material body, and my conscious self was now looking down on both.

The crash of my fall brought old Peter running up. I watched him at first with a mild curiosity, bathing my forehead and dashing water on my face and pouring a few drops of whiskey into my mouth; then a kind of pity seemed to inspire me for that body which after all had served me well, and I first hoped and then resolved that his efforts should be successful; as I consciously tried to assist him, the blood came back to the cheeks, I could feel it surge through heart and brain, the eyes opened, and I looked up at Peter with something of a wild stare.

"Where have I been?" I said.

"Eh! laddie; that's more than I can ken", said Peter. "Ye just fell down in a faint, so soon as ever ye put foot into this little room; come awa wi' ye noo. Weel I wat ye've been among some of them. I warned ye, ye mind, but ye would na heed me."

"O Peter," I said, "I've been where sure never man was before, I've been down to the gates of death."

I leant on the old man as we descended the stair. In the hall I paused for a moment to look at the picture; it had faded into its old dimness, but there was the remains of a wicked gleam in the eyes.

"Peter," I said. "That man or devil is not gone, his wicked soul haunts this place."

"Sorrow o' me kens," replied Peter. "Mony's the time I've seen him, ill fa' his lean wicked face; but whether he's alive or dead I canna tell. Sair did he plague puir Mistress Dalrymple, but I think she's wen to a place noo where she has the victory over him. Whiles I've seen him come gliding across the hall just as he used wi' the smile on his lips, that he aye had when he had ony special deviltry afoot, and I've seen my leddy stay her foot just there by the seventh step, and take that cross hilted dagger from her bonny breast, and he just cowered and fled, as the Devil always does from the sign of the cross." Here old Peter who in his earnestness had lapsed almost into pure English in a deep and solemn tone, crossed himself devoutly, and opened the door to let me pass out.

The fresh evening air revived and restored me, and passing down Dundas Street to my lodgings, I suddenly heard myself hailed from a window by an old fellow-student. "Come a wa' in, mon!" he called. "I've got a book here that will just delight your soul."

"What is it?" I answered, feeling, truth to tell, much more inclined to go home and sleep than to stay up talking books.

"The writings of Fergus Fergusson, the auld Scots Wizard," he replied. "I dug it out of the University Library today; they didn't know they had it."

I was up my friend's stair in a twinkling, and seizing the book turned eagerly to the frontispiece. There sure enough were the lineaments so firmly imprinted on my mind as those of Signor Hernandez; the date was 1670, but a note in the preface stated that it was printed from an MS. of 1430. My acquaintance with the old world lore of Edinburgh, instantly connected the latter date with the presence of a considerable Spanish colony in Edinburgh. Of the book itself I need say nothing here. It was of much the same character as the writings of Cornelius Agrippa, of Michael Scot, and other old world wizards; and I am bound to say at that time looked to me, who had not the key thereto, like a farrago of nonsense, though here and there a phrase caught my eye which seemed like an exact description of my experience of that afternoon.

Utterly tired out at last, I borrowed the book from my friend, and returned to my lodgings, where I soon fell into a deep and dreamless sleep. Next morning I took the book and the scrap of paper which I had found in the little octagon room, and again called on Mr. Dalrymple, anxious to hear the completion of his story.

As soon as Mr. Dalrymple came into the room I handed him the old book I had borrowed. He opened it with great interest and looked long and attentively at the engraved portrait. "Yes!" he said at last. 1430, a curious likeness; it is strange how these family features are transmitted. Signor Hernandez must have been a direct descendant of that old wizard, if indeed he were not — but no! that would be too impossible. I think Hernandez had some of his powers too. Look here! do you see this figure of a pentacle? well that is exactly the figure I have seen Hernandez trace, and he had it engraved on a brass instrument; but what is that paper you have in your hand?" "A scrap," I replied, "which I found in the little octagon room yesterday afternoon." And I told him something of my experience there.

"Strangel most strange!" he said, "I thought I was abnormally sensitive. You are far more so. Never fail, my young friend, to thank God that your path has been through clean and wholesome ways, and let the experience of this old house be a warning to you, as doubtless it was intended to be, of the dangers which lie close over the threshold of our ordinary five senses. This fragment of a letter was my poor wife's, and written as I think to Hernandez, but how or why written, and how it came to be where you found it, I can only guess. Now light a cigar and sit down, and I will finish my story as briefly as I can. After your second visit to the house you will perhaps follow it more easily.

"I will not weary you with any account of my journey to Seville, nor with any descriptions of that beautiful city, which you know as well as I, probably. Enough to say that I got there in ample time, and spent the intervening days in visiting friends and relatives, of whom I had a few living there at the time. You may guess my state of feverish excitement when the day dawned which my beloved Mercedes had appointed. I betook myself betimes to the Cathedral, but not a vestige of her could I trace, not even the faintest indication of her presence. In fact ever since I left Scotland it seemed as though the magnetic chain were broken, and Mercedes had passed out of my life for ever. I ought to mention that, before I left, my engagement to Edith Challenor had been definitely broken off. Blame me as you will for this, I was the sport of stronger influences than my own will could control, and could no more help myself than a straw can help being carried on the current. Had it been otherwise, had I strengthened and exercised my own will as I now, too late, know how to do, and used it to carry out the dictates of my conscience, none can say what misery might have been saved. There are few more disastrous things in life than to know the right, and from a weak fluctuating will to be unable to do it.

"The evening was drawing in fast, vespers were just beginning. I knelt in the Cathedral, praying with all my soul that whatever power had guided my steps thus far would enable me to help and rescue my darling from whatever trouble or peril she might be in. All at once a strange flutter came to my heart, a warm glow spread all over me, the well known scent of sandal wood almost overpowered the incense, and instinctively I turned to a dim chapel on the right hand side where only two candles burnt before a small altar of the Mater Dolorosa. There, in the well-known amber robe and the black lace mantilla, knelt a figure. I looked intently, all my soul in my eyes, she looked up: it was Mercedes, as I had seen her at Lady Scott's ball, only now it was a crimson covered prayer book in place of the fan. — The great dark eyes were raised one moment in piteous pleading, and seemed to say 'come and help me!' — there was a little rustle of a dress — she was gone — whither? I rushed from the Cathedral. All was dim without in the ill-lighted streets, I ran aimlessly up and down, peering down every alley, but in vain, and now there chanced something which I can only explain on the theory known to the Hebrews as Bath-kol, or an appropriate answer given in some apparently chance way to a query in one's mind. As I went in great agitation past a chemist's shop, the scent of sandal wood floated out — no uncommon thing you will say in a chemist's shop — but it arrested my steps in a moment. A plan of Seville was in the window, and a jagged line of light, thrown from a cracked glass, lay exactly on certain streets, and pointed right out of the map, and on a piece of printed paper beyond I started to see the name Mercedes. It is as you know a common enough Spanish name. This printed paper set forth that a certain face powder was used by a popular actress of that name, but as it was folded and covered by other goods it merely displayed the words in Spanish, 'Straight forward, Mercedes.' It flashed to my mind in a moment, I must take the streets indicated by the line of light, and go straight on beyond the parts shewn in the map in the same direction.

 I took it all in as rapidly as possible, and started as fast as I could thread my way along the streets, over the Guadalquivir and out into the suburbs, straight on and on till I came to where the road turned at right angles right and left. I paused a second in doubt; then upon my ear came a sort of strange chant. I listened intently; where had I heard that weird music before? Then my mind recalled the uncanny witchcraft my uncle had practised with my cross-hilted dagger. It was the same chant — so far as I could hear, or as I could remember, it was the same words. I looked straight ahead. Over a low wall fronting me was a graveyard — an old disused place. I had often heard that the natives would not on any account go there at night, and hardly by day. Some old stories hung about of some terrible butchery of Christians by the Moors perpetrated there — or it might have been the other way, I am not sure — anyhow infidels had been buried there, and some horrible cruelties had profaned it, and unquiet spirits wandered there, so it was said. A strange fright caught my breath for a moment, thinking of those old stories, as I saw what seemed a faint blue light, and heard that weird chant, but calling on the name of Mercedes, and nerving myself to a supreme effort, I went forward to the low wall, and saw a solitary figure waving its arms in strange gesticulations, as though mesmerizing somebody; the chant, which now came clear on my ear, was the same which I had heard my uncle singing. I put my hand on my dagger, to feel if it were still there; the touch of the metal, though it felt like a magnetic shock, gave me fresh vital force and resolve. I bounded over the wall and strode straight to the figure, and with a start I recognised Hernandez; around him, cut on the turf, was a double circle about eighteen feet in diameter; a chafing-dish with live coals was at his feet, on which he had apparently sprinkled some incense, for a fragrant smoke curled upwards; other strange shaped vessels were about, one containing what looked like blood.

"Instantly I felt the same feeling of giddiness which had overcome me in the old house in the Canongate, when I first saw Hernandez; involuntarily I felt drawn towards him and into the magic circle in which he stood, as though invisible hands pushed me, till I stood beside him. As I did so he lowered his hands and ceased the mesmeric passes for a moment; then he held his right hand steadily pointed towards the city with some bright short instrument, rather like a stiletto, in it. 'You have come?' he said quietly. 'It is well; I told you we should meet in Spain. You want your sweetheart; well! she is coming; patience, she comes over fields, and ditches and hedges. I called her from the Cathedral an hour ago. I have need of you both. Be good children and all shall be right.' He spoke placidly, slowly, almost like an automaton, without accentuation, and as though he were afraid the least effort or movement would destroy the stern concentration of will that was on every feature.

"My feelings were horrible to look back upon; for the moment I looked on Hernandez as a dog might look on his master; his strength and his will seemed the only firm things in a world of wavering shadows; the most dreadful fate seemed to be separation from him. I know not by what chance or providence it was that, as I stood besides Hernandez within the magic circle, my hand should fall instinctively on my cross-hilted dagger, and I should draw it out and gaze hard upon it. But as I did so, the thought sprang like lightning to my mind that this man, by some subtle power of evil, had drawn me and was drawing Mercedes within his toils, and as I thought of this his hand quivered — the fixity of will in his face was crossed by a shade of doubt, and in an instant all became plain to me, and I sprang upon him like a wolf, and wrenching the little steel wand from his hand I flung it far away. With a horrible curse he closed upon me, and for one awful minute we wrestled within the charmed circle; only once did my right hand pass beyond it, and that moment I felt an agony like tongues of flame, and became aware of thousands of presences — spirits, call them what you will, circling round like a rushing mighty wind; and over all one single huge eye. Since then I have learned something of the occult sciences, and the construction of many pentacles has been shown to me, but I have never fathomed exactly the rite which Hernandez was practising there. I may be describing it wrongly, for at that time I knew nothing about the matter, and can only tell you the circumstances as they appeared to me. By a strange intuition I knew that outside of the pentacle were a mob of howling demons, who would probably kill me if I ventured outside, and that no one but Hernandez who had summoned them could dismiss them to their own place. At last I got him in my power — my hand was on his throat. 'Dismiss your foul crew,' I said, 'or by the Devil who will certainly claim your accursed soul, I will send you to him before your time'. How I obtained any power over him I know not — it seems to me now contrary to all the occult laws I know. But the thing was even as I have told you, and I know that my dagger was a powerful charm, and altogether I am convinced that the whole occurrence followed some laws which I have never fathomed. Anyhow Hernandez, almost choked by my fingers on his throat, gasped out some words in either Hebrew or Arabic, and instantly the air grew clear and fresh as on a Spring morning in Scotland, and leaning over the churchyard gate I saw my beloved Mercedes looking wild with terror, wearied to death and travel-stained, but, thank God! safe. I flew towards her, and just as she fell almost fainting in my arms, I saw Hernandez gathering up his various implements, departing with a sinister look of hatred which burnt itself into my memory for ever.

 The after events are very dimly outlined on my mind now. It was early dawn: many hours must have gone by while I stood with Hernandez within that pentacle, during the terrible fight, but they seemed like a few moments only. A countryman passed with cart laden with fragrant hay; on this soft couch I gently placed the fainting form of Mercedes, and a liberal gratuity induced the man to go a considerable distance out of his way, to the house of an old lady, a distant relative, to whose care I proposed to entrust Mercedes. My relation was not up when we go there, but she soon appeared, and hearing the fragmentary story, which was all I could give here then, she readily undertook the kind office.

"Mercedes, so long a vision was now to me a living and breathing reality. But it was weeks before she was sufficiently recovered to tell me anything of her story, and even when I learnt it, it was vague and imperfect. It was however, clear that she was what is called a natural sensitive. She had, I imagine, been stolen by gipsies in early childhood, for she had been brought up by them – not, however, in the squalid way and with the vulgar associations belonging to the English or Scottish idea of gipsies. The tribe with whom she had lived, had their home away in the Basque mountains, where, though shunning houses, as is the manner of all their race, they seem to have maintained an almost regal magnificence. Like all their race, they were deeply skilled in the occult sciences, and had, as I suppose, stolen Mercedes, who I fancy from various indications must have belonged to some noble Spanish house, for the sake of her remarkable gifts. It seems she lived happily enough with the gipsies, never dreaming that she was not what she was reported to be – the daughter of the chief. But for the last year her sleep had been haunted by strange visions. A house unlike anything she had ever seen, indeed, very few houses were ever seen by this dweller in tents and caves, an evil haunting presence, her description of which tallied curiously with my own impression of Hernandez and someone to whom she always fled for protection, and in whom she seemed now to recognize myself. In her dream the evil figure seemed to be dominating both her own life and mine, and it was in obedience to an uncontrollable impulse that she had come a considerable distance to the Vesper Service in Seville. After kneeling at the altar she became absolutely unconscious, and only recovered to find herself wearied out, and terrified near to death, beside the Churchyard gate. The little I then knew of spiritualism led me to a definite conclusion, viz., that Hernandez, who, whatever other powers he might possess, was clearly a very strong mesmerist, had long known the wonderful clairvoyant faculty of Mercedes, and determined to avail himself of it; meeting me he had recognized in me a similar power, and had laid his plans with diabolical coolness and cunning to bring us both under his will, that the mediumistic force of two sensitives acting and reacting in reality on each other, might produce results beyond what could be achieved by one. So it seemed to me then – but I confess to you that spiritualism and the phenomena of mediumship never attracted me much; when not utterly trivial they seem to me fraught with risks too grave to be lightly faced, so I have never read much of the literature of the subject, and my conclusions may be widely erroneous. But it seemed to me that without, or even against his will, the power of his mesmeric influence had drawn the astral form of Mercedes to the old house in the Canongate, and thus magnetic connexion was established between her and me, which his subsequent mesmeric experiments on me had deepened and intensified, till at last bringing us together had defeated his own ends, but what those ends were, or who or what was Hernandez, I am wholly unable to hazard even a guess.

"There is no particular interest for a stranger in this part of my story. I will therefore hurry over it as rapidly as I can. Suffice it to say that I married Mercedes, as of course you will have guessed, after some opposition, but at last with the full approval of the gipsy chief who had been as a father to her. He was utterly reticent as to her history, but in every other respect no prince of the blood could have met me with greater courtesy, and to all the details of my strange experience he listened gravely with a slow wise smile as one who knows all about it, looking from time to time at the palm of my hand, but saying no word. Never in this world I think were married lovers so happy as we during a long summer holiday in the beautiful Basque provinces which, unknown to nearly every traveler, were as familiar to my half-gipsy bride as the streets of Edinburgh are to us today.

"At last we bent our steps homeward, and it was with a feeling of pride that I took Mercedes to the old house. Her first exclamation was, 'How familiar it all is'. Like a merry child she ran from room to room, exploring every hole and corner; the old house was very bright then, and as I have told you some of my happiest days belong to this period. Now and then a dark shadow would pass over in consequence of a certain delicacy of health of my beloved Mercedes, but this the doctors assured me would pass away; a tendency to hysteria they called it; but from time to time she would fall in to deep trances, in which sometimes she would say strange and startling things. It had been a great grief to us that we had no children, but one day in one of these deathlike trances she suddenly looked up and said, 'It is well we have no child. You are the last of your race, the old curse will break with me.' At another time she said, 'I grow stronger, he grows weaker, he will not succeed again.' These and many other sentences of the kind, whose meaning was entirely beyond my power to fathom. I had told my uncle, who, by the way, still resided with us, of my experiences in Spain and my encounter with Hernandez, of which he gave a totally different explanation from that which had commended itself to me.

'It was not Signor Hernandez himself that you saw,' so he said to me one evening. 'If you go to a spiritual séance you will very likely see Shakespere or Julius Caesar, or some other great personage called up and materialized before your eyes, but directly they write, as they sometimes do, or rap out communications, it becomes at once evident that not the spirit of the mighty dead, but a very vulgar and illiterate spirit is manipulating the form which you see. So it was here; some low and evil spirit put on the aspect of Hernandez to deceive you; his actions prove it. Had you been more advanced in occultism you would have recognized this at once.' Nevertheless I was not satisfied, and I seemed to have so fully recognized Hernandez, not by the outward shape, but by the personal influence which surrounded him, that I felt no manner of doubt that it was himself. My uncle, however, grew so urgent on the point that after a while I became convinced against myself, and ready to admit that what I had seen was some mere delusive shade.

"It was about this time that old Peter, the old servant who shewed you over the house, came back. I had not seen him before; he was originally as a boy in my father's employment, and had been picked up by him somewhere, I believe, in the West Indies. Peter is said to be a half-caste, but what his particular breed is I can't tell you; I suspect he has a good deal of Spanish blood in his veins and more than a dash of negro; anyhow Peter has always from a boy been curiously sensitive and directly he was employed, I think as a page or boot boy or something, about the old house he seemed almost to become a part of the house; it had a strange fascination for him, and he was never happy away from it; but shortly before my return to my ancestral home Peter had been ill, and my uncle sent him away for rest and change, and so it was that until my return from Spain with Mercedes I never saw Peter. I must notice here, what you have remarked, the singular way in which most of the people intimately connected with the old house have been peculiarly sensitive. My uncle unquestionably was so in some directions, in fact, I have no doubt of his having been a spirit medium, either naturally or by cultivation; so from what I can learn was my grandfather who married a Spanish lady. She by the way played him false, and learning of her treachery at the supper table one evening, in a fit of sudden madness he flung a dagger which struck her on the chest and went straight to the heart, killing her instantly; the story was hushed up, my grandfather went abroad and died very shortly after of apoplexy. Criminal justice was, as you know, very uncertain in Scotland a hundred years ago, and while poor wretches in the Cowgate were hanged for petty thefts, high placed murderers like my grandfather escaped scot free sometimes. Then my father, who had nothing of the sensitive about him, never lived in the house at all; he married a douce pious Scotch lady, when he was pretty well on in life, but only knew of the Canongate house by tradition. I must have been born a sensitive I think, though the powers only developed when I came to the old house. My darling Mercedes was exceptionally so, old Peter also, and now you who are also sensitive, whether you know it or not, must needs go rummaging and exploring about the place, and catching all its weird influence. It seems as though the old house, like a living creature, had some almost conscious power of attracting to itself those whom its wicked influences can affect. You will remember how you, a total stranger, were impelled to go in and explore it, and unless Providence had guided you to me you would have been caught like a fly in a spider's web, or rather what seems to me a better simile, like some poor insect attracted to a carnivorous plant which absorbs and destroys it. Soul and body, will that accursed house destroy all sensitives who come within its influence, unless they have great powers of resistance.

"Very shortly after our return, I met Hernandez in the hall. I started on seeing him; my uncle who was with me said, 'Now nephew! you've been telling me various cock and bull stories about Signor Hernandez; he has in fact never left this house since you went away. Look at him carefully now, and you will see how little like he is to the astral that you saw at Seville.' I did so, and Hernandez gazed full into my eyes; as he did so the scene in the churchyard sprang into sudden vividness, and to my utter amazement the wizard who had been making those mesmeric passes in the magic circle was a totally different person from Hernandez who stood before me.

"I felt bound to offer him an apology, but I was not satisfied. No sooner however, did Mercedes set eyes on him than she fell into a dead faint and was ill for a long time. Peter also conceived the most extraordinary repulsion for him. 'Mr. Dalrymple,' he said to me one day, 'yon man is the devil — or if he's no himself, I'm thinking he's no vera far awa' kin. And look ye, sir, if I'm no much mistaken he's just practicing his uncanny arts on the young mistress, puir thing! and it's truth I'm telling ye, gin she should make a moonlight flitting wi' him, she'll no be to blame; it'll no be her fault, puir leddy, but just against her will and through the deviltries of that black sorcerer.' I remembered his strange influence over Mercedes, and altogether made up my mind that Hernandez must go. I was just beginning to say to my uncle that I intended to tell him so, when Hernandez himself came up with his travelling valise in his hand. 'I find I have to leave you suddenly,' he said, 'but we shall meet again ere long.' I answered somewhat stiffly that I feared I should not be able to receive him as a guest for the present, owing to private arrangements. He was not in the least put out, but simply replied, 'Oh! of course, not here. I understand, exactly, but you will be my guest soon, in the land of the olive and wine — your uncle comes with me to-night.' Another moment and he was gone. 'What does he mean, uncle?' I said. 'You are not going to leave us.' 'No! no!' said my uncle with a nervous little laugh, quite foreign to him. 'Signor Hernandez mistook. I don't know what he was thinking of.' I noticed, however, that his jolly red face was very pale.

"That night the house was full of strange noises. I have heard similar sounds in other houses sometimes and was told they were rats; it may be so. I saw nothing. Peter told me afterwards those that he calls "them as walks" were all about that night, far more manifest and more wicked than usual. About 3 o'clock in the morning, as nearly as I could time it, I heard a long, wailing cry which sounded like that of a person in utter terror, then several choking sobs mixed with a stertorous kind of snoring, and a rattling noise as of a person breathing with great difficulty through an obstruction: then a stillness as of death. I sprang out of bed and on to the stairs, and called several times. At last old Peter came; in answer to my inquiries he had heard nothing; troops of phantoms according to him had been flitting up and down the stairs, but he had not heeded them and had gone to sleep. We took candles and searched everywhere, but in vain. My uncle's bedroom was locked as usual. We knocked, and he answered from within in his usual cheery tones; the little vaulted room was locked as it always was. At last we went to bed. Next morning we found my uncle's room empty. The bed had not been slept in, and on breaking open the door of the little vaulted room, there lay his body stiff and cold. He must have been dead many hours. The face was swollen livid, the tongue protruded and bitten through, on either side of the throat two long black marks. 'Apoplexy,' the doctor said, an old family physician with a grave face and a gold-headed malacca cane. 'Apoplexy, my dear sir. His father, your grandfather, died of the same; hereditary tendency I fear; a little blood-letting might have saved him.' The marks on the throat he accounted for in some way which I forget, pressure of a tight collar or something; but I am ascertain as that we sit here, that my uncle was strangled by some hand, physical or not, and that Hernandez had something to do with it. But what ghost or spirit or human being it was that mimicked my uncle's voice, and replied to our knock, probably no one will ever know."

THE END OF MR. DALRYMPLE'S STORY
While Mr. Dalrymple was talking he had been carelessly turning over the leaves of the old book containing the writings of Fergus Fergusson. After telling the tragic story of his uncle's death his eye fell on a passage which attracted him, and he read eagerly and in silence for some time. "This is very remarkable," he said at last. "Listen! here is a short account, about two pages long, of the old wizard—this is the end of it: 'He (the wizard) was a man of notoriously profligate character, his last exploit being to elope with a noble lady of Spanish birth, the wife of a good gentleman of fortune in Edinburgh, whose name was Dalrymple; the populace were so enraged at this, that he was seized and with brief shrift condemned to be burnt alive. He was drawn on a hurdle to the place of execution, but on being bound to the stake, and the faggots lighted, it

was found that he had vanished; but whether preserved by his curious arts, or whether as some assert, the Devil, who was his master, at that moment claimed his wicked soul as the prize of his misdeeds the chronicler knoweth not. Yet are there not wanting, even now, some who assert that Fergus Fergusson was seen alive and well in the streets of Edinburgh long after this occurrence; yet he could not be apprehended of any man.'

"The old curse", continued Mr. Dalrymple, "goes deeper and further back than I knew; three hundred years ago, you see, here were the same fatal elements of tragedy present in my own family, and in the same old house, and still that same infernal face appearing as the evil genius of the family. I must hurry on with my story — but one circumstance after my uncle's death was so curious in the light what followed, that I must tell it you here. Mercedes, despite the doctor's assurances, grew weaker, and her trances more frequent and lasting longer, and sometimes when wearied out and ill at ease, she has stopped in front of that picture in the hall and sighed deeply. 'I wish he would come back,' she sometimes said, 'it was so pleasant when he was here.' I would have done anything in the world to pleasure my darling, even to the inviting of Signor Hernandez, much as I detested him, to my house; but always in the morning when I mentioned the subject to her, she would entreat me with a shudder never to let him come near to her. I concluded that her desire to see Hernandez was merely a fantasy bred of a weak and overwrought brain, which cool reflection and waking strength turned into the natural loathing her pure soul felt for a bad man.

"Several times about this period old Peter startled me by saying he had seen 'yon auld deevil', as he always called Hernandez, about the house. At such times every corner was searched, but without result; only now and then an echo, that sounded like the sneering laugh characteristic of him, seemed to sound through the hollows down below the foundations. 'He's after the mistress, puir leddy,' said Peter to me once, 'an ye'll no catch him, the foul devil-dealing brute — gin ye could catch him, and wring the ill-fared neck o' him ye wad do the world a guid turn; but I reckon he can go invisible and pass through closed doors as easy as open anes by some of them wicked cantrips o' his.'

"One night I was just thinking of going to rest, when Peter suddenly beckoned to me, and led me to a window, you probably remember it, which commanded a partial view of the Canongate. 'Whisht!' he said, 'yon black deevil has bewitched the puir mistress — see ye there.' Sure enough down the Canongate was walking my beautiful Mercedes. You will remember the Canongate was a very different place fifty years ago from what it is now. A fashionable street it had been in old times, and there were still some families of distinction living there. She had simply the tartan plaid drawn over her head after that graceful fashion which our rulers once thought fit to forbid by sumptuary laws, and in wearing which she adopted our old Scottish fashion and added to it all the grace and beauty of her native land. By her side was a figure I knew only too well — it was Hernandez. Immediately under my hand lay a sword-cane which I had found useful in some of my travels. I caught it up and followed the pair. Down the Canongate they went and past the old front of Holyrood, I after them; and as I passed, crowds of ghosts of the old historic personages seemed to be thronging the windows of Holyrood. On they went past Muchat's cairns, past the ruins of St. Anthony's Chapel, I panting after them. Just as they paused for a moment beside the end of Hunter's Bog I grasped my cross-hilted dagger. One mad moment I poised it, meaning to fling — the next the story of my grandfather flashed through my mind. I should miss Hernandez, I should kill my darling wife; the haunting sense of the old tragedy was upon me. Over and over again must the scene be re-enacted, so some inner voice seemed to be saying — over and over again till — then it became silent; but the brooding curse settled down on my spirit, and the consciousness that I myself had been through this very scene before forced itself very strongly upon me.

"I drew the blade from the sword cane and rushed madly at the pair; I could almost hear their low whispers. I made a wild lunge at Hernandez; my foot slipt as I did so and the blade passed clean through him — aye! but with no resistance even as though it passed through a cloud — and that moment like a cloud the unclean form dispersed. A wraith of pale blue vapour floated up the side of Arthur's Seat, but Mercedes lay at my feet as one dead. I had the fullest confidence in the absolute purity of my wife and I gently raised her in my arms and carried her home, where for weeks she lay unconscious. When at last she came to herself she remembered no word of the nocturnal adventure — only that her sleep had been troubled by hateful and impure visions which she seemed unable to drive away or flee from. I thought of the obscene forms conjured up by my uncle in the little vaulted room, and shuddered at the idea of such foul shapes invading the pure sleep of my darling; but at last she recovered and seemed her old girlish self once more, delighting to throw herself down into a lounge in our room in front of the old mirror in amber, satin, and black lace, with the dear old sandal wood perfume about her, and enact the part of my dream love of olden days. Happy days were these, and old Peter used to say 'them as walks' had never been so peaceful as then, though he met wraiths on the stairs and hovering round, yet all ever benignant and well disposed towards us, and of Hernandez nothing whatever was seen or heard by anyone. Happy days but all too few, and the calm was ominous. Very soon alarming symptoms began to show themselves in my darling Mercedes; not only now was it physical weakness and the persistent recurrence of the long death-like trances, but mental aberration; often she did not recognize me, and would fall into fits of uncontrolled and violent passion, as unlike herself as could well be imagined.

"One night as I sat watching by her bedside a strange drowsiness crept over me, very much like that which had affected me when first I wooed her as the lady of the mirror. I could see the room and all its surroundings, but of sitting there myself I was utterly unconscious; I seemed to be everywhere and as it were part of everything, and in this state I saw plainly what I took to be the spirit form of Mercedes, herself, yet glorified and purified and transfigured, and her message to me, though I must needs translate it into words, yet came not in that form, but as it were flashed from soul to soul in an instant. 'Mourn not for me,' she seemed to say, 'I am here no longer but happy and at rest at last. The poor body you look upon contains my spirit no longer. I died weeks ago according to the time of earth. It is an evil spirit, or creation of him who persecuted me, that now animates that frame of flesh and blood.' At this mention of Hernandez I felt an irresistible wave of wrath rise in my soul; but the gentle message came again: 'Nay, be not wrath, we are not angry with the medicines that bring us health, nor with the exercises that bring strength to our bodies. I was weak and sickly; it was my trial and my task to meet and overcome him. I failed, and over and over again in infinite kindness was the same task set me, and over and over again I failed, but with each failure I gathered new strength. So long as I failed his will could chain me to this old house; but now I am free, and in winning my freedom, I have won release for you too, my beloved; in a few days you will leave this house, accursed as it is for all your race, and you will enter it nevermore. He whom you know as Hernandez was once in earth-life the ancestor of your family. He now embodies all that is evil in the inherited tendencies of that family. He and you and I have enacted the same scenes together but with a different result many times — but now you, O my beloved, have crushed out your inherited tendencies, have fought successfully against the characteristics you derive from your family, and your strength has been strength in me, and by repeated opposition we have conquered Hernandez; and we can now recognize that it is he who supplying a force to oppose our own has developed our strength and to whom we must be grateful. The ancient curse is broken.' So saying the lovely vision faded away and the feverish form of Mercedes was left tossing restlessly on the bed. In the morning I did not remember the vision, nor did it come back to me for long afterwards. I knew, however, when it did come back, when and where I had seen it.

"The doctor who came daily told me that Mercedes was developing a tendency to suicidal mania, and cautioned me to keep everything of a dangerous nature out her reach, and to watch her carefully. This I did: but one night I presume I must have slept at my post, for I suddenly became wide awake, and the great funeral bed was empty. Mercedes was nowhere to be seen. 1 called, but no answer. In an agony of mind I rushed to the little landing. There at the head of the stairs lay my darling — her night dress stained and dabbled with blood, my cross-hilted dagger in her breast — dead and cold. The blank terrible despair of that moment was almost more than flesh and blood can bear. I cried an exceeding bitter cry and fell in a dead faint beside the corpse.

"How long I was unconscious I cannot tell, days, weeks, months, I know not. I heard afterwards that there had been some enquiry, that I had been found in a swoon beside the body of my darling, and that the Crown with its usual intelligence had come to the conclusion that I might have killed her — I who would have given every breath in my body to shield her from the slightest pain. Of all this, however, I was mercifully unconscious, and Peter took me abroad, when I first recovered myself, and then I remembered the visit, and I knew, though of course your scientific men would jeer at such an idea, that my pure and holy Mercedes had never been guilty of the sin of suicide; long before, she had left the poor frail body she used to inhabit, and it was but the foul elemental conjured up by Hernandez to take possession of it which had grown wrath with its material dwelling-place, and plunged the dagger into that sweet breast from which the angel spirit had long flown; but how the dagger came there I never knew. I have never parted from it since.

"Leave me now, my young friend, my story is done. I have never before told it to mortal man, and would not have told it to you had you not come within the spell of the old house. It is but the evil magnetism which lingers there now: the spirit of Mercedes has met and conquered the spirit of evil, and very soon no stone shall be left on another to mark where stood a place accursed of God and man."

THE WRITER'S LAST WORDS.

But little now of my story remains to tell. Business took me out of Edinburgh almost immediately after my last interview with Mr. Dalrymple, and it was some weeks before I saw the old house again; when I did the workmen had been some time in possession and but little of the old fabric remained, all the walls were laid bare, the floors and timber were gone: only the ground floor in fact remained, and that was open to the sky, and excavations were going on below. No secret passages or unknown rooms had been discovered, it had been simply a solidly built old-fashioned mansion, some of its lower parts, from their strength and solidity, apparently belonging to a fortified place of old time. I closely questioned the workmen and learnt that at the seventh stair, the place where, according to Peter, the ghost of the lady with the dagger in her breast had always disappeared, there was an evident trace under the plaster of an old door, but the aperture had been bricked up solid some time very long ago and no man could say what had been its original purpose, for if opened it would have led out on an outside wall with a drop of some twenty feet to the ground. This I suppose must ever remain an unknown mystery.

On two points only did any interest attach to the excavations; below the old stair leading from the Laird's room to the kitchens they had pierced down to the solid rock, and had found there a curious cleft or hollow leading apparently to the bowels of the earth, up which had floated a vapour of so deadly and noxious a character that two of the men had fainted and been carried off in a perilous state to the infirmary; and below the little vaulted room was some curious arched masonry; something like a very primitive crypt, on the floor of which they had found a stone which now lay loose, though when discovered it was firmly bedded in the masonry, carved with a rude serpent and some other emblems; on the wall, under one of the vaultings, was cut with a chisel, a pentagram, but roughly done as though by an amateur. I was looking curiously at this, when I became conscious that someone was watching me; I looked up, and standing just above me was a slim handsome man of about forty, very dark, and dressed in some foreign fashion. I looked curiously at him. Where had I seen that face before? Then in a moment it flashed across me, "Signor Hernandez". I said. "You have mistaken me," he answered tendering his card. "Count Bernstein." I heard the voice of old Peter close behind. "God save us a', yon's that auld Deevil."

"You seem to have mistaken me for a friend," he said, with slightly melancholy accent; "permit me to give you a hand out of that pit. I think I can show you who I am." I extended my right hand mechanically; my left was resting on the wall against the pentagram, and I stood on the carved stone. As his hand touched mine a vision flashed across my mind. I saw Hernandez in habit like some ancient Druid offering a human sacrifice, and the victim was a gipsy girl, who, as some inner sense seemed to tell me, had been unfaithful to his savage semi-animal passion; and onwards over and over again I saw the same scene repeated, and I heard his deep enunciation of undying hate and pronouncement of a curse so terrible that my blood congealed and the roots of my hair stirred. Not as a succession of pictures did these varied scenes appear, not even as a number of pictures seen all at once, but with a consciousness that each one was the same, all apprehended as one, all seen and understood in a flash, quicker far than thought, and borne in upon my mind, as I knew, by the fact of my completing some mysterious magnetic circles by standing on that stone, with one hand on the pentagram, the other in that of Hernandez.

Yet it was only during the interval between my placing my foot on a fragment of broken wall and stepping off the carved stone. All the events of many centuries seemed flashed into my mind in that instant;

the next I saw him again clearly. "Mysterious being," I said, "are you man or devil ?" "I am to you," he replied, "as you shall take me. Adam and Eve yielded to the tempting of Satan, and for them and their offspring to the last generation Satan is an ever-brooding curse. Job resisted the power of Satan, and for Job Satan appeared as one among the Sons of God. Which is the true aspect, think you? Through the attachments of family, through specious calls of duty, through wealth and through misery, Job fought with Satan and overcame. He saw Satan clearly; your friend Mr. Dalrymple sees me clearly now. Call me Satan if you will. You and all of earth have to meet with those like me, and sometimes we appear as angels of light: when there is a clear duty, we shall show you that your circumstances are exceptional; the stronger you are, the wilier must the trial be; but learn once to go fearlessly along the path, though all pleasure and vanities have to be thrown overboard; straight on though father and mother, wife and children, seem to block the way; straight on though obedience to the command seems to imply a moral guilt; straight on though it seems to be the destruction even of your very higher self; and you shall know us for what we are, angels of light," his voice grew deep, and his figure seemed transfigured as he spoke: "But fail in any of the tests, and you shall also know us; or what we are to you, eternal and undying curses, lamentation, and woe." The last words were hissed like the tone of a serpent in my ear, and he was gone.

"Who was that ?" I asked a workman next me.

"No man here but ourselves," was his answer, "what are ye thinking of master ? "

"Whisht!" said old Peter, "They can't see, but he was here for all that—his last visit I'm thinking."

[Reprinted from *Lucifer*, Vols. 5 & 6, November 1889 to May 1890]

THE GOLDEN DAWN COMPANION
By R.A. Gilbert

The Hermetic Order of the Golden Dawn epitomized the paradox of an intellectual élite who rejected orthodox religion and yet remained within the social establishment of its day. The colourful story of these would-be magicians is well known to students of nineteenth-century social history, but the private archives on which the definitive history of the Order (Ellic Howe's *The Magicians of the Golden Dawn)* was based have only recently become accessible for study by scholars.

In this new edition of *The Golden Dawn Companion* the texts of both official and unofficial documents are made available for all. Here are the full texts of the Order's Constitution, Rules and Regulations, the Obligations of candidates for both the Outer and Inner Orders, the 'General Orders' of the R.R. et A.C., and the complete membership lists from the official Address Book, the Order Rolls and other lists compiled within the various branches of the Order up to 1914. There also detailed descriptions of the Temples, the Grade rituals, and the manuscript collections that comprise the archives.

In addition, the original texts of the various theories of origin of the Golden Dawn are brought together, and there is a comprehensive, updated and annotated bibliography of printed material relating to the Order.

R.A. Gilbert read Philosophy and Psychology at the University of Bristol and later received his doctorate from the University of London, for a thesis on esoteric publishing in the Nineteenth Century. He is a retired antiquarian bookseller, and the author and editor of many books on Western Esotericism, including studies of the Golden Dawn and its members.

ISBN 978-1-913660-12-3

SECRETS OF A GOLDEN DAWN TEMPLE
Book 1: Creating Magical Tools
By Chic Cicero and Sandra Tabatha Cicero

From its inception over 100 years ago, the Hermetic Order of the Golden Dawn continues to be the authority on magic. Yet the books written on the Golden Dawn system have fallen far short in explaining how to construct the tools and implements necessary for ritual. Now, with *Secrets of a Golden Dawn Temple, Book I: Creating Magical Tools*, the practicing magician has access to a unique compilation of the various tools used, all described in full: wands, ritual clothing, elemental tools, Enochian Tablets, altars, temple furniture, banners, lamens, admission badges and much more.

"The Hermetic Order of the Golden Dawn has been both praised and criticized by various 'authorities' over the years. However, when all is said and done, its work remains a foundation stone and springboard for most modern magical training and experiment.

"Chic and Tabatha Cicero, as representatives of a stalwart band dedicated to preserving [The Golden Dawn's] teaching and powers intact, deserve praise in developing such specific instruction as an aid to any modern student, experienced or beginner, who seeks to tap into this important mag ical current".

— Gareth Knight
Author of *A Practical Guide in Qabalistic Symbolism*

"Here is a superb do-it-yourself book that tells you every step to take in the construction of any GD wand, implement, or temple furnishing. Constructing such implements from scratch is a spiritual path of its own".

— David Godwin
Author of *Godwin's Cabalistic Encyclopedia*

ISBN 1-870450-64-7

DION FORTUNE AND THE INNER LIGHT
By Gareth Knight

At last – a comprehensive biography of Dion Fortune based upon the archives of the Society of the Inner Light. As a result much comes to light that has never before been revealed. This includes:

Her early experiments in trance mediumship with her Golden Dawn teacher Maiya Curtis-Webb and in Glastonbury with Frederick Bligh Bond, famous for his psychic investigations of Glastonbury Abbey.

The circumstances of her first contact with the Masters and reception of "The Cosmic Doctrine". The ambitious plans of the Master of Medicine and the projected esoteric clinic with her husband in the role of Dr. Taverner.

The inside story of the confrontation between the Christian Mystic Lodge of the Theosophical Society of which she was president, and Bishop Piggot of the Liberal Catholic church, over the Star in the East movement and Krishnamurti. Also her group's experience of the magical conflict with Moina MacGregor Mathers.

How she and her husband befriended the young Israel Regardie, were present at his initiation into the Hermes Temple of the Stella Matutina, and suffered a second ejection from the Golden Dawn on his subsequent falling out with it.

Her renewed and highly secret contact with her old Golden Dawn teacher Maiya Tranchell-Hayes and their development of the esoteric side of the Arthurian legends.

Her peculiar and hitherto unknown work in policing the occult jurisdiction of the Master for whom she worked which brought her into unlikely contact with occultists such as Aleister Crowley.

Nor does the remarkable story end with her physical death for, through the mediumship of Margaret Lumley Brown and others, continued contacts with Dion Fortune have been reported over subsequent years.

ISBN 1-870450-50-7

www.ingramcontent.com/pod-product-compliance
Lightning Source LLC
Chambersburg PA
CBHW031133160426
43193CB00008B/128